Roma in Europe

Migration, Education, Representation

Roma in Europe
Migration, Education, Representation

Anca Pusca, editor

International Debate Education Association
New York, London & Amsterdam

Published by
International Debate Education Association
105 East 22nd Street
New York, NY 10010

For permission to reproduce in whole or in part, please contact idea@idebate.org.

Library of Congress Cataloging-in-Publication Data

Roma in Europe : migration, education, representation / Anca Pusca, editor.

p. cm.

ISBN 978-1-61770-059-0 (alk. paper)

1. Romanies--Europe--Social conditions. 2. Romanies--Government policy--Europe. 3. Romanies--Legal status, laws, etc.--Europe. 4. Romanies--Migrations. 5. Romanies--Ethnic identity. 6. Europe--Emigration and immigration--Government policy. 7. Discrimination in education--Europe. 8. Europe--Ethnic relations. I. Pusca, Anca.

DX145.R64 2012

323.1191'49704--dc23

2012024431

 IDEBATE Press

Composition by Richard Johnson
Printed in the USA

Contents

Introduction:
Representing the Roma in Europe

Roma in Europe: Migration, Education, Representation builds on a previous volume, *Eastern European Roma in the EU: Mobility, Discrimination, Solutions*. While that volume focused on the achievements and failures of the EU institutional frameworks set in place to negotiate the Roma position in Europe, this anthology focuses on how Roma are represented and perceived in Europe. The various authors argue that perception plays a key role in the continuing promotion and enforcement of discriminatory policies, focusing in particular on views about Roma migration, education, and representation expressed in the media. The volume offers a framework by which to understand the continuing discrimination against Roma despite strong commitment and sustained effort by various EU institutions, national governments, Roma rights groups, and NGOs. The issues of representation and perception are key to this framework, helping us comprehend how different Roma groups become visible or invisible and how the relationship between Roma and non-Roma groups is negotiated in diverse settings, including Roma camps, schools with a large Roma presence, and local government policy meetings.

As the title suggests, the book is divided into three sections, each presenting a series of prominent contemporary case studies that have brought the issue of the Roma to wide media attention. These cases include: the controversial Roma evictions from Italy starting in 2008 and France starting in 2010; the *D.H. and Others vs. the Czech Republic* case argued before the European Court of Human Rights and the impact of the Court's ruling on Roma education across Europe. They also include the portrayal of Roma and Travelers in the media of the United Kingdom; and the 2004 case of arson at a Roma settlement in Vilnius, which was portrayed by the Lithuanian press as a Roma-led terrorist attack.

Each of these contemporary cases points to a worrisome negative trend in the representation and perception of Roma, one that is increasingly coupled with security issues and criminalization. More and more, Roma are portrayed as an "outsider" group that resists "normalization" or "integration" into majority life, hence justifying policies that effectively seek to permanently quarantine them to less visible yet easily watched spaces: Roma camps, special schools, Traveler sites. This trend is especially worrisome given that it coexists with what has perhaps been a period of the greatest sustained commitment—both financial and institutional—to the Roma cause in Europe since 1990. The striking correlation between a significant rise in financial, institutional, and rights investments in the Roma cause at the EU and local levels, and the increasingly negative representation of Roma both "at home" and "abroad"[1] suggests that these investments have had neither the desired effect nor have been able to allay the fears of the non-Roma majority (often expressed in dangerous stereotypes).

While Roma festivals, exhibits, and presence at Art Biennales are all good initiatives, their reach is often limited and fails to counteract significant negative stereotyping. Why? Because they rarely directly address key issues surrounding nomadism, poverty, criminality, migration, and segregation or engage with a wide enough audience to promote a broad debate on these issues. The current economic climate in Europe and pervasive fears about a potential disintegration of the eurozone and even the EU are not helping. With the decline of economies throughout Europe, all minority groups, including Roma, are likely to become an even more vulnerable target for attacks from a majority that is desperate to find a scapegoat for their economic woes. Increasingly associated with other migrant groups whose different cultures are perceived as permanently resisting the possibility of assimilation, Roma groups, despite generally holding EU or European passports, risk being labeled not only as a difficult minority but, increasingly, as non-Europeans.

With poverty in Europe likely to increase, now is the time to cultivate empathy rather than exclusion, to explain the economic necessity of the cyclical migration within Europe that the Roma have been following for centuries, to engage the media, and to focus on Roma projects that develop partnerships with neighboring communities. Unfortunately, what is required is both an institutional and financial effort that could become increasingly difficult in the coming years as priority is given even more to appeasing and protecting majorities. The increased social tension and criminality that usually occur at times of economic distress could again lead to greater criminal activity in vulnerable groups, including Roma—thus further contributing to negative stereotypes. If many Eastern European Roma return to their home countries in response to the continuing economic decline, guarding against increased tensions "at home" is essential.

THE ROLE OF THE MEDIA

The media play a key role in determining how Roma and other minority or migrant groups are portrayed. Thus, unless a more targeted and significant attempt is made to actively engage the media and hold them responsible for what is effectively, in many cases, a social destruction project,[2] we are likely to see a further increase in the negative stereotyping of Roma. Holding the media responsible for wrongful accusations and smear campaigns that reinforce dangerous stereotypes and oftentimes lead to violent reprisals is essential for changing negative perceptions of Roma. Academics have conducted extensive research on how these stereotypes are reinforced, yet have attracted only a limited audience. Paying closer attention to their findings could help focus anti-smear campaigns and potentially even support criminal charges that can be brought against media sources directly responsible for inciting violence. Such judicial actions could significantly affect current reporting practices and inflammatory news making.

STEREOTYPES

The current perception of the Roma in Europe is increasingly influenced by powerful stereotypes that dominate the popular imagination, making discussions on Roma inclusion difficult. These include:

- the conflation of Roma migration and Roma nomadism with crime;
- the conflation of Roma presence with mess and cost, particularly around Roma Traveler sites and Roma camps;
- the translation of Roma socioeconomic disadvantages into psychological disorders that warrant "special treatment" at schools, in hospitals, in housing, in confinement, etc.;
- the representation of Roma identity as fake, largely attributable to inconsistencies in how it is depicted by different activist and interest groups.

Each of these stereotypes serves to justify different kinds of discriminatory policies, from illegal evacuations of Roma camps and Traveler sites, to imprisonment and mistreatment under false accusations, to hostility from local authorities and hesitation to treat Roma elites and other Roma rights groups as legitimate or effective representatives of Roma communities. Each of these stereotypes also relies on an assumption of essential difference, cultural *and* physiological, a large part of which is a direct result of how Roma visibility or invisibility is managed by both different Roma groups as well as representations of these groups by others.

Conflating Nomadism and Crime

Academics such as Nando Sigona[3] and Giovanni Picker[4] have long pointed to the controversial treatment of many Roma (including Traveler groups) as "nomads" or migrant groups and the extent to which this has influenced policymaking and legislation. In fact, nomadism, perceived as a form of cyclical migration that is unique to the Roma, follows patterns similar to other forms of economic migration. Yet, by associating nomadism solely with Roma and Traveler groups, their migration begins to be considered unique, with a separate treatment under the law. The assumed dichotomy between a fixed-place culture (sedentarism) or way of life and a nomadic culture[5]—while seemingly used to provide the protection and cultural preservation of a particular lifestyle under the law—in fact, serves to ensure and even promote Roma presence as only temporary and make settlement rights difficult, if not impossible. This is particularly the case in Western European countries, especially Italy, France, and the United Kingdom, where limits to nomadism are written into law.

Unlike sedentarism, nomadism is perceived to promote isolated, family-based communities that shun outsiders and do not form particular attachments to the areas they inhabit temporarily. The perception of all Roma groups as nomads thus removes the possibility that these groups could ever become part of a wider community. Other migrant groups can, in time, claim hyphenated identities, but Roma integration into wider communities can seemingly occur only through a renunciation or denial of their identity. With nomadism historically associated in the popular imagination with crime and Roma nomadism in particular increasingly associated with brutal crimes—rapes, murders—Roma migrant groups stand little chance of getting equal treatment under the law. Debunking such strong stereotypes will take time, creativity, and increased willingness among different Roma groups to make parts of their lives more visible—and hence potentially more vulnerable—to the wider community.

Conflating Roma Presence with Mess and Cost

The mess and cost stereotype is in many ways directly connected to the Roma nomadism stereotype. Because Roma are only temporarily settled, their investment in the spaces they inhabit is perceived to be minimal, often leading to destruction of property and improper disposal of trash—which presumably the local governments, and hence local taxpayers, must pay for. Given that aesthetics plays such an essential role in the economic valuation of property, the presence of Roma groups is automatically perceived as undesirable.

While other migrant groups have managed their different aesthetics to their advantage by entering the local economy, selling culturally specific items, opening ethnic restaurants, and allowing others into their places of worship, the Roma have, for the most part, not done so. Recent trends do, however, suggest the possibility of new openness. TV shows such as *My Big Fat (American) Gypsy Wedding*, photographic tales of Roma contemporary life that offer a peek inside the new Roma palaces, or social media sites seeking to connect Roma groups from across the world offer a much-needed, albeit in many cases highly stereotypical, insight into this community.

With increased visibility comes not only the potential for increased vulnerability, but also the opportunity for others to connect and empathize. Seeing obsessively clean interiors, learning of the difficulty in negotiating basic services (e.g., trash collection) with local governments and the necessity for a strong culture of improvisation may, in time, help disassociate Roma groups from the stereotype of mess and cost.

Associating Poverty with Backwardness

Extreme Roma poverty has often been associated with social and, in some cases, psychological backwardness—with Roma groups often associated with a distant past that no longer corresponds to current social relations, conventions, and expectations. Reminiscent in many ways of the colonial treatment of "primitive" groups, current state practices toward Roma groups display a similar level of distrust and discrimination based on an assumed inferiority. This is reflected in school segregation; hospital mismanagement leading to mistreatment and decisions made on behalf of an individual or families with permanent effects; threats by social services to remove children from their Roma families; housing segregation; and other forms of documented mistreatment.

Even empathetic educators and social and health workers rely on this perceived connection between poverty and backwardness to explain how different Roma groups approach such issues as family planning and balance education and work. Well aware of these stereotypes, many Roma fear that revealing too much about their specific situation will result in unwanted state interference. Accordingly, they purposely keep social and health workers in the dark, only disclosing what they think will most likely grant them access to the services they immediately need. Educating state employees who are in charge of offering essential services to vulnerable groups takes time, personal commitment, and a government willing to invest in such services.

Data collection is key to providing these services, yet data collection on vulnerable groups, particularly Roma groups who participate in cyclical migration, is tedious and difficult work. This becomes even more challenging when, for some Roma groups, their situation can change daily—with the data then requiring updating. The fear of increased surveillance and policing through data is also legitimate given that many data collection attempts involved practices such as fingerprinting. The balance between the benefits and drawbacks of increased visibility of Roma groups is difficult to achieve; in the wrong hands, greater access to data could help justify more discriminatory policies, increased police surveillance, and further segregation.

Questioning Roma Identity

All Roma stereotyping is ultimately based on a particular understanding of Roma identity. Unlike groups whose identity is based on a specific nationality, Roma identity is not fixed, varying from place to place, time to time, and group to group. Thus, representing Roma is particularly difficult as Roma political parties and lobbying groups across Europe have shown. Roma elites are rarely seen as representative of Roma majorities and often fail to gather the necessary constituency support to truly represent them. The deep distrust of the state and acute awareness of discrimination make many Roma hesitant to show open allegiance to a Roma party; poor resources, as well as at times self-interested Roma elites, make reaching out to their constituencies difficult for Roma parties.

Defending a Roma identity becomes a political issue in itself, with different groups seeking particular forms of labeling for different reasons. While Roma parties have an interest in presenting Roma groups as united as possible, some Roma groups might have an interest in separating themselves from particularly controversial communities or only admitting to be Roma when it is in their favor. This ability to present your Roma identity as either fixed or fluid or periodically to step out of it altogether makes it particularly difficult for Roma groups to follow the typical path of representation by political party. Many studies have remarked on the difficulty of representing the Roma at the national level vs. the local level—where flexible identities can be more easily negotiated.

ABOUT THE BOOK

Roma in Europe addresses the implications of each of these stereotypes in influencing policies surrounding Roma migration, education, and media representation. Each of the three sections explores a series of prominent contemporary case studies that consider specific underlying stereotypes that can lead to violent practices, policies, and reactions. These articles also debate the sources of, consequences of, and possible solutions to addressing such stereotypes.

Migration

This section discusses whether the increased criminalization of Roma migrants in France and Italy is unique or is part of a larger trend of greater politicization of migration across Europe in general.

In Chapter 1, "Sarkozy's Law: The Institutionalization of Xenophobia in the New Europe," Dominic Thomas[6] argues that current attitudes toward Roma in France are part of a wider trend that has seen the issue of immigration shift from an integration policy to a discourse on securitization and protection of citizens, particularly under the Sarkozy administration. Right-wing supporters of Sarkozy believe that France has too many immigrants. Thus, most immigrants are increasingly seen as risks to be kept at bay, with only the best and brightest allowed in. According to Thomas, increased criminalization of migrants in general has caused many of them to move from a legal to an illegal status, leading to increased economic barriers and disparities that only feed further into the perception that many immigrants are criminals. Thomas sees this increased aversion to immigration and certain types of migrants in particular as increasingly reflected in new EU treaties. One such treaty is the Union for the Mediterranean, which promotes the circulation of goods but frowns on migration of people from certain areas of the Mediterranean who are perceived as threatening and non-desirable. He also associates the increased criminalization of Roma migrants with a wider European turn to the political right.

In Chapter 2, "The Politics of Roma Migration: Framing Identity Struggles Among Romanian and Bulgarian Roma in the Paris Region," Alexandra Nacu[7] takes a more moderate stance in regard to the perception of migrants, particularly Roma migrants in the EU. She argues that a large part of the problem of perception is that East European Roma migration is poorly understood in Western Europe by both citizens and decision makers, with the media playing a large role in distorting the image of the Roma. A further issue is the Roma's circular migration, which is often caught in the intricacies of electoral politics in France as well as in the EU-related discourses in their home countries. Roma migrants are often depicted as a culprit in both places: in France, for their perceived criminality, in their home countries for giving the entire nation a bad reputation. The treatment of the Roma is thus worsening at every point in their cyclical migration, with economic conditions also on the decline in the Roma camps in France (and other places in Europe) as well as in their home countries. With policymaking often driven by reaction to crimes committed against and by the Roma, policies are often extreme and overreactive, looking for short-term rather than long-term solutions. Focusing on the issue of health care in particular, Nacu seeks to show how local, national, and NGO actors in France are ill-prepared to deal with Roma migrants, and how even the little goodwill there is often is wasted because of erroneous assumptions about the perceived backwardness of Roma groups.

In Chapter 3, "The Roma in Italy: Racism as Usual?," Claudia Aradau[8] looks at the case of Giovanna Regianni, the 47-year-old Italian robbed and murdered in northern Rome on October 30, 2007. This horrific crime sparked the expulsion of thousands of Eastern European Roma from Rome and saw increased violence against Roma and their property across Italy. Aradau uses this case to highlight not only the dangers of misguided accusations—the Romanian Roma accused of the robbery and murder was later found innocent—and the media frenzy that surrounded them but, more important, the way in which these accusations—even when proven false—were used to promote extreme government policies and popular violence. To Aradau, this case points both to an entrenched ongoing racism that is often masked by a rhetoric of security and to the development of a neoliberal state that has long prioritized citizens and powerful majorities as the most successful entrepreneurs and given short shrift to minorities, who are perceived as less entrepreneurial and most costly for the state. The state has then sought to protect economic gain over individual and minority rights. For Aradau, the violent criminalization of the Roma is part of a wider trend in Italy as well as across Europe that sees certain groups—poor migrants and asylum-seekers—as particularly threatening. Only by acknowledging the racism of many neoliberal European states can this issue be addressed directly, according to Aradau.

In Chapter 4, "Gender as a Catalyst for Violence Against Roma in Contemporary Italy," Shannon Woodcock[9] looks at the rape case of a 14-year-old Italian in Rome and the wrongful accusation of two innocent Roma-looking Romanian men. The accusations resulted in violent reprisals against the two, leaving them beaten and hospitalized. Although the two accused were innocent, the Roma population in Rome once again became scapegoats, experiencing increased violence and discrimination fueled by a media and poster campaign sponsored by Forza Nuova, a radical right-wing group that depicted an Italian woman screaming in terror while being assaulted by a brown-skinned long-haired man. Unlike Aradau, who focuses on the relationship between the neoliberal state, racism, and immigration policy, Woodcock focuses on how gender stereotypes are vital to the mobilization of violent racism against the Roma in contemporary Italy.[10] With increasingly powerful right-wing political groups promoting and playing on potent stereotypes of Romani men as sexually aggressive toward Italian women and Romani women as baby thieves, wrongful accusations and disproportional violence toward Roma groups in Italy is on the rise. Playing on the old trope of the nation protecting its women and children, the Italian state is also using these stereotypes to justify increasingly violent actions toward Roma migrants, including evictions, expulsions, demolitions, and imprisonment.

In Chapter 5, "Locating 'The Gypsy Problem.' The Roma in Italy: Stereotyping, Labelling and 'Nomad Camps,'" Nando Sigona[11] looks at yet another strong stereotype—nomadism—surrounding Italy's Roma populations and how it is used to legitimize segregation policy. Focusing on the Scampia suburb of Naples and an arson at the Roma camp (in response to a car accident involving a Roma driver and two Italians on a motorbike), Sigona seeks to show how the label of *nomadism* is often applied indiscriminately to all Roma groups—Roma, Sinti, Camminanti, citizens, noncitizens, itinerant and non-itinerant. The label serves to justify policies of relocation that seek to push Roma camps further out where their interactions with Italian counterparts is likely to be increasingly limited. The stereotype of nomadism and practices of relocation also turn Roma camps into makeshift locations, with little investment in infrastructure or help from social services. The increased surveillance and policing of these camps turns what, in many cases, is a residual population into a forced "nomadic" one, inhabiting spaces that are by definition designed to be "temporary." This, according to Sigona, is nothing but an attempt to effectively deny the Roma a right to exist as a settled group and as equal members of the society.

Education

This section assesses the wide-ranging effects of the 2007 European Court of Human Rights ruling in D.H. and Others v. Czech Republic, *which addressed the discrimination against Roma children in the Czech educational system.*

In Chapter 6, "Solving the 'Gypsy Problem': *D.H. and Others v. The Czech Republic*," William New and Michael Merry[12] question the extent to which court rulings by themselves can lead to decreased marginalization and segregation of Roma, especially in schools. For them the case, which brought together the complaints of 18 Roma parents who argued that their children were discriminated against by being sent to special schools for children with learning disabilities, emerges as an important "discourse moment" that was able to open an essential debate on Roma parents' choices and how these are affected by cultural and social limitations as well as institutional racism. This "discourse moment" alone however, cannot solve the larger problem of a lack of what they call "social and cultural capital" essential for negotiating the Czech Republic's complicated and highly constrained education system whose structure is unlikely to change anytime soon. According to the authors, until Roma parents learn to "command a mode of speech that would allow them to communicate as equals with school authorities,"[13] their claims will not be recognized as legitimate and they will not have the power to advance their children's cause. Consequently, they see the positive ruling at the European Court of Human Rights as limited in its effect, at least when it comes to the Czech Republic.

Lilla Farkas,[14] from the European Roma Rights Centre, adopts a more positive attitude. In Chapter 7, "The Scene After Battle: What Is the Victory in D.H. Worth and Where to Go From Here?", she argues that the European Court of Human Rights ruling was path-breaking in a number of respects. The ruling recognized patterns of discrimination against and lack of equal access to education for Roma as a persistent problem throughout Europe. The Court accepted indirect discrimination as a violation of the European Convention on Human Rights and acknowledged the relevance of statistics to prove such discrimination. It also accepted a no waiver of the right to nondiscrimination argument and recognized the Roma as an ethnic minority group requiring special protection. Farkas argues that despite the prohibitive cost of litigation—in excess of $250,000 (which very few plaintiffs could otherwise afford without outside help)—the ruling has already positively influenced other similar rulings in Hungary, Bulgaria, and Greece. In addition, it has opened the way for NGOs to bring *actio popularis* claims in front of national courts in Romania, Bulgaria, and Hungary. Farkas thus sees this ruling as not only promising but as a potential future avenue to address other forms of Roma discrimination and segregation.

Representation

This section builds on the previous two, addressing the increased criminalization and segregation of Roma through the lens of Roma stereotyping and Roma identity. Articles question the extent to which there is a fixed Roma identity, lifestyle, and culture and whether the majority resistance to accepting this culture can be blamed on negative stereotyping.

In Chapter 8, "Talking About Gypsies: The Notion of Discourse as Control," Joanna Richardson[15] argues that most discourses and debates on the Roma serve to justify different forms of control. For her, "words and terms often used in the discourse around Gypsies and Travellers are not passively describing a situation but instead they are interpreting them,"[16] leading to increased pressure on Roma to conform to norms of settlement and the policing and welfare strategies required to reinforce these norms. Concentrating on media portrayals and on interviews with Roma and Traveler focus groups in Colchester, United Kingdom, Richardson seeks to identify the nature and power of the specific discourses of "mess and cost" surrounding these groups and how local politicians use them to justify limited site provision and facilities. She argues that Roma stereotyping is employed not only by local media but also by local councilors and neighbors in policymaking, welfare distribution, and in attempts to settle disputes and claims over land. For her, Roma identity is negotiated by outsiders in close connection with these stereotypes, which are, in turn, used to justify discriminatory practices.

In Chapter 9, "Ethnic Minority Identity and Movement Politics: The Case of the Roma in the Czech Republic and Slovakia," Peter Vermeersch[17] discusses how Roma identity is shaped by Roma activists and Roma elites in the Czech Republic, Slovakia, and beyond. He argues that their conception of Romani identity is often more closely tied to their political strategies than any attempt to represent particular Roma groups. This, to him, becomes particularly obvious in the mixed success that Roma activists and Roma elites have had in advocating on behalf of the Roma in the Czech Republic and Slovakia. While they have succeeded in getting the term *Roma* adopted in mainstream politics and have gained increased access to the domestic policymaking process, they have failed to attract large constituencies or effectively organize into single-interest political parties. Vermeersch argues that this is largely the result of competing understandings of Romani identity and increased pressure from national and transnational institutions to get the Roma to represent themselves as a united group. While unity in identity and discourse is key for political success—as the backing of the International Romani Union by the Organization for Security and Co-operation in Europe and the Council of Europe proves—because Roma identity is so closely connected to negative stereotypes, it often fails to effectively mobilize people around their ethnicity. The dilemma, as Vermeersch explains, is that "the more they emphasize their ethnic identity, the more they appear to be held responsible for what is typically called the 'Romani problem.'"[18]

In Chapter 10, "Chimeras of Terror: Disciplining Roma Identity in Lithuania," Jurate Kavaliauskaite[19] picks up on Richardson and Vermeersch's arguments about the negative effects of current discourses on Roma by focusing on a 2004 incident of arson at a Roma settlement in Vilnius. A local Roma was wrongly accused and increasingly portrayed as a "terrorist" threat. By examining the evolution of how the incident was portrayed in the local media, Kavaliauskaite seeks to understand how Lithuanian authorities were allowed to provocatively label Roma as "terrorists" without major public dissent. She argues that it was largely the result of how "their collective identity is permanently molded by scandals, police reports and repeating stereotypes"[20] by self-interested agenda-setters. These individuals, who maintain the greatest influence on the media, seek to justify the necessity for an increased marginalization, silencing, and invisibility of Roma groups.

Roma in Europe seeks to show how different forms and techniques of Roma representation and Roma stereotyping in particular are often used to justify discriminatory, violent, and segregationist practices against Roma in migration, education, health care, and housing. By focusing on some of the most prominent stereotypes that have emerged across Europe and the extent to which these stereotypes are often reinforced by the very people who are charged with protecting the Roma, the articles in this volume reveal how dangerous these stereotypical discourses are and the importance of addressing them on a wider scale.

As with most forms of discursive control, unraveling the power of these stereotypes is not an easy task; the power of the discourse does not lie in any one particular hand but in many. From the police, state authorities, local councilors, Roma activists and elites, and right-wing movements to news writers, neighbors, and readers, we are all implicated. A simple nod in one direction versus another is sometimes all it takes for violence to erupt as a result of this discourse. How the Roma are represented by others or represent themselves is thus no small matter. Increased Roma visibility, understanding, and access to otherwise completely secluded parts of Roma life, although dangerous, is perhaps the only way to create the possibility for a connection and empathy—the fundamental pillars for a community of different people to coexist peacefully.

NOTES

1. "At home and abroad" is a phrase often used in Roma literature. It refers to their home countries and the other European countries to which they travel.

2. Ivan Leudar and Jiri Nekvapil, "Presentations of Romanies in the Czech Media: On Category Work in Television Debates," *Discourse and Society* 11, no. 4 (2000): 487–513; Marco Solimene, "'These Romanians Have Ruined Italy': Xoraxane Roma, Romanian Roma and Rome," *Journal of Modern Italian Studies* 16, no. 5 (2011): 637–651.

3. Nando Sigona, "The Governance of Romani People in Italy: Discourse, Policy and Practice," *Journal of Modern Italian Studies* 16, no. 5 (2011): 590–606; Nando Sigona, "Locating 'The Gypsy Problem.' The Roma in Italy: Stereotyping, Labelling and 'Nomad Camps,'" *Journal of Ethnic and Migration Studies* 31, no. 4 (2005): 741–756.

4. Giovanni Picker, "Welcome 'in.' Left-Wing Tuscany and Romani Migrants (1987–2007)," *Journal of Modern Italian Studies* 16, no. 5 (2011): 607–620.

5. Ibid., 613.

6. Dominic Thomas, "Sarkozy's Law: The Institutionalization of Xenophobia in the New Europe," *Radical Philosophy* 153 (January/February 2009): 7–12.

7. Alexandra Nacu, "The Politics of Roma Migration: Framing Identity Struggles Among Romanian and Bulgarian Roma in the Paris Region," *Journal of Ethnic and Migration Studies* 37, no. 1 (2010): 135–150.

8. Claudia Aradau, "The Roma in Italy: Racism as Usual?," *Radical Philosophy* 153 (January/February 2009): 2–7.

9. Shannon Woodcock, "Gender as a Catalyst for Violence Against Roma in Contemporary Italy," *Patterns of Prejudice* 44, no. 5 (2010): 469–488.

10. Ibid., 469.

11. Sigona, "Locating 'The Gypsy Problem,'" 741–756.

12. William New and Michael Merry, "Solving the 'Gypsy Problem': D.H. and Others v. the Czech Republic," *Comparative Education Review* 54, no. 3 (2010): 393–414.

13. Ibid., 397.

14. Lilla Farkas, "The Scene After Battle: What Is the Victory in D.H. Worth and Where to Go from Here?," *Roma Rights Journal* 1 (2008): 51–62.

15. Joanna Richardson, "Talking About Gypsies: The Notion of Discourse as Control," *Housing Studies* 21, no. 1 (2007): 77–96.

16. Ibid., 79.

17. Peter Vermeersch, "Ethnic Minority Identity and Movement Politics: The Case of the Roma in the Czech Republic and Slovakia," *Ethnic and Racial Studies* 26, no. 5 (2003): 879–901.

18. Ibid., 898.

19. Jurate Kavaliauskaite, "Chimeras of Terror: Disciplining Roma Identity in Lithuania," *Alternatives* 33 (2008): 153–171.

20. Ibid., 160.

REFERENCES

Aradau, Claudia. "The Roma in Italy: Racism as Usual?" *Radical Philosophy* 153 (January/February 2009): 2–7.

Farkas, Lilla. "The Scene After Battle: What Is the Victory in D.H. Worth and Where to Go from Here?" *Roma Rights Journal* 1 (2008): 51–62.

Kavaliauskaite, Jurate. "Chimeras of Terror: Disciplining Roma Identity in Lithuania." *Alternatives* 33 (2008): 153–171.

Leudar, Ivan, and Jiri Nekvapil. "Presentations of Romanies in the Czech Media: On Category Work in Television Debates." *Discourse and Society* 11, no. 4 (2000): 487–513.

Nacu, Alexandra. "The Politics of Roma Migration: Framing Identity Struggles Among Romanian and Bulgarian Roma in the Paris Region." *Journal of Ethnic and Migration Studies* 37, no. 1 (2010): 135–150.

New, William, and Michael Merry. "Solving the 'Gypsy Problem': *D.H. and Others v. The Czech Republic*." *Comparative Education Review* 54, no. 3 (2010): 393–414.

Picker, Giovanni. "Welcome 'in.' Left-Wing Tuscany and Romani Migrants (1987–2007)." *Journal of Modern Italian Studies* 16, no. 5 (2011): 607–620.

Richardson, Joanna. "Talking About Gypsies: The Notion of Discourse as Control." *Housing Studies* 21, no. 1 (2007): 77–96.

Sigona, Nando. "The Governance of Romani People in Italy: Discourse, Policy and Practice." *Journal of Modern Italian Studies* 16, no. 5 (2011): 590–606.

———. "Locating 'The Gypsy Problem.' The Roma in Italy: Stereotyping, Labelling and 'Nomad Camps.'" *Journal of Ethnic and Migration Studies* 31, no. 4 (2005): 741–756.

Solimene, Marco. "'These Romanians Have Ruined Italy': Xoraxane Roma, Romanian Roma and Rome." *Journal of Modern Italian Studies* 16, no. 5 (2011): 637–651.

Thomas, Dominic. "Sarkozy's Law: The Institutionalization of Xenophobia in the New Europe." *Radical Philosophy* 153 (January/February 2009): 7–12.

Vermeersch, Peter. "Ethnic Minority Identity and Movement Politics: The Case of the Roma in the Czech Republic and Slovakia." *Ethnic and Racial Studies* 26, no.5 (2003): 879–901.

Woodcock, Shannon. "Gender as a Catalyst for Violence Against Roma in Contemporary Italy." *Patterns of Prejudice* 44, no. 5 (2010): 469–488.

Section I:
Roma Migration to France and Italy

The question of Roma migration has once again been put at the top of the European agenda in the wake of the violent Roma expulsions from camps across France and Italy in 2008 and 2010 and tense discussions over the legality of such actions.. Yet what has been largely presented as an issue unique to France and Italy might turn out to be part of a much wider European antidiscriminatory trend that increasingly sees and treats certain migrants, Roma among them, as criminals—thus leading to what has been labeled as increased politicization and securitization of migration across Europe.

This section debates the extent to which such increased politicization and securitization involves Roma migrants in particular or is part of a more general trend that considers most forms of immigration to be threatening. Focusing on the specific events that led to the Roma expulsions in France and Italy and the Roma stereotypes through which they were initially addressed, the authors in this section discuss the potential sources of these stereotypes, their dangerous effects, and potential solutions.

Chapter 1: Sarkozy's Law: The Institutionalization of Xenophobia in the New Europe

*by Dominic Thomas**

France's recently elected hyper-president, Nicolas Sarkozy, assumed the presidency of the European Union on 1 July 2008 under acrimonious conditions triggered by the 13 June 2008 Irish 'no' vote on the Lisbon Treaty. Nevertheless, France has been able to obtain virtually immediate consensus on two significant and connected initiatives: the European Union Pact on Migration and Asylum and the Union for the Mediterranean project. Closer scrutiny of these French priorities provides interesting insights into broader debates on the contested parameters of a European identity.

Recent developments in Europe shed new and disquieting light on the original organizing principle of the European Union, according to which the EU was to become a 'family' of democratic European countries. EU membership has continued to grow (adding new members in 2004 and 2007) and this growth has been accompanied by the liberalization of internal frontiers. These measures have also coincided, however, with heightened concerns over border control and the vulnerability of 'Fortress Europe'. At the same time, assertions of national sovereignty have taken on an increasingly shrill and reactionary intensity, raising important questions about belonging, cohesiveness, and the sanctity of the original structuring aspirations and objectives.

France has, historically, played an extremely important role in defining EU identity, and policies and measures concerning migration and security precede the Sarkozy administration. In the Third Annual Report on Migration and Integration (2007), the EU emphasized the point that the 'integration of third-country nationals is a process of mutual accommodation by both the host societies and the immigrants and an essential factor in realizing the full benefits of immigration'.[1] However, French determination to impose and extend a key domestic policy agenda item throughout the EU zone must be understood as the outcome of electoral campaign promises made by then-candidate Sarkozy to his extreme right-wing constituencies. Polls conducted during the 2007 French presidential elections revealed that a majority of Sarkozy supporters believed there were 'too many immigrants in France'. In turn, this has resulted in a shift away from policies concerned with the integration of migrants towards an emphasis on protecting its 'own' citizens from migrants through more restrictive laws, regulations and restrictions.

THE POLITICS OF 'CO-DEVELOPMENT'

The creation in 2007 of the new Ministry of Immigration, National Identity, Integration and Co-Development essentially completed a project Nicolas Sarkozy started as minister of the interior (2005–07). In that capacity, he had already made the fight against illegal immigration a priority, resulting in dramatic increases in expulsions during both this period (35,921 in 2005, 34,127 in 2006, and 20,411 during the first six months of 2007, a 19 per cent increase over the similar period in the previous year) and in the last couple of years.[2] Under the leadership of his close friend and political ally, Brice Hortefeux, the new ministry has endeavoured to capitalize upon the widespread belief that national identity has been eroded. For example, DNA testing has been proposed as a 'scientific' way for 'foreign families' to prove their ties to France, but instead has served to support prevalent assumptions that *visible* minorities and immigrants belong to a distinct social configuration, outside the dominant order of things. Likewise, reforms to immigration policy have overlapped with the consolidation of extreme right-wing positions in Europe or at the very least their mainstreaming by right-wing political parties; calls for increased border control, heightened security, and the expansion of police powers have become routine in many European countries. The new preoccupation with border security, while reviving discussions on European identity and integration, have encouraged monolithic interpretations of history that fail to account for the fact that European populations are more intimately related to non-European ones than some European people wish to believe.

The structure of the new French ministry is organized around four main priorities: chosen/selective immigration based on certain skill sets; the fight over illegal immigration, the introduction of integration contracts (comprising language proficiency tests and a commitment to respecting Republican values and ideals); and measures aimed at co-development partnerships with sending countries. The key objective has been to reduce dramatically family-related immigration (i.e. reunification) in favour of economic migration (i.e. exploitation).

To this end, domestic policy and foreign policy can no longer be decoupled, since they unambiguously concern both facets of immigration: namely, the dynamics of internal race relations and policies aimed at controlling the entry of migrants into France. Naturally, these mechanisms reinforce existing paradigms concerning the criminalization of poverty in the *banlieue*, and these have been transferred to economic models that essentialize the criminality of immigrants. These labels emerge as inseparable components of the illegal migrant's 'clandestine' status in the EU, a presence that is therefore assumed *a priori* as a 'risk' factor, while also being structured around comfortable and shared negative representations. (A similar trend applies to the United States, where immigration discourse has moved away from seeing it as a positive historical phenomenon to viewing it as an undesirable component of globalization.)

The politics of 'co-development', meanwhile, essentially reproduce age-old patterns of labour acquisition in the global South; all that has changed is that the coordinates of human capital exploitation have shifted from the healthiest and the strongest (slaves) to the best and the brightest (employees). Brice Hortefeux defends this dimension, arguing that these mechanisms do not entail a 'brain drain' but rather a 'circulation of competence'.[3] This position entails consideration neither for the nature of neo-colonial relations and the circumstances that trigger migration, usually in the guise of perilous Mediterranean crossings whose recalibration echoes an earlier *middle passage*, nor for the broader unidirectionality of the process of labour circulation. In fact, France has been actively establishing *quotas* with African-sending countries, agreeing for example on 25 February 2008 with Senegal to issue 'competence and skills cards' to young Senegalese workers in return for assistance in fighting illegal immigration, improving border control, and streamlining the process of repatriating illegals (similar deals are being pursued with Benin, Congo Republic, Gabon, Morocco, Togo, etc.).

Before we look at the ways in which the French government has sought to extend these policies to the EU, we should briefly consider earlier EU initiatives. In October 1999, EU leaders at a European Council meeting in Tampere, Finland,

> called for a common immigration policy which would include more dynamic policies to ensure the integration of third-country nationals residing in the European Union. They agreed that the aim of this integration policy should be to grant third-country nationals rights and obligations comparable to those of citizens of the EU. The European Union is keen to promote economic and social cohesion throughout its territory. As such, integrating third-country nationals has become a focal point of the European Union's immigration policy.[4]

For many years, EU leaders have underscored the importance of fostering *prosperity*, *solidarity* and *security* alongside immigration. These guidelines have been both augmented and redefined, however, under the aegis of the new European Union Pact on Migration and Asylum, presented to the European Council of Ministers of Home Affairs/Interior and Justice on 7 and 8 July 2008 in Cannes, France. Brice Hortefeux underlined the imperative of achieving uniformity among the disparate national mechanisms currently in place and the need to regulate legal immigration and asylum policy concerning third-country migrants (i.e. any person who is not a national of an EU member state). Proposed measures were targeted at developing a common and coordinated policy, one that would endeavour to harmonize approaches to legal and illegal immigration: the first to proceed through a European Blue Card Scheme designed to address internal labour shortages, the second to be controlled through a newly integrated series of 'security measures', consisting of deportation, detention, expulsion, regularization, repatriation, return directives. Approved in principle in July, these measures were voted on at the October 2008 EU summit meeting.

In some cases, at least, these tougher regulations have been counterproductive. In recent years it has become harder for immigrants to achieve regularization; expulsions are accompanied by a five-year ban from the EU, which, rather than solving the initial problem, merely ensures the illegality of returnees; many workers find themselves reduced to the status of illegals when they are made redundant; and, finally, 'returning' illegals to third-party states merely transfers their status, vulnerability and problems to another space. At the same time, the kinds of economic disparities long observed in the global South are also increasingly in evidence in the economically prosperous regions of the North; riots in France during the autumn of 2005 underscored the class and racial marginality of disadvantaged populations.

WITHOUT PAPERS, OR RIGHTS

Economic migrants, faced with these new pressures, have recently become increasingly vocal in their demand for social and political rights. 'Illegals' around the world are slowly beginning to emerge from the dubious 'safety' of legal invisibility, and have begun to press more directly for public representation. During April and May 2008, several French businesses (with support from the CGT and other trade unions) went on strike to support the illegal workers known as the *sans-papiers*, and called for regularization. This action also served to counter popular misconceptions and stereotypes concerning illegals, bringing attention to the 'legal' work they perform and contributions they make, but also signalling the dangers of restrictive employment laws in exposing workers to exploitative employment practices that European workers would find unacceptable.

EU laws designed to punish abusive employers exist, notably Article 5 of the Charter of Fundamental Rights that concerns the *Prohibition of slavery and forced labour*: (i) No one shall be held in slavery or servitude; (ii) No one shall be required to perform forced or compulsory labour; (iii) Trafficking in human beings is prohibited.[5] The European Court of Human Rights in Strasbourg is also committed to protecting human beings from slavery, servitude and forced or compulsory labour. Nevertheless, abusive practices have been widely tolerated, and extensively documented. Hugo Brady has shown that

> The Commission estimates that there are around 8 million illegal immigrants in the EU, and that this number increases by 500,000 to 1 million every year.... These workers are drawn to Europe mainly by the knowledge that they can find work illegally in the construction, agriculture, cleaning and hospitality industries. Many end up doing under-paid or dangerous work.[6]

Fabrizio Gatti, the recipient of the 2006 award 'For diversity—against discrimination' has provided a compelling account of the glaring failure of the EU to address exploitative labour practices. Gatti equates current employment conditions with slavery:

> In order to pass a week undercover amidst the slave labourers it is necessary to undertake a voyage that takes one beyond the limits of human imagination. But this is the only way to report on the horrors that the immigrants are forced to endure.... They're all foreigners; all employed as so-called 'black workers', the name used to describe illegal, untaxed and underpaid work scams.... Down here they also ignore the Constitution: articles one, two and three, as well as the Universal Declaration of Rights.[7]

Considerable disparities persist in the EU concerning integration and the required degree of adherence to national codes and values. The Union for the Mediterranean (in effect the culmination of the Barcelona Process that began back in 1995) was agreed on 13 July 2008 in Paris, and signed by the 27 EU members and 43 non-EU countries (except Libya): it extends both the economic and the social priorities of the EU Pact on Migration and Asylum, while simultaneously promoting the circulation of goods but not people. (France's support for the Union for the Mediterranean project and its implicit position that Turkey's proper role should be confined to this body rather than the EU itself, serves as a strong indicator as to what they will be prepared to accept in terms of future EU membership.) Efforts at defining a common or shared European identity have been informed by such categories as *desirable* and *undesirable* subjects, and Eurosceptics and repeated 'no' votes (France, the Netherlands, Ireland) have also contributed to feelings of disidentification alongside rising xenophobic tendencies aimed at non-EU members. The very concept of 'integration contracts' reveals the degree to which the French authorities continue to subscribe to and embrace a long-held belief that such a European identity either exists or can be achieved. What is less clear is the degree to which any such identity will depend on an increasingly rigid polarization of 'insiders' and 'outsiders', on the increasingly paranoid resentment that divides privileged members of the 'family of democratic European countries' from their extra-European cousins.

Repeated attempts have been made to connect the fight against illegal immigration to a discourse of human rights concerned with the protection of vulnerable subjects from fraudulent traffickers and employers. Abundant evidence of growing insensitivity to migrants demonstrates their ineffectiveness, as do the findings of demographers who have demonstrated Europe's long-term need for cheap labour. Instead, obsessive concern with the apparent need to delineate a European identity in a newly 'uncertain' global landscape has encouraged legislators to approach immigration exclusively in terms of security and economic policy, without adequate mechanisms for ensuring that basic standards of equality and justice apply to the new global migrant working class. The resulting dehumanization of migrants and their characterization as economic burdens (immediately scapegoated during downturns in the global economy) have made it easier to expel them and to dissociate such harsh measures from any reference to the migrants' own experience. Additionally, the commitment to a dramatic reduction of family reunification in favour of the economic migration needed to build a more cohesive 'European family' ignores and occludes the collective migration experience over a much longer historical time frame. If more attention were paid to this history, debates about European identity and singularity would be less distorted and short-sighted.

'New Europe', Old History

In the absence of such attention, questions about the nature of 'Europeanness' are difficult to address. Current talk about the emergence of a *new* Europe remains exceptionally vague. EU member states have denounced evidence of ultra-nationalism and human rights abuses in countries seeking EU membership, but do not always adhere to those standards themselves. Proposed measures in Italy to fingerprint and register Gypsies (communities who were previously expelled by Mussolini in the late 1920s and subsequently exterminated during the Second World War), along with the similar treatment of Roma populations in Portugal, France and elsewhere, are a case in point. European immigration policy increasingly depends on multilateral and non-reciprocal Euro-Mediterranean agreements and partnerships that serve to restrict population movements and duplicate age-old historical patterns of exploitation and uneven exchange. French–African relations were conceived from the beginning in terms of racist and culturalist supremacy, and they continue to shape patterns of neo colonial domination and exploitation that contribute directly to the very problems of destitution and emigration that France bemoans. EU subsidies and biased trade policies ensure that 'co-development' policies serve largely to perpetuate African poverty. EU immigration policies pay obsessive attention to the problems associated with poverty in the global South, yet, as Philippe Bernard has shown, for every migrant who tries to move illegally from Africa to an OECD country there are more than four people who migrate illegally from one African country to another (4 million and 17 million people respectively).[8]

A speech delivered by President Sarkozy in Senegal last summer ('The tragedy of Africa is that the African has never really entered history...') drew liberally on racist stereotypes recycled from colonial times. Much of the language used to describe today's clandestine and 'illegal' immigrants was first developed, in the nineteenth century, in response to those *indigènes* of Algeria or the Ivory Coast who stubbornly refused to appreciate the virtues of the French *mission civilisatrice*. Today, as Mauritanian filmmaker Med Hondo has argued, 'seeing Africans chained together like criminals prior to forceful repatriation is a spectacle that does little to honour those states who claim to embrace the rights of Man and democratic ideals. Nothing is worse for a person than humiliation. This has become the daily lot of immigrants in the countries of the North'.[9] Drawing on more recent historical memories, the French government has also established target figures for the expulsion of illegal migrants that have resulted in often arbitrary *rafles* (round-ups) of subjects—a term that evokes the 1942 *rafle du Vel d'Hiv*, for starters, which led to the deportation of French Jews to Nazi concentration camps.

Europe cannot afford to ignore such antecedents when its leaders have recourse to terminology and procedures of this kind. The racial profiling of 'insiders', the return of biology and race, rising Islamophobia and anti-Muslim sentiment, the demonization of asylum-seekers—all these measures are directly related to the most troubling sequences in European history. Any searching genealogy of the European family yields a lesson, first and foremost, on the institutionalization of xenophobia.

Notes

1. Communication from the Commission to the Council, the European Parliament, the European Economic and Social Committee and the Committee of the Regions, *Third Annual Report on Migration and Integration*, Brussels, 11 September 2007, p. 3.

2. *Les Orientations de la politique de l'immigration*, La Documentation Française, Paris, 2007.

3. www.immigration.gouv.fr/article.php?id_article=640, 19 June 2008.

4. http://ec.europa.eu/justice_home/fsj/immigration/integration/fsj_immigration_integration_en.htm, September 2007.

5. Available at www.europarl.europa.eu/comparl/libe/elsj/charter/art05/default_en.htm#6.

6. Hugo Brady, *EU Migration Policy* (2008), www.cer.org.uk/pdf/briefing_813.pdf, p. 27.

7. Fabrizio Gatti, http://espresso.repubblica.it/dettaglio/I%20was%20a%20slave%20in%20Puglia/1373950, 4 September 2006.

8. In any case, though Europe has been and remains actively complicit in the destitution of large parts of Africa, the defenders of Fortress Europe cannot directly govern the behaviour of the people they exclude: 'in spite of all the obstacles, xenophobia and expulsions, when one considers the multiple forms of migration, Africans emerge as the most mobile inhabitants of the planet'. Philippe Bernard, 'L'autre immigration africaine,' *Le Monde* 26 June 2008, p. 2.

9. Cited in Ibrahima Signaté, *Med Hondo: Un cinéaste rebelle*, Présence Africaine, Paris, 1994, p. 72.

*Dominic Thomas is professor of French and Francophone studies and Italian at the University of California at Los Angeles.

This article first appeared in *Radical Philosophy* 153 (January 2009) and is reprinted here with permission from the publisher.

Chapter 2: The Politics of Roma Migration: Framing Identity Struggles Among Romanian and Bulgarian Roma in the Paris Region

by Alexandra Nacu*

The aim of this paper is to understand how identity shapes the politics of Roma migration at European, national and local scales. I studied Romanian and Bulgarian Roma migrants living in slums around Paris through participant observation and in-depth interviews. I analyse the interplay of political and social intervention concerning this population, with an emphasis on humanitarian medical intervention. In these interactions, the Roma identity is often ethnicised, and the Roma in turn use this identity construction in their daily struggles with public institutions in order to gain more control over their lives. Their migration is the source of a new form of urban marginalisation, which continues despite both Romania's and Bulgaria's EU accession.

INTRODUCTION

Through featuring periodically in Western European media in spectacular images of police interventions, breaking news of criminal activity or shocking scenes of extreme poverty, East European Roma migrations are often poorly understood by ordinary citizens and decision-makers. In the last few years, Roma migrations have become increasingly politicised, both at an international and a local scale—facing popular protest and becoming the target of electoral politics in Italy in the 2008 municipal elections, or undergoing more-downplayed local politicisation in France.

My hypothesis is that questions of identity—especially involving struggles over the legitimate definition of the migrant group—are central to the way in which Roma migrations are managed by national and local actors and also to how the Roma respond to these actions and construct their own local struggles. My study looks at how identity impacts on the politics of migration at European, national and local scales. The particular angle of my fieldwork led me to become interested in the Roma as a target of public health policies—healthcare, and especially the doctor–patient interaction—allowing me to observe how identity is embodied in them.

The place of the Roma in the building of national identity has been well documented in Eastern European countries (Stewart 1997), where the Roma represent an important—and often discriminated against—ethnic minority (European Commission 2004; Guglielmo 2004), though less so in a migration context. Therefore, I demonstrate in this article how perceptions of the Roma also affect politics in the target countries, especially in the Paris region. I show that, although the Roma are often perceived as alien, their migrations share multiple features of other East European migrations to the West.

This paper is based on a five-year period of sociological fieldwork which began as part of a doctoral study in two Roma districts in Bucharest and Sofia, and then went on to follow contemporary Roma migration paths to slums and camps around Paris—the temporary homes of several thousand migrants from Romania and Bulgaria, most but not all of whom are Roma. I undertook participant observation with the organisation 'Médecins du Monde' (hereafter MdM) in Paris, conducting interviews with migrants, local authorities and health professionals. The main fieldwork for this article was carried out between 2003 and 2007, although observation is still ongoing.

ENLARGING BREACHES: ROMA MIGRANTS WITHIN CHANGING EUROPEAN IMMIGRATION REGULATIONS

The first Eastern European Roma in this migration wave arrived in the Paris region at the beginning of the 1990s. More followed at the beginning of the 2000s, a turning-point being the suppression of Schengen visa requirements for Romania (in 2001) and Bulgaria (in 2002) which opened the way to a three-month stay as a tourist, provided possession of a required amount of money was proved. These are circular migrations between the regions of origin and Paris, people migrating for several months at a time then returning to their home towns or villages for short time spans. The fact that citizens of Romania and Bulgaria no longer needed visas in order to travel to France did not mean that the status of these migrants was legal: indeed, before their countries' EU accession in 2007, many migrants used to shift between a legal and an illegal status, regularly going to their home countries to 'clean' their passports (a term used in Romanian and Bulgarian). This further increased migration circularity.

Since the beginning of the 1990s, the presence of Eastern European migrants, and specifically that of the Roma, has been a sensitive issue in the European Union accession process for Romania and Bulgaria. The migration of poor Roma also raised issues of identity for the home-country populations: not being assimilated, and being perceived by the media and important sections of the non-Roma population as a 'deviant' group, have become crucial issues for the population in both countries—very acutely so in Romania, home to Eastern Europe's largest Roma minority.

EU accession marked a change in security and immigration policy regarding the Roma (as was the case with all Eastern migrants), whereas it meant no notable change in the everyday plight of the Roma, as we shall see later. Suffice to say that, before 2007, the management of Roma migration was chiefly a national matter (often that of the home countries) whereas, since 2007, it has become an increasing issue of local politics for the target regions, especially the Parisian region.

Before EU Accession: Mobility Despite International Regulations

Indeed, the pre-accession period is a time when 'control at a distance' (Bigo and Guild 2005) characterises Western European states' migration policies, relying on the countries of origin to filter the arrival of migrants. Thus, the task of controlling and sorting migrants, or of sanctioning overstayers, was passed on to the countries of origin, who thus had the chief role in repression. When a Romanian or Bulgarian migrant outstayed the three-month period, not only remaining in the Schengen area but also going back to the country of origin became problematic, as the home-country authorities could confiscate passports or issue an interdiction on leaving the country for several months or years. However, there were breaches in these regulations: returning migrants could use informal payment at the border, or chose a different way back—for example through Istanbul for Bulgarian Roma.

Thus control at a distance translated into an increased arbitrariness and inequality between migrants at the border. An example was the sudden enforcement of passport control at the Romanian border in the summer of 2005, leading to the confiscation of several thousand passports in three days.[1] Among these policies one can also mention the agreements—signed in 2004 between the then French Minister of the Interior, Nicolas Sarkozy, and the governments of Romania and Bulgaria—for the return and reintegration of Roma migrants, or IOM's voluntary return programmes[2] which were generally used by migrants to return to their home countries for short periods of rest before heading back to France (FIDH and MdM 2003).

Social inequalities and ethnic discrimination also played an important role in this 'control at a distance' and, thus, in Roma's access to international mobility. Informal payments lay a heavier burden upon poorer migrants. Several interviews I carried out with Roma and non-Roma migrants indicate that Roma were more often asked for informal payments. Today, still, they are also more liable to face identity controls in the streets of Western cities. But inequalities in mobility were also resented at the scale of the two emigration countries: their delay (compared to other Central European countries) in accessing visa-free travel to the West, and later a right to work in the EU, has been a subject of choice in the national press and a recurring electoral issue.

Simultaneously, the EU promoted Roma-targeted measures in the candidate countries through pre-accession programmes such as PHARE,[3] in close conjunction with international agencies such as the UNDP and the World Bank. Whereas these efforts did put the Roma on national agendas, the way the question was framed in the national contexts was ambiguous and contributed to creating competition between the Roma and other more-or-less impoverished groups (Nacu 2006). The actual impact of these programmes has been widely criticised as having no real effect on the plight of the Roma (Guglielmo 2004). This competition also takes place within the respective migration frameworks where avoiding being lumped together with Roma migrants has become an important concern for Romanian and Bulgarian migrants. This is reflected in interviews with non-Roma migrants, through constant stigmatisation of Roma migrants as offenders or beggars and praise of non-Roma migrants as hard workers.

Thus, an internal tension emerged in EU pre-accession requirements: on the one hand, the EU was promoting equal rights for the Roma, who faced discrimination in the accession countries. On the other hand, it pressurised those countries to keep the Roma within their borders (for example by enforcing border control, requirements for travelling etc.), thereby denying their equality with other citizens (Castle-Karenova 2003). Pointing to human rights violation in the candidate countries was, however, a doubled-edged sword for Western states, as it amounted to supporting claims for granting the Roma asylum (Castle-Karenova 2003). Thus, progressively, EU emissaries replaced human rights language with that of the fight against inequalities.

After EU Accession: Towards Migration Control at the Local Level

Since their countries' EU accession in 2007, Roma from Bulgaria and Romania, and their fellow citizens, have a right to travel and reside for a limited period in France (as in all EU countries); however, the French labour market did not open for the newly entered countries. Moreover, a government regulation[4] states that Romanians and Bulgarians are liable to receive notification to leave the country (*'Obligation de Quitter le Territoire Français'* or *OQTF*) in case they become an 'unreasonable burden for the French social assistance system', a somewhat unclear notion that makes Roma liable to be fined if they are caught begging in the streets. It is under this regulation that, from 2007 on, many Roma living in camps were collectively given *OQTFs*. These were followed by collective 'voluntary returns' by plane or bus, organised by the IOM, even as their camps were being destroyed by the police.[5] Even if many receive such *OQTFs*, or sign 'voluntary return' documents, they tend to return to France after a short stay in their home country.

Thus, although officially Roma are no longer deported to their native countries, their plight has not much improved and remains uncertain and precarious. If a police control no longer means deportation with no possibility of return, it still entails threats on their precarious habitat and a break in social links (family, housing, work, school).

As we shall see later, post-EU integration means that the management of this population was increasingly passed from national authorities to local authorities. The management of sometimes large groups of illegal immigrants and squatters has become an issue for many municipalities, especially those in the former 'red belt'. This region comprises mostly communist and socialist mayors in the north and east of Paris, and contains many industrial wastelands and deserted areas which attract squatters. Migrants have to juggle between visibility and discretion in order to be tolerated for as long as possible.

ROMA MIGRATION TO PARIS: ENTERING A NEW SOCIAL ORGANISATION SYSTEM

Becoming 'Nomads': Constrained Mobility

Roma migrants in the Paris region earn their living mostly from begging and other activities reminiscent of 'hunting and gathering' (Stewart 1997)— collecting scrap metal, selling flowers or playing music on public transport; sometimes a minority resort to petty theft and prostitution. There are currently several thousand Eastern European Roma in France, among whom 3,000–4,000 living in the Paris region according to Médecins du Monde (2004). Most are Roma from Romania and Bulgaria. There also exists a minority of non-Roma engaging in similar activities.

These migrations have specific features: they very often involve family members or close neighbours. Migrants create specific forms of habitat such as slums or sometimes live in squatted buildings. Slums are temporary and fragile settlements—usually made of second-hand caravans or wood cabins—housing between 50 and 500 people in each complex. Most slums are regularly evacuated by the police, often at the request of the owners or of the municipality—which makes Roma into 'nomads' against their will, since they can seldom occupy one site for more than a few months. According to a Romanian Roma woman:

> I'm not used to this, the dirt, the rats, the other people here [in the camp]. This is not the way we live back home (in Romania). Now with this newborn baby it's very hard, if I were home we would give her a bath every day—here we cannot. But here we can earn our living, back home I would not be able to feed my children (Interview December 2007).

Like other migrants, the Roma in Paris are organised in networks: a few 'pioneers' migrate towards a city and then others follow. This feature explains the highly contingent character of these migrations: there are large concentrations of migrants from a few regions in both Romania and Bulgaria. The social profile of the migrants follows the network logic: the first ones accumulated a relatively greater social or financial capital, whereas subsequent migrants may come from all the sub-layers of the group. Eventually, the migration process feeds on itself and a large percentage of the members of the group eventually leave—sharing another classic feature of contemporary migrations (Massey 1988). Like other migrations from the Balkans, Roma migrations involve a high degree of mobility and of co-presence in both the host and the home countries (Diminescu and Lagrave 1999).

Becoming Beggars: Real and Missed Opportunities

Throughout changing regulations, Roma have continued migrating between their home towns or villages to the Parisian suburbs, learning by trial and error to exploit niches in juridical and administrative regulations. In contrast with African or Asian migrants, they have taken advantage of the above-described border porosity and of the relative proximity of their countries of origin: they do not have to cross multiple borders or to travel large distances, the price of a Sofia–Paris or a Bucharest–Paris bus ticket never exceeding 100 euros. Many migrants use privately owned vans, which allows them to travel directly from their region of origin.

Several other factors affect their migrations—such as the possibility to squat a building or to beg in the street—and vary according to the host country or region. Migrants communicate about the different possibilities that are open to them, even though information is sometimes unreliable. Their mobility is accentuated by the technological arsenal of globalisation, such as mobile phones or money transfer. Here, a Bulgarian Roma living in a squat near Paris and earning a living through begging, gives his own vision of the spectrum of possibilities a Roma has in different European countries:

> How did we decide to come here? Well, everyone runs away from P.
> [his home town], all that is left there is sick people, crazy people... All
> those who could have already left. My mother and brother are in Italy,
> my cousin in Belgium. P. is now the whole world. [...]If I'd been able to
> leave earlier, I would be my own man now, I would have a job, I would
> live normally. My cousin in Belgium, that's what she did. But look at
> me, I was stupid, I left too late, and now we are sentenced to begging. In
> 1992 I had an opportunity to go to Germany, but see how stupid I was,
> I got off the bus before it left. At that time, in Germany, they gave you
> asylum, a house, assistance, everything! I did not dare to leave, and look
> at me today...(interview December 2005).

As the excerpt shows, many of these migrations are failed work migrations (potential black-market workers failing to enter the illegal jobs circuit and resorting to begging as a viable and often lucrative alternative). The low social status of most of the Roma in their home countries explains both the lack of social capital allowing them to enter these migrations and the relative ease with which they adopt the begging solution—which, however, entails a great deal of personal suffering obvious in the interviews (Travers 1999).

> It wasn't easy for me [to become a beggar]. I waited for 6 months trying
> to get work, spent all my money, ate at the soup kitchen, got robbed by
> contractors ... At the end, I had to do it, everyone around me was beg-
> ging, so why not me? And I got to become very good at it, a real special-
> ist (laughing) (Bulgarian Roma, Interview December 2005).

Work regulations introduced at the time of the home countries' accession to the EU in January 2007[6] are liable to let very few Roma enter the legal job market. These migrations have much in common with other illegal work migrations: their network logic; the semi-legal status of the migrants; and their impact on the home communities, involving a great deal of ostentatious consumption and expenses, and seldom longer-term investment (Potot 2003).

Roma in the Midst of Local Politics: Issues of Definition and Participation

Although their status in France is extremely marginal, migrants' contacts with the rest of society are numerous, and outsiders frequently visit the camps. Many of these visitors belong to NGOs that support the Roma (MdM is one of the most active). In the few municipalities where they are tolerated, migrants become an issue of local politics among local authorities, rival political parties, NGOs, local support groups, local inhabitants often hostile to their presence, and the police. Thus municipalities find themselves in a situation of double-bind, between inhabitants' protests, and support for—or at least tolerance towards—the Roma migrants.

The status of the Roma makes legal working papers an almost impossible option. Therefore, these local actors have to reach compromise deals which often imply rehousing a small minority in temporary projects and evicting the others (another source of unequal treatment or highjacking of the majority's interests). On these occasions, the interplay in discourses is very interesting, paradoxically the migrants becoming more an object of public attention than they have ever been in their home countries.

Support for Roma groups can allow left-wing municipalities to manifest their criticism of government migration policies, as was traditionally the case for slum eradication in the Paris 'red belt' in the 1950s and 1960s (Masclet 2005). Decisions concerning the residence of Roma groups are often contingent upon tragic events: a fire or an accident can be the opportunity for a municipality to launch a re-housing project—or, on the contrary, to decide on an eviction from what is labelled a 'dangerous site'.

Dilemmas of 'Participation'

In several negotiations I witnessed, issues such as 'victimisation discourse', 'participative approaches' (promoted in the treatment of diverse issues such as slum sanitation, schooling, healthcare, family planning etc.) and involving people in what is labelled a 'development' process, were differently understood and reshaped in the power struggles between various actors. Thus, municipalities that engage in resettlement projects often seek Roma 'representatives' in order to address Roma groups, although the persons who are thus chosen are not generally acknowledged by other group members as such. Similarly, medical NGO members tend to promote group approaches on some issues such as family planning. The term 'participative approaches' (Crochet 2000) also belongs to

NGO vocabulary promoted in the access to healthcare. It is differently defined according to the necessities of the situation:

> We used to think that, on contraception issues, it was better to have women's group discussions, because it allows women to feel more confident, to ask more questions, to share each other's experiences, instead of one woman facing the doctor and the translator. However, we noticed that sometimes, in one group in a camp, we had women coming from different regions, who didn't trust each other at all and didn't want to discuss their sexuality in the open, so we concluded that, in some cases, it's better to go back to individual consultations (Midwife, November 2007).

These are recurrent issues confronting NGOs working with undocumented migrants in France. Often, these concerns go beyond the local level to political-semantic struggles involving the definition of these migrants and their motivations to migrate. This is one of the numerous avatars of the inextricable distinction between 'real asylum-seekers' and 'economic migrants' (Vasecka and Vasecka 2003). Struggles of definition over the sociology of the Roma group are also a way of framing the Roma issue: for example, municipalities who do not want to accept the Roma would tend to define them as 'nomads', whereas others, who developed resettlement projects, point to the fact that Roma have been settled for centuries in Eastern Europe and that they are simply 'migrants' in search of a better life.

Framing 'The Roma'

Individuals involved have their own (often implicit) definition of the 'Roma question'. The Roma cause is *par excellence* a 'heretic cause' similar to that of illegal migrants (Siméant 1998). The Roma do not always comprehend the interplay of different stakes and interests around their presence. For some NGOs, Roma are the perfect victims, allowing the adoption of a stance of denunciation towards French public authorities, and even more so towards the authorities of the country of origin (especially Romania). The marginal status of the Roma population allows it to crystallise these projections, from the figure of the 'good savage' to that canvassed by Günter Grass, for whom the Roma are the 'true Europeans' (1992).

The presence of the Roma is also an opportunity for persons in a relatively marginal social position (i.e. retired healthcare workers, leftist activists or students) to gain considerable power over the destiny of other individuals, power which becomes obvious when an NGO team enters a slum. This power is even greater when it also adds the very strong symbolic power of the doctor in contemporary societies. This is what allowed, for example, a voluntary doctor at MdM to carry out an unasked-for and unannounced condom distribution in a Roma camp, in the midst of the embarrassed sniggers of the Roma, most of whom perceived this gesture as humiliating. The language barrier and extreme social inequality between healthcare workers and their target population made such a misunderstanding common. As a translator, I tend to be sensitive to the often intrusive presence of the NGOs in the slum, whereas many medics are sincerely surprised when I voice such concerns. However, some of them explicitly distance themselves from the search for power, preferring to define their role as 'being socially useful': 'It is the only place where I can still see real sick people, unlike when I had my town office' (former liberal general practitioner, interview September 2005).

Access to healthcare is an everyday problem for many migrant Roma. The health of the Roma population is poorer than that of the countries of origin in terms of life expectancy and the types of disease to which they are prone— diabetes and high blood pressure are not uncommon in people as young as 30. Harsh living conditions, poverty, and early and numerous pregnancies (by Western European standards) affect the health of women, who often use abortion at the local hospital as a means of birth regulation. Tuberculosis is also frequent in Roma camps. Because of the threat of an epidemic, it is among the rare diseases that prompt local health authorities to send teams into the field.

The lack of medical insurance[7] and of the ability to speak French are obvious barriers to healthcare access, and most Roma only seek medical attention in emergency situations, usually at the nearest hospital. Most pregnant women only go to hospital when they are in labour.

ROMA AND HEALTH POLITICS: NEGOTIATING HEALTHCARE CHOICES
Healthcare for the Undesirable

MdM's 'Roma mission' is part of a trend that appeared amongst French humanitarian NGOs in the 1980s. In order to attract public attention to the 'new poverty' and 'social exclusion' affecting increasing sections of the population in Western counties, NGOs that used to work essentially in Third-World countries decided to target some of their actions towards these new groups in the home countries of the NGOs themselves. However, the problem for these NGOs is to avoid usurping what they consider to be a government role. Not becoming 'a hostage of the state', 'a subcontractor' or 'the poor's social security' is a concern voiced by MdM workers, who repeatedly urge the government to 'fulfill its role'.[8]

However, public care structures—mostly dispensaries and hospitals—usually tend to rely on NGOs for liaison services, translation or even healthcare. This dilemma is all the more acute in that it is all about caring for officially undesirable populations. Indeed, will the government choose to 'fulfill its role' for a population with such an ambiguous status? This situation leads NGOs to become *de facto* substitutes for the public system. Therefore, for many Roma, the entry-point into the health system would be through MdM.

In public health institutions, the Roma often are, from the point of view of healthcare professionals, an unsettling presence disrupting medical routines. They often resort to emergency-ward care, as such facilities increasingly have to admit patients who are not medical, but rather social, emergencies. Indeed, the accident and emergency ward is one of the few facilities that cannot refuse to take in the destitute patient, even if he or she has no medical insurance.

> When Roma girls began to come to give birth at the hospital a few years ago it was a shock for us, we didn't understand what was happening, why we suddenly had all those pregnant teenage girls who showed up at the emergency ward in labour. I think they are born under a lucky star, really, because one would expect such cases to have complications at delivery, and usually things go on OK. But for us it's very stressful, just imagine: the girl drops in to the emergency ward and we have nothing on her, no blood group, no ultrasound; she doesn't speak French so we have no information. We have to ask for emergency tests and, as the hospital is overbooked, it's a pain for everyone (Midwife, public hospital, interview February 2008).

'Poor People's Medicine'

For a person in a situation of acute deprivation, health is seldom a priority. This leads many Roma to miss appointments, refuse their children's vaccinations or disregard doctors' nutritional recommendations. This often causes dismay among health professionals. However, the latter might not see that the Roma's apparent disregard for their health is sometimes a response to the inadequacy of the healthcare they are offered.

One paradox of MdM's work lies in its endeavour to ensure the follow-up of a population whose contrived mobility makes this a perpetual challenge. Each eviction from a residential site results in lost medical documents and missed appointments. Thus the Roma's actual access to medical treatment is severely delayed, some patients waiting for months or even years before receiving appropriate care. This creates a situation of permanent frustration for MdM medics: 'It's really poor people's medicine' or 'This is veterinary medicine', are not uncommon comments by doctors. Moreover, the mobility of the Roma contradicts a contemporary evolution that requires NGOs to account for all their activities.

For example, the repeated loss of vaccine booklets or the refusal by a non-negligible minority of parents to have their children vaccinated may also be interpreted as a silent form of protest in regard to the second-class medicine they are offered. Thus, in one camp, a child was vaccinated three times by three different medical teams who were unaware of each other's identity. The child's parents, who had lost the vaccine booklet after an eviction, refused to pursue the vaccination programme, the proof of which was needed for the child to be registered for school. During one of the MdM visits, the child's mother told the doctor: 'We are Born-Again Christians [pocaiti in Romanian, i.e. members of a neo-Protestant church] and therefore I refuse to allow the child to be vaccinated' (interview, December 2007). I later understood that the family was not against vaccination but they were afraid that repeated doses of vaccine may be dangerous. The religious argument was considered by the grandmother to be the ultimate unopposable argument and, indeed, it was accepted as such by the MdM doctor. As we shall see below, Roma often use others' perceptions of the Roma 'culture' as a means to gain more control over their lives.

Financial constraints and social domination make it more difficult for the Roma to negotiate their treatment with the doctor. For example, MdM and hospital doctors are reluctant to prescribe contraceptive pills to Roma women who ask for them, arguing that their low education and the instability of their way of life make them more liable to forget the pill and thus lead to unwanted pregnancies. These were indeed very common, with the number of abortions being very high for Roma women, a majority of women in their 20s having already experienced at least one abortion, according to the Roma mission. Doctors unilaterally recommended intrauterine devices—a common practice in humanitarian medicine in Third-World countries (Gautier 2002)—or hormonal implants, although many women are defiant towards these contraceptive methods. Thus, many family-planning consultations end up with Roma patients' 'orientations' (referrals) to family-planning services never actually being visited by them.

There is also a gender bias in access to healthcare: domestic violence and male domination sometimes make it difficult for women to have control over their fertility. 'My husband does not want me to use contraception' is a repeated complaint on the part of some Roma women. The doctor's or midwife's presence in the camp may be seen by some husbands as an intrusion, usurping their authority over women's bodies: it was common to hear comments such as 'If she gets pregnant she can go and get cleaned up' (i.e. get an abortion) on the part of angry husbands whose wives had contacted MdM to obtain contraception.

Despite the procedural, universal claims of the humanitarian NGO, access to healthcare for the Roma is often contingent and conditional upon the involvement of voluntary workers. If there is no one to explain, translate for or assist the Roma in healthcare institutions, it is very likely that they will not receive appropriate care.

Performing and Interpreting 'Culture'

The Roma are a novel minority group for many health professionals. In some doctor–patient interactions, perceptions of ethnic difference or otherness seem to overrule all other motivations, becoming the only source of understanding. Thus problems in access to healthcare tend to be viewed as hindered by 'cultural barriers' which are seen as among the most difficult to lift. Thus, in situations as different as a woman forgetting her medication, a man with high blood pressure continuing to smoke and drink alcohol despite medical advice, or a destitute woman having several children, 'cultural barriers' would be uniformly invoked by medical professionals.

'Culture' often functions as a euphemism for ethnic or racial difference, summing up everything that is seen as an obstacle or as problematic. That 'culture' seems a handy euphemism for large ethnic entities is not specific to healthcare workers but quite common in France, where the social sciences have only recently begun to reflect on notions such as 'ethnicity' and 'culture' (Vinsonneau 2002). One doctor in a dispensary, who had trouble explaining to a patient that she had high cholesterol, summed up the situation to me (the translator) thus: 'Culturally, they are unable to distinguish a benign symptom from cancer. For them it's all the same' (interview, February 2008). Similarly, for a Roma woman to have five or six children is seen by the medical professional as 'cultural', as opposed to an 'individual choice': 'It's in their culture to want many children'. The Roma woman's behaviour would be interpreted as compliance to tradition, whereas using birth control and having one or two children for a French-born patient would be seen by the same professional as 'individual choice'.

This very perception is used by Roma in their interaction with healthcare professionals: 'We Roma are thus, we want many children'. A woman who wanted to become pregnant but did not manage to told the doctor: 'Some people have too many children and some have none' (interview, August 2005). In this case, 'too many children' refers to what she believed was the perception French people, or *gadje* (non-Roma) had of people like her. This is not without recalling the 'return of the stigma' phenomenon in which the stigmatised individual uses the stigma in order to face the outside world (Goffman 1975).

'Culture' also constitutes a meaning-granting framework: it allows, when one lacks information about someone's circumstances, to interpret an individual's situation by referring it to the group to which the individual is supposed to belong. If one lacks information, there is often a transfer of perceptions from previous experience with other ethnic groups. Thus, a midwife described migrant women's behaviour during labour by comparing it to a different type of population she was used to: 'Older Roma women [who give birth], they are like older African women: they give birth easily, they give birth well. But the younger ones, they are scared, crying' (interview, March 2008). What appears here is that healthcare workers tend to consider the Roma patient as primarily a member of a group (as the use of the plural shows) and that 'culture' is often a shortcut to ethnicity.

A common misconception by medical professionals results in their interpreting as 'cultural' attitudes and behaviours which are simply engendered by poverty. For example, one day, as I was accompanying an elderly woman in a hospital, she stopped to wash her face and drink water in the public toilets. Like many older Roma women, she wore a headscarf—a common garment in the Balkans, especially in rural areas where it has no religious meaning. However, in France, women wearing headscarves are usually perceived as Muslim even though most Roma women are Christian.[9] A nurse who passed by scolded us: 'Please tell them not to perform their ablution rituals here, this is a public hospital. I am also a Muslim but I do not do this in here'. The nurse did not have time to listen to my explanation that the woman was not performing rituals but that she simply had no running water in the slum where she lived.

Attention to ethnic diversity is recent in French public policy, including health institutions, and its legitimacy is seen as problematic (De Rudder *et al.* 2000). This raises questions about the emerging field of migrant medicine and the role that 'cultural differences' can be made to play in healthcare. This can be observed in emerging programmes in the French system set up to train 'health mediators'— teaching health professionals to deal with patients belonging to 'different cultures'. In my study, I found that health professionals are often polarised between a minority who are interested in a 'culturalist' approach and a larger group which is more supportive of a 'social' stance. Thus, a gynecologist, who was asked why Roma women keep using abortion as a method of birth control, answered:

> Why are they like this? Because they are like our grandmothers. They haven't been informed, they haven't been given access to different means of contraception. How did our grandmothers cope [before abortion was legal in France]? They went to see midwives who could help them. It is just that Roma women are 30 years late in comparison to us (interview, March 2008).

Healthcare can thus be a locus of empowerment as well as of domestication of an exoticised 'other'. Paradoxically, for some Roma ill-health can become an advantage, as it is for them the only way to obtain a regular permit to stay in France.[10] In the context of the restriction of migrants' rights, and of a concomitant financial crisis of the social security system, 'culture' is a socially constructed category 'justifying' various problems in the interaction between marginalised migrants and the healthcare system.

CONCLUSION

This paper has highlighted the limits of local management in a situation where the main obstacles to integration are not in the hands of local authorities. Previous observations show that the management of this population, which is often 'by default', tended to increase its marginalisation. The Roma are the subject of struggles of definition and framing, where they seldom have the upper hand, but where they use everyday strategies—including playing on the way they are essentialised or ethnicised—to try to turn the situation to their advantage.

However, this often has ambiguous effects, with short-term benefits for the Roma and the long-term reinforcement of stigmatisation schemes. The case of healthcare, which I highlighted as being one of the main approaches of NGOs and local authorities towards the Roma, epitomises these effects. As we have seen, healthcare can be a locus of empowerment as well as of domestication of an exoticised 'other', by the service providers refusing to acknowledge the migrants' right to choose, but blaming the individual for the 'bad' choices. Roma migrants are particularly vulnerable to this kind of labelling. Thus, Roma migrations are both a short-term solution to the problems of poverty and unemploy-ment which the Roma face in their home countries and the source of new types of marginalisation on the fringe of Western European cities.

An update. In the summer of 2010, in a context of sinking popularity for President Nicolas Sarkozy and of national economic crisis, migrant Roma in France were the target of an unprecedented campaign of public defamation by the French authorities. In an official address on 30 July, the President lumped together *gens du voyage* (travellers), Roma immigrants and French citizens 'of foreign origin', and linked, at the same time, migration and crime. Further ut-terances from members of the government described migrant Roma as offenders and beggars. This was followed by a wave of protest on the part of major political personalities (including some belonging to the ruling party), anti-racist NGOs and academics. The protest also came from international organisations such as the EU and the UN. Observers pointed out that it was the first time in de-cades that the French authorities had adopted an extreme-right-wing position on immigration—using the rhetorics of xenophobia—in line with a supposedly menaced French identity.

Announcing the destruction of illegal Roma camps and the deportation of the Roma to Romania and Bulgaria, the government framed the situation of Roma migrants as a crime issue calling for urgent measures. The speed with which the Roma were framed into the new governmental security agenda was startling. However, nothing in the announced 'security measures' was new: for years, Roma had been evicted from their camps and the inhabitants sent back to their countries of origin, with no other consequence than the further mar-ginalisation of migrant Roma in ever-moving suburban slums. The newly an-nounced measures could not meet their target, given that the Roma were now EU citizens with the right to travel freely across Europe. Indeed, evicted and repatriated Roma expressed their desire to return to France, where most of them saw their future and where many had been living for years.

Whereas the actual management of migrant Roma camps is increasingly left to local authorities, the rhetorical use of 'the Roma question' has been taken up by central government in line with a general politicisation of immigration issues. Thus, securitarian policies are liable to aggravate the previous situation of constrained mobility and identity-misframing that had been the lot of Roma migrants for years, maintaining them in a state of marginality.

NOTES

1. See, for example, 'Bucarest durcit le contrôle aux frontières pour ses propres ressortissants', *Le Monde*, 10 August 2005.

2. The International Organization for Migration provides assistance for the 'voluntary return' of migrants to their countries of origin.

3. Poland and Hungary: Assistance for Restructuring their Economies, a programme originally set up in 1989 to assist accession countries during a period of massive economic restructuring and political change.

4. Circulaire INT/D/06/000115/C du 22 décembre 2006 relative aux modalités d'admission au séjour et d'éloignement des ressortissants roumains et bulgares à partir du 1er janvier 2007.

5. See 'Les "retours humanitaires" de Roms se sont accélérés', *Le Monde*, 30 December 2007.

6. Since January 2007, Romanians and Bulgarians are theoretically entitled to work in France in 62 professions facing workforce shortages. However, obtaining a work permit is a painstaking bureaucratic procedure in which the employer is supposed to fill in a form, pay a tax and wait for two months for the employee's work permit, so that being hired becomes very unlikely, all the more so for the Roma, who lack the social connections allowing them to find a job.

7. Illegal immigrants in France are entitled to a form of medical coverage called the *Aide Médicale État*, but current regulations state that immigrants have to prove their presence in France for at least three months, which the Roma seldom can.

8. See the article 'On n'a pas vocation à être la Sécu du pauvre', *Libération*, 25 September 2004.

9. Moreover, in recent years, some Roma women took advantage of this misperception. They choose to wear, when they are begging, a style of distinctive Muslim garment such as the *hijab*, which allows them pass as Muslims. It was a way, one woman explained to me, to escape from being perceived as Eastern European Roma in the districts where they were begging and also to appeal to the generosity of Muslim inhabitants.

10. In France a 1999 law allows provisions for granting temporary residence permits to individuals whose very serious health condition would represent a threat to their lives should they have to return to their home countries.

REFERENCES

Bauman, Z. (1998) *Globalization, the Human Consequences*. New York: Columbia University Press

Bigo, D. and Guild, E. (2005) 'Policing at a distance: Schengen visa policies', in Bigo, D. and Guild, E. (eds) Controlling Frontiers. Aldershot: Ashgate, 233–63.

Castel, R. (1999) *Les Métamorphoses de la Question Sociale: une chronique du salariat*. Paris: Gallimard.

Castle-Karenova, M. (2003) 'Round and round the roundabout: Czech Roma and the vicious circle of asylum-seeking', *Nationalities Papers*, 31(1): 13–25.

Crochet, S. (2000) 'Cet obscur objet du désir: la participation communautaire', in Brauman, R. (ed.) *Utopies Sanitaires*. Paris: Le Pommier-Fayard, 47–76.

De Rudder, V., Poiret, C. and Vourc'h, F. (2000) *L'Inégalité Raciste: l'Universalité Républicaine à l'Épreuve*. Paris: Presses Universitaires de France.

Diminescu, D. and Lagrave, R. (1999) 'Faire une saison: pour une anthropologie des migrations roumaines en France. Le cas du pays d'Oas?', *Migrations Études*, 91(11–12): 1–14.

European Commission (2004) *La Situation des Rom dans une Union Européenne Élargie*, http://europa.eu.int/comm/employment_social/fundamental_rights/pdf/pubst/roma04_en.pdf, last accessed August 2005.

FIDH [Fédération Internationale des Ligues des Droits de l'Homme] and MdM [Médecins du Monde] (2003) *Mission d'Evaluation en Roumanie*. http://www.fidh.org/europ/rapport/2003/rom0107f.pdf, last accessed March 2008.

Gautier, A. (2002) 'Les politiques de planification familiale dans les pays en développement: du malthusianisme au féminisme?', *Lien Social et Politiques—RIAC*, 47(4–6): 67–81.

Goffman, I. (1975) *Stigmate: les usages sociaux des handicaps*. Paris: Minuit.

Grass, G. (1998) 'True Europeans', *Index on Censorship*, 27(4): 51–3.

Guglielmo, R. (2004) 'Human rights in the accession process: Roma and Muslims in an enlarging Europe', in EURAC Research (ed.) *Minority Protection and the Enlarged European Union: The Way Forward*. Budapest: Local Government and Public Service Reform Initiative, Open Society Institute, 37–59.

Masclet, O. (2005) *La Gauche et les Cités. Enquête sur un rendez-vous manqué*. Paris: La Dispute.

Massey, D. (1988) 'Economic development and international migration in comparative perspective', *Population and Development Review*, 14(3): 375–97.

Médecins du Monde (2004) *Rapport Annuel de la Mission Roms*. Paris: MdM.

Nacu, A. (2006) La Construction Sociale de la Pauvreté en Roumanie et en Bulgarie après 1989. Paris: Sciences-Po, unpublished PhD thesis.

Potot, S. (2003) *Circulation et Réseaux de Migrants Roumains: Une Contribution à l'étude de nouvelles mobilités en Europe*. Nice: Université de Nice-Sophia Antipolis, PhD thesis, http://tel.ccsd.cnrs.fr/documents/archives0/00/00/34/80/tel-00003480-00/tel-00003480.pdf, last accessed August 2005.

Siméant, J. (1998) *La Cause des Sans-Papiers*. Paris: Presses de la FNSP.

Stewart, M. (1997) *The Time of the Gypsies*. Boulder: Westview Press.

Travers, A. (1999) 'The face that begs: street begging scenes and selves' identity work', in Dean, H. (ed.) *Begging Questions, Street-Level Economic Activity and Social Policy Failure*. Bristol: The Policy Press, 121–43.

Vasecka, I. and Vasecka, M. (2003) 'Recent Romani migration from Slovakia to EU member states: Romani reaction to discrimination or Romani ethno-tourism?', *Nationalities Papers*, 31(1): 27–45.

Vinsonneau, G. (2002) 'Le développement des notions de culture et d'identité: un itinéraire ambigu', *Carrefours de l'Éducation*, 2(14): 2–20.

*Alexandra Nacu is a postdoctoral researcher at the Centre de Sociologie des Organisations, Sciences-Po Paris.

Alexandra Nacu, "The Politics of Roma Migration: Framing Identity Struggles Among Romanian and Bulgarian Roma in the Paris Region," *Journal of Ethnic and Migration Studies* 37, no. 1, (January, 2011).

Chapter 3: The Roma in Italy: Racism as Usual?

*by Claudia Aradau**

On 30 October 2007, Giovanna Reggiani, a 47-year-old Italian woman, was robbed and murdered in a deserted area of northern Rome. The man accused of murdering her was a Romanian Roma, Nicolai Romulus Mailat, who had been living in one of the 'unauthorized' settlements in Rome. The media immediately reported horrific stories of torture and rape, raising the 'spectre of "monsters" arrived from Europe'.[1] The crime became more than a crime; it was a crime against the nation. The wife of a naval officer, Reggiani sparked the protective and militarized anxieties that help constitute and reproduce the legitimacy of nation-states. And the nation reacted. The ex-communist mayor of Rome, Walter Veltroni, requested an emergency decree for the deportation of European citizens deemed to be a threat to public security. While the settlements at the margins of Rome and other Italian cities were being evacuated and bulldozed, the government of Romano Prodi, former president of the European Commission, was busy fast-tracking a decree on 'urgent provisions for removals from Italian territory for reasons of public safety'. The decree was openly aimed at Romanians and particularly the Romanian Roma, who had rights of mobility and residence since 2007 when Romania joined the European Union. The incident was followed not only by new security legislation but also by vigilante violence against Roma and Romanian citizens. Occasional instances of physical violence gave way to more systematic attacks on the camps. The media continued reporting details of the violence as emblematic of the 'discontent of the nation' with the government's policies on immigration and security.

Despite the urgency with which the Prodi government passed security legislation, and Veltroni's reassurances of firm action against crime perpetrated by Romanians, the government lost a vote of confidence in parliament and was swiftly replaced by a new Berlusconi right-wing government. In an alliance with the parties of the extreme Right, the Alleanza Nazionale (National Alliance) and Lega Nord (Northern League), Berlusconi came back to power on promises to crack down on crime and change immigration policies. Two weeks after his electoral victory, for the first time since the Second World War, Rome elected a right-wing mayor, former youth leader of the neo-fascist Italian Social Movement, Gianni Alemanno. Alemanno's 'Pact for Rome', which sailed him to power, had promised the expulsion of 20,000 immigrants in Rome and the destruction of the camps inhabited by the Roma. The government's 'security package' also envisaged the criminalization of undocumented migrants, the demolition of 'unauthorized' camps and the fingerprinting of the Roma. In the meantime, violence against the Roma continued unabated: arson, physical attack, insult and injury. In May 2008, a Roma camp in Naples was set on fire with Molotov cocktails. A few days later, another was burnt to the ground after a teenage Roma woman was arrested for allegedly trying to steal an infant.

The events were subject to widespread denunciation from all corners of the political spectrum. Liberals and radicals, capitalists and anti-capitalists, NGOs and governments, the Catholic Right and the secular Left reacted with declarations, appeals and press conferences, condemning the fascist turn in Italian politics and the ethnic profiling of the Roma undertaken by the new Berlusconi government. Alemanno's election as mayor of Rome reinforced suspicions about the rise of neo-fascism and an extreme Right whose security policy had gone 'out of control'. Liberal activists and NGOs focused on showing the falsity of the reports that had allegedly sparked the violence against the Roma and Romanians. The Roma represent only about 0.3 per cent of the Italian population. The teenager accused of trying to steal a baby was not Roma and did not try to steal the baby. Romanians are not criminals, but care for the elderly and clean the streets of Rome. Crime is not disproportionately the responsibility of foreigners. Rather, statistics show that crime has not increased over the past decade and Italy continues to have one of the lowest murder rates in Europe.[2] The Roma were not even foreigners, but more than half were European and Italian citizens. They were driven to live in makeshift camps by the lack of housing. Italy has a systematic and publicly funded system of camps that ignores the Roma's demand for adequate housing and continues to call them *nomadi*, despite their sedentary lifestyle. Many of the camps were set up to shelter refugee Roma from ex-Yugoslavia. Other camps have an even longer history. Campesina 900 in Rome dates back to the 1960s.

Exposing false perceptions did not make much of a dent in government policies or abate popular violence. Other voices continued denouncing the anti-Roma measures as racist and fascist and appealed to the universal prescriptions of law, democracy and human rights. *Famiglia Cristiana*, Italy's most widely read Catholic paper, suggested fascism was resurfacing in the government and drew parallels between the treatment of the Roma by the Berlusconi government and that of the Jews by the Nazis. The Council of Europe referred to 'historical analogies which are so obvious that they don't need to be spelled out'.[3] The financier George Soros sent a letter to Berlusconi demanding urgent measures to protect the Roma from racist aggression. Médecins du Monde, the French NGO founded by Bertrand Kouchner, Sarkozy's minister of foreign and European affairs, described the situation of the Roma as a 'state of exception' which should no longer be covered in silence.[4] The European Network against Racism denounced the Italian authorities for 'conducting arbitrary detentions and expulsions, making provisions for discriminatory anti-Romani and anti-Romanian laws and measures and openly inciting its population to racially motivated violence'.[5]

A state of emergency had been declared, executive powers were passing decrees that directly targeted particular sections of the population, and European citizens were losing their rights. The situation should have been indisputable. Nonetheless, the accusations of fascism and racism remained largely ineffective. Despite the rhetoric, few measures were taken by international institutions to try and halt racist discrimination against the Roma. The Italian situation appeared extraordinary, beyond the bounds of normal politics. However, rather than being something new, racism has long been constitutive of the normal politics of modern states. The problem with the accusations of racism and fascism was that they did not make sense of the government's measures against the Roma as part of the ordinary fabric of liberal politics. This was compounded by the gradual incorporation of anti-racist movements into a liberal discourse of culture and prejudice. Yet neither cultural nor biological difference was immediately at stake in the exclusionary reproduction of infra-humanity in Italy. The measures were part of a much more insidious and entrenched racism whose workings have been largely neutralized by the rhetoric of security. As Franco Frattini, Italian Foreign Minister and former European Commissioner for Freedom, Security and Justice, put it: 'These things are done by many other countries in Europe without causing any scandal'.

ORDINARY RACISM

Faced with accusations of racism and fascism, the Italian government reacted with indignation. 'Macché que razzisti, Italia e in regola' ('What racism? Italy is in order!') was the headline of one of the Italian dailies in the wake of the European debates about Berlusconi's 'security package'.[6] After all, when Berlusconi came to power, his 'security package' could rely on the emergency legislation brought in by Prodi's centre-left government. The Communists themselves, who had taken part in Prodi's twenty-month government, had been supportive of these measures. The government claims that all the measures it has taken are legal. In the wake of concerns voiced by the European Commission, Italy 'reassures the EU that fingerprinting Gypsies is legal and not racist'.[7] According to the government, the measures are actually compassionate, driven by a desire for social integration. The Italian interior minister Roberto Maroni justified the new state of emergency instituted nationally in July 2008 by the Berlusconi government as being 'better to assist the illegal immigrants by accommodating them in buildings rather than tents, and guarantee them more humane treatment'.[8]

In rejecting accusations of racism regarding the fingerprinting of the Roma living in camps, Maroni argued that 'I must be able to know who is in Italy, where they live, what they do, what they will do in coming months.' That fingerprinting will also entail the deportation of undocumented migrants appears as collateral damage of a policy that presents itself as genuinely striving for social integration. What better way to govern populations than by gathering adequate knowledge about their life? Furthermore, the 'security package' is not much of a novelty in the European security landscape. Maroni had, after all, pointed out that making irregular migration a crime only brings Italy into line with other European countries such as Britain and France, which have long had similar laws.

In Italy itself, accusations of racism did not stand before the law. In March 2008, the Court of Cassation passed a judgment on six defendants, including the mayor of Verona, who had signed a leaflet demanding the expulsion of all Roma from the city. The court decided that it was not a case of racism but of 'deep aversion [to Roma] that was not determined by the Gypsy nature of the people discriminated against, but by the fact that all the Gypsies were thieves'.[9] In the court's judgment, racism is defined by ideas of superiority and racial hatred and not by criminal statistics. As the mayor and the other defendants were found to be prejudiced against the Roma's criminal behaviour, rather than cultural or racial differences, such racial prejudices were not deemed to amount to racism.

Eventual anti-racist measures by EU institutions did not fare any better. Jacques Barrot, the European commissioner for justice, freedom and security, also declared: 'The measures being carried out by Italy to tackle the Roma emergency do not violate EU law'. In the wake of a report submitted by the Italian government, the measures envisaged in the 'security package' were found not to contradict European legislation since fingerprinting only targets persons who cannot be otherwise identified, rather than particular ethnic or racial categories.

The outbursts of violence and the vigilante patrolling of the streets of Rome appeared as expressions of popular discontent, which were justified by some voices on the extreme Right as responses to state indifference and inaction. The population, who have supported the anti-Roma anti-immigrant policies of successive right-and left-wing governments, do not see themselves as racist, fascist or in any other way extreme. Those who started anti-Roma vigilante patrols on the street of Italian cities call themselves 'Circolo della Libertà' (The Freedom Circle) and claim to be acting against growing insecurity in urban areas.[10]

The widespread accusations of racism have ignored the discourses of law, freedom, liberalism and order that underpin both popular and governmental reactions. They share the liberal view that racism is a problem of individual prejudice and misguided perceptions and they are formulated in the liberal terms of the rule of law and universal rights. But by trying to find recourse in liberal law and universal rights, anti-racist accusations have inhabited the same space as the legal theory that condones it. What none of these accusations has come to terms with is the liberal justification of 'protective measures' within the confines of the law.

What is really at stake in Italy is not the rise of extremist language, but liberal politics as usual. Rendered more visible through the spectacular state interventions in the wake of the murder of Giovanna Reggiani, Italian government policies harbour many continuities and similarities with European policies already in place. The demand to introduce DNA tests for assessing demands for family reunification by refugees, the criminalization of illegal immigrants and the increase in prison time for migrants who have committed a crime are not new, but have already been introduced in several other European countries. Similarly, fingerprinting is not a novel measure, reminiscent of the 1930s. Rather, the fingerprinting of asylum-seekers is common policy in the European Union, where the Eurodac database aims at preventing asylum-seekers from applying for asylum in different countries. At the same time as the Italian government was undertaking the fingerprinting of the Roma, including children, the EU drafted legislation requiring the fingerprinting of all children over 12 years of age (after an initial proposal of fingerprinting everybody older than 6) for the purpose of fighting child trafficking. In the context of the 'war on terror', fingerprinting has become a much more extended device than denunciations of the Italian case care to admit.

What the Italian case should highlight is a more insidious and less striking form of racism that is already at work in Europe and whose effects often remain unnoticed: the increasing use of 'security' discourse to divide humanity with the commonsensical measure of a need for social protection.

Security as Liberal Politics

By ignoring the co-constitution of racism and the modern state, liberal anti-racism is not only ineffective but can become a dangerous force in the perpetuation of state racism. The anti-racist discourse that emerged at the end of World War II understands racism as a matter of individual prejudice and proposes cultural rather than political responses to it.[11] From this vantage point, the accusation of anti-racism can be uttered by virtually anybody. State institutions can therefore become involved in an anti-racist struggle that is oblivious of the perpetuation of state racism through the use of security measures. Yet security has been constitutive of the biopolitical aspect of modern states, which place both the welfare and protection of populations at their core. Within the larger rationality of welfare and the betterment of populations, racism introduces a split in the continuum of life, differentiating the assurance of life from its denial. According to Foucault, the function of racism is to fragment and create caesuras within the biological continuum addressed by power. Yet racism becomes invisible as immediate cultural or biological coding through the separation between state and society brought about by the security *dispositif*.[12]

The security *dispositif* treats populations as 'natural objects' with their own laws of functioning and self-regulation. It is thus no surprise that the Italian government relied on laws that allowed for emergency measures in situations of natural disasters, calamities and other events. With the development of biopolitics, it is not the relation between state and citizen that is at stake, but the relation between state and population as an object of government. While contractual relations to the state require the legitimation of sovereign power in relation to right, governmental interventions are assessed in terms of their utility or non-utility for this new object of government, the population.[13] State measures become justified by the principle of efficiency and integration in the 'natural' functioning of societies. Limits to what the state can do are no longer primarily established through the contractual negotiation of rights between the individual and the state, but in relation to the objectives of governing society.

It is the definition of society and population as independent realms of knowledge which should not be destabilized that provides the most insidious justification of the anti-Roma measures. As the social becomes naturalized, the state holds individuals and groups of the population accountable for the proper use of their freedoms. Those who do not conform to the limits and conditions set by the state become dangerous, disorderly excesses that disturb the good functioning of society. As they pose a risk to the good functioning of society itself, their neutralization or elimination can only be a logical corollary. With the neoliberal representation of society on the model of economic markets, which only need framework conditions to do their self-regulative work, policing excesses and disorderly disruptions of the well-functioning societal organism become a necessity without immediate biological or cultural inscription.

The Italian government has justified its measures in relation to intrusions upon the 'natural' functioning of society. The presence of the Roma is seen as being of an 'extreme critical nature' and as a cause of 'serious social alarm'. The Roma disrupt the security and 'nature of things' in Italian society. Therefore the 'security package' only aims at restoring the self-governance of society and does not necessarily apply to particular ethnic or cultural categories. As such, it can apply indiscriminately to both the garbage situation in Naples and to the Roma, using similar measures to restore the proper functioning of cities. Soldiers are deployed to fight both crime and the garbage crisis.

In the biopolitical state, law has changed its function and itself become a site of racism. Legal interventions make decisions dependent upon standards of efficiency and appropriateness 'naturally' contained in the characteristics of society. Thus, fingerprinting is an appropriate intervention for correctly identifying all members of a community. After all, the Red Cross joined the government's fingerprinting process, arguing that it was done by respecting rights. And how could a database managed by a humanitarian organization not be respectful of human rights?

In the terms of neoliberalism, the kind of individual to be fostered through law and other social measures is the entrepreneur. Legal interventions no longer attempt to palliate the effects of the market, but to create subjects as entrepreneurs and to regulate the unavoidable conflicts that emerge among competing entrepreneurs.[14] Those who cannot become self-governing are to be preventively neutralized. And while these categories can become culturally and racially reinscribed, their exclusion is nonetheless rendered in the preventive terms of protecting society and securing its way of life.

NOTES

1. 'Lo spettro dei "mostri" venuti dall'Europa', *Corriere della Sera*, 1 November 2007, www.corriere.it/cronache/07_novembre_01/spettro_mostri.shtml.

2. Marco Brazzaduro, *Italy's Choice: Risk from Roma vs Roma at Risk*, Open Democracy, 2008, www.opendemocracy.net/article/risks-from-roma-or-roma-at-risk.

3. Council of Europe, Press Release, 27 June 2008, https://wcd.coe.int/ViewDoc.jsp?id=1315385 &Site=DC&BackColorInternet=F5CA75&BackColorIntranet=F5CA75&BackColorLogged= A9BACE.

4. 'Les Roms craignent une "contagion" de la "vague de racisme" italienne', *L'Express*, 7 August 2008, www.lexpress.fr/actualite/societe/les-roms-craignent-une-contagion-de-la-vague-de-racisme-italienne_546904.html?p=2.

5. European Network Against Racism, Press Release, 19 May 2008, http://cms.horus.be/ files/99935/MediaArchive/pdfpress/2008=05=19%20anti-Roma%20events&20Italy.pdf.

6. *Il Giornale*, 5 September 2008.

7. 'Italy Reassures EU that Fingerprinting Gypsies is Legal and Not Racist', *International Herald Tribune*, 24 July 2008, www.iht.com/articles/ap/2008/07/24/europe/EU-EU-Italy-Roma.php.

8. www.wsws.org/articles/2008/aug2008/ital-a06.shtml.

9. ERRC et al., 'Security a la Italiana: Fingerprinting, Extreme Violence and Harrassment of Roma in Italy', 2008, www.errc.org/db/03/21/m00000321.pdf.

10. http://circoloromaliberale.splinder.com/post/14621530/contro+1percent27insicurezza+galoppant.

11. Alana Lentin, 'Racial States, Anti-Racist Reponses. Picking Holes in "Culture" and "Human Rights"', *European Journal of Social Theory*, vol. 7, no. 4, 2008.

12. Michel Foucault, *Security, Territory, Population*, Palgrave, Basingstoke, 2007, p. 245.

13. Michel Foucault, *Naissance de la biopolitique. Cours au Collège de France, 1978–1979*, 'Hautes Etudes', Gallimard/Seuil, Paris, 2004, pp. 42–3.

14. Jacques Donzelot, 'Michel Foucault and Liberal Intelligence', *Economy and Society*, vol. 37, no. 1, 2008.

*Claudia Aradau is senior lecturer in international relations at the Department of War Studies, King's College, London.

This article first appeared in *Radical Philosophy* 153 (January 2009) and is reprinted here with permission from the publisher.

Chapter 4: Gender as Catalyst for Violence Against Roma in Contemporary Italy

by Shannon Woodcock*

Silvio Berlusconi's use of ethnicity and immigration as national security issues in his successful campaign for election to the Italian presidency in 2008 was by no means unique in contemporary Europe. What was surprising was the speed of his right-wing government's legislative restriction of migrants in the form of the so-called 'security package', first introduced just five weeks after the election. Woodcock explores the striking fact that this 'security package', and the intense wave of racist violence by Italians against Roma that it legitimized and encouraged, was proposed and justified in response to media reports of Italian babies being stolen by 'Zingari' from the 'nomad camps' and of Italian women being raped and beaten by Romanian men of 'Zingari' ethnicity. Gender and ethnicity are the twin constitutive discourses of modern European society, and racialized subjects are necessarily gendered. The stereotype of 'dangerous black men sexually threatening white women' has been mobilized in a vast range of European and colonial nationalist projects in order to justify the policing of both racialized masculine subjects and women as objects of the patriarchy. Similarly, the depiction of women as hysterical, sexually vulnerable objects in need of (white) masculine protection is an old story that the Italian media recognize as a fairy tale even as they reproduce the discourse. Woodcock explores what has not been mentioned thus far, namely, that gender stereotypes are vital to the mobilization of violent racism against the Roma in contemporary Italy, and how conservative gender binaries are strengthened and policed in a time of social crisis through the stereotyping of Roma as racial threat.

Since the early 1990s Italian government policy has segregated migrants identified as Roma in the peripheral socio-economic spaces formally known as *campi nomadi*. It is this policy that forces both contemporary asylum-seekers and economic migrants into a much older stereotype, that of pejorative Gypsy/*Zingari* nomadism with its constitutive elements of sorcery and criminality.[1] Since Silvio Berlusconi was elected to a fourth term as prime minister with a right-wing coalition government in 2008, state-sanctioned and media-fuelled violence perpetrated by Italians against people identified as Roma has increased. With a shifting conflation of racial and gendered stereotypes, Berlusconi's government validates acts of violence against racial Others, regardless of their citizenship, as acts of 'the Italian people'.

Berlusconi's reliance on ethnicity and immigration as a national security issue is by no means unique in contemporary Europe. What was surprising was the speed of his government's legislative restriction of migrants in the form of the so-called 'security package', approved by the cabinet just five weeks after his election. This article explores how this 'security package', and the intense wave of racist violence it legitimized and encouraged, was fuelled by media reports of Italian babies being stolen by 'Zingari' women from the 'nomad camps' and of Italian women being raped and beaten by Romanian men of 'Zingari' ethnicity. Gender and ethnicity are the twin constitutive discourses of modern European society, and racialized subjects are necessarily gendered. The stereotype of 'dangerous black men sexually threatening white women', which has been central to European and colonial nationalist projects, is being invoked again in order to justify the policing of both racialized masculine subjects and women as objects of the patriarchy. Similarly, the depiction of women as hysterical, sexually vulnerable objects in need of (white) masculine protection is an old story that the Italian media recognize as a fairy tale even as they reproduce the discourse. This paper explores gender as central to the mobilization of violent racism against the Roma in the Italian case, and how conservative gender binaries are strengthened and policed in a time of social crisis through the stereotyping of Roma as racial threat.

As a specialist in anti-Romani discourses, specifically in Romania, I came to write on the Italian case in response to the shocking levels of violent state intervention and the fact that, although 'rape' (and ethnicized masculinity and femininity) was used to mobilize the violence, this vital factor was often elided in both English and Italian sources.[2] While an analysis of Italian political and media responses requires recognition of regional divides, and attention to the nuanced differences in political positions, this paper attempts to analyse the trans-regional mobilization of gendered racial stereotypes, across the political spectrum, from the left to the right. Indeed, an increasing number of Italian scholars point out that anti-Romani policies of the last decade have been mobilized in similar ways and intensities by both the left and the right, especially in Rome and in Florence, where large communities of Roma were living prior to recent deportations.[3] This paper summarizes the main points of the Italian case and draws on the dominant images circulated throughout the public sphere in media, on posters and on websites. It traces the mobilizing power of gendered ethnic stereotypes throughout Italian society, including in online blogs and forums, virtual spaces where those without public space in which to speak can give voice to their experiences.

A History of Romani Peoples in Italy: Stereotypes and Anxiety

Since the fifteenth century, those who have lived in the Italian lands have stereotyped Romani peoples as embodying certain taboos and anxieties. Indeed, Roma have consistently been treated by the majority population in ways that force them into fulfilling stereotypical expectations. Historically, Roma who sought to settle down while trading were constantly expelled from towns as 'nomads': the first recorded expulsion of Roma was from Milan in 1493. The stereotype of nomadism is a powerful discursive frame that persists at the core of contemporary anti-Romani prejudice. This stereotype is linked to a discourse that imagines the entire people as criminal, irreverent towards religion, harbouring sinister magical powers and primitive, as evidenced in promiscuity, dancing and baby-snatching. This cluster of stereotypes has simultaneously enabled those who project them to remain settled, God-fearing and civilized, and be recognized as citizens within local administrative structures. In 1876 Cesare Lombroso's chapter about the pejoratively named *Zingari* in his book *L'Uomo delinquente* linked these historical stereotypes to the physical constitution of the Roma as a race, thus building anti-Romani stereotypes into the foundation of western eugenics.[4] The stereotypical discourse was also intrinsically gendered: it was Romani women who, then and now, were portrayed as stealing babies and practising witchcraft.

Italian colonialism, like other European colonialisms, was shaped by these pre-existing racial and gendered discourses. In Eritrea, for example, the Fascist regime's policy, and expectation, upon invasion in 1935 was that colonized women were both objects of liberation and desire for Italian soldiers: semi-pornographic photographs of African women were distributed, and the colonies were made available for popular consumption in songs such as 'Faccetta nera' ('The Little Black Face').[5] The Fascist racial hierarchy of course did not support the prospect of inter-racial marriage (sex was another story) and, on 19 April 1937, Vittorio Emanuele III prohibited 'conjugal relations' between colonial subjects and Italian citizens. In this way, while rape and non-conjugal sexual relations between Italian men and African women were sanctioned, the Italian state relied on gendered and ethnicized legislation to define and police Italian (as European and colonial) identity. In the course of the Second World War, Italian Roma and Sinti were also persecuted as racial Others, the previously articulated range of social behaviour stereotypes located in their supposed biological difference to ethnic Italians, even though Romani Italians fought in the Italian army.[6]

After 1945 Sinti and Roma in Italy were segregated and marginalized by state institutions and understood primarily through a consistently racist discourse in the broader community. By the 1980s Italy had radically changed from being a source of emigrants to being a host society for migrants from Eastern Europe (including Roma) and Africa. This caused various social upheavals. Migrants found work in industries that suffered from the out-migration of young Italian men, and newly arrived women found work as carers and in traditionally female roles that catered to the needs of an ageing population at a time when extended families were becoming increasingly uncommon. Italian legislation did not keep up with the flow of migration, especially for those claiming refugee status after 1990. Even as migrants to Italy were easily incorporated into the employment market, the government did not formalize, in popular discourse or in policy, this incorporation, resulting in a situation that one author referred to as 'permanent social emergency'.[7] Throughout the 1990s, Romani migrants arrived in Italy seeking asylum from the wars in Bosnia, Croatia, Serbia and Kosovo. From 2002 (when Romanian citizens no longer required Schengen visas) onwards, further European Union (EU) accession changes made it easier for Romanian Roma to migrate to Italy. Following Romania's full accession to the EU in 2007, in particular, there was a visible wave of Romani migrants to Italy (and western Europe in general) who were often conflated with Italian Roma and Sinti, to the detriment of the latter.[8]

While Italian political culture must be approached with a recognition of regional divides, right-wing political groups *across the country*, including the Lega Nord and Movimento Sociale Italiano (MSI, later Alleanza Nazionale), all sought to mobilize intolerance against migration in the name of 'the Italian people'.[9] The stereotypes of migrants that were widely available in everyday life and in the media in the 1990s were racialized and gendered in historically continuous ways. For example, Albanian migrants, who were predominantly men, were stereotyped as racially predisposed to violent criminality, while Nigerian women were seen as 'synonymous with being a prostitute'.[10] Institutional and violent acts of racism in the decade prior to 2008 are documented in a range of reports.[11] In turn, stereotypes of Roma informed legislative decisions that further entrenched the treatment of Roma as embodiments of pejorative, historically developed images

As hostility to the eastern European and African migrants grew stronger in the 1990s, so too did anti-Romani sentiment, often the result of the slippery categories of identity wherein Romanian Roma and ethnic Romanians could be conflated or differentiated according to the (racist) discourse of the speaker. The clear targets of a core part of Berlusconi's 2008 'security package', for example, were 'nomads'. This term could be understood as referring to anyone living in the authorized and unauthorized 'nomad camps' throughout Italy, regardless of their citizenship status. Even Romani refugees from settled communities were called 'nomads' by the authorities because they were Roma and allowed no option but to settle in the makeshift camps on the peripheries of cities. These camps were—and continue to be, where they remain—rarely serviced with water, electricity, rubbish collection or public transport by the Italian state; they are policed and perceived as sites of illegal activity rather than of enforced poverty and social segregation. There are an estimated 130,000/160,000 Roma and Sinti in Italy, of whom some 18,000 people—the official Italian government figure is 12,346—are non-Italian Roma living in camps.[12] Italian Roma and Sinti are also part of the camp population, and they are often treated as badly as non-Italian Roma.[13] The 'nomad camps' were originally manifestations of the Italian government's unwillingness to grant refugee status to the influx of Roma fleeing wars in the former Yugoslavia. Italian policy towards non-Romani refugees from those wars, and from Romania and Albania in general, made the acquisition of legal residency papers difficult for those wanting to claim refugee status.[14] Policy, rather, encouraged individuals to work without permits in the private care industry, out of sight in private homes and without state protection. These carers now form a huge workforce supporting Italy's ageing population, comprised of millions of (specifically female) migrants from Romania and Albania.

Nando Sigona, an academic and activist for Romani rights, explains that the discursive construction of Romani refugees as 'nomads' effectively precludes them from being understood as 'refugees' or 'citizens'.[15] In the very term 'nomad', a Romani survivor of war is made into the stereotypical ancient wanderer who is directed by primitive instinct. Italians also project older stereotypes of Roma—as uncivilized, musical, violent, sexual or without loyalty to state or religion—on to those categorized as 'nomads' today. As the 'nomad camps' forced Roma to live in dire poverty, without access to schools, and working piecemeal jobs without registration papers, the Italian government created a population against whom the ancient stereotypes could be employed once again, and to great effect.

BERLUSCONI'S 'STATE OF EMERGENCY'

Italian nationalism and society has been gendered and racialized in intensely unique ways since the formation of the Italian state. Today, Berlusconi's government harks back to recognizable modes of inter sectionality between gender and race. While there is a vast literature analysing gender, race and nationalism as inseparable, constitutive identity discourses,[16] scholarship and activism focused on race and gender *vis-à-vis* policy and community in Italy since the establish-ment of the European Union have failed to address these twin discourses as interdependent.[17]

The radical and rapid intensification of anti-Romani legislation and hate speech in the early months of Berlusconi's government in 2008 continued the focus of his election campaign. In October 2007 the press reported that a wom-an it repeatedly described as 'the wife of a retired Italian admiral' had been raped and murdered by a Romani Romanian man in Rome. This sparked an in-tense wave of Italian legislative activity and citizen violence against Romanian, Albanian and Romani individuals across Italy, as well as the reinvigoration of specifically anti-Romani racism. The description of the victim as the wife of a military man signified to the broader society that 'even' middle-class, married, older women were not safe: all white Italian women were potential victims of sexual violence by non-Italian men.

On the first day of November, two days after the attack, the Italian govern-ment passed Law Decree 181/2007 entitled 'Espulsione di cittadini comunitari per motivi di pubblica sicurezza' (Expulsion of local citizens for reasons of pub-lic security). This decree gave local representatives of the interior ministry the power to expel any European citizen identified as a threat to public security.[18] Expulsions were to be decided by prefects without a hearing, and approximately twenty individuals were expelled in the first twenty-four hours after the law's implementation, forty were expelled within the week, and hundreds over the next three months.[19] All Romani men were identified, and vilified, as sexually aggressive threats to Italian women and, as such, to Italian society in general. One survey published in *Corriere della Sera* reported that 70 per cent of Italian respondents said they didn't think co-existence with Roma was possible,[20] but it was Romanian citizens—perceived to be linked to Romani ethnicity—who were specifically targeted.[21] On 4 November 2007 'several hundred Italians marched in Rome declaring that they were giving all Romanian immigrants ten days to leave Italy'.[22]

This is the context in which Berlusconi fought his election campaign: in the midst of media-fuelled and organized racist rhetoric and actions against the ex-aggerated sexual threat of Romani men against Italian women in public space. Throughout the campaign, the Italian media continually reported stories of Ital-ian citizens, mostly groups of young men, beating and even killing random and innocent men identified as ethnically Romani or eastern European.[23] Since the October 2007 case of the admiral's wife, sexual violence against Italian women in public space has been the relentlessly-referred-to rallying cry driving the media, government and popular vigilante frenzy. In that case, the issue of class was also raised in the press, and discussion focused on how the victim was a working middle-class woman, at home in public space and yet, clearly, still vulnerable to rape and murder therein. This single case was taken up by Berlusconi and his colleagues across the political right as a sign of the times, as a demonstration that 'even' the secure middle classes were being figuratively and literally 'attacked' by migration.[24] To the working classes, who had already been experiencing the belt-tightening, stressful effects of new economic and employment measures, a single threat, that of non-Italian men to Italian women, that could be shared across regional and class divides enabled a new sense of solidarity on the basis of masculine ethnic nationalism.

In May 2008 Berlusconi assumed his fourth term as Italian prime minister, supported by a right-wing coalition that had campaigned on the claim that irregular migrants were causing a 'national security emergency' in Italy.[25] Berlusconi was already well known for Law 189/2002, the so-called Bossi-Fini law of 2001 that tightened regulations on foreign residents. This legislation made a standing job offer a requirement of the 'entry for employment' category, and abolished permits for employment-seeking migrants, thus linking the residence permit to the working contract and increasing the number of cases in which expulsion was justified.

On 21 May 2008 the Italian cabinet unanimously adopted the even more restrictive provisions known as the 'security package' (Law Decree 92/2008), proposed by Interior Minister Roberto Maroni (of the Lega Nord).[26] In brief, the package has four sections. The first enabled the expulsion of EU and non-EU citizens in Italy sentenced to more than two years' imprisonment, and made being an 'illegal' resident an aggravating offence subject to a jail sentence one-third longer than would be applicable to Italian citizens. Renting property to a 'foreign citizen illegally residing in the Italian territory' became an offence punishable by imprisonment and property confiscation. In addition, Article 6 amended Law Decree 267/2000 to give mayors 'the competence to adopt "urgent regulations for security reasons"', and municipal police access to databases of the interior ministry.[27] Article 7, 'participation of the Army in territorial control', was used by the Minister of Defence in July 2008 to deploy 3,000 soldiers across Italy in operations of population surveillance and control.

The second section of the package brought in tougher measures and higher costs for EU citizens and Third Country Nationals (TCNs) applying for residence and seeking work in Italy. European citizens now needed to register with the authorities after showing evidence of 'sufficient economic resources ... to sustain themselves' on arrival. The entry of EU citizens and their family members might be limited 'for reasons of state security [or] preemptory reasons of public security'.[28]

A draft law proposed by the government on providing public security was the third section of the 'security package' and included the recommendation of prison sentences for those who used children for begging, as well as for 'illegal entrance in the Italian territory'.[29] It made it compulsory for money transfer agencies to obtain a copy of the residence permits of TCNs, and extended the length of detention in a centre for 'irregular immigrants' from 60 days to 180 days.

The final section was the declaration by the Council of Ministers of a 'state of emergency in relation to the settlements of nomad communities in the regions of Campania, Latium and Lombardy', which had immediate and violent consequences for Roma. As highlighted by many NGO reports, the power to declare a state of emergency (under Article 5 of Law 225/1992) is restricted to cases of 'natural calamities, catastrophes or other events that according to their intensity and reach need to be faced by extraordinary powers and means', a condition that the Italian government applied to the very existence of the so-called 'nomad camps' in the regions stipulated.[30] As Massimo Merlino points out, the 'emergency ordinances' that were included authorized local prefects to implement various measures as well as to use police and military personnel in doing so,

> in light of 'the extremely critical situation generated by the presence of numerous irregular and nomad foreigners who are permanently installed in the urban areas'. The government holds that 'the precariousness of those camps has caused situations of serious social alarm [among] the local populations'.[31]

On 26 May, five days after the 'security package' was approved, Maroni announced that a census of all 'nomads' would be conducted. It was clear, therefore, that Romani people, labelled and stereotyped as 'nomads', and socially and spatially segregated as such, were the primary targets of the legislation. It is vital to examine how gender stereotypes and roles functioned as a catalyst for the development and implementation of this legislation.

BERLUSCONI'S ITALY: WHITE MEN PROTECTING WHITE WOMEN FROM 'OTHER' MEN

On 10 May 2008, in the first days of Berlusconi's new government, an Italian woman in Naples claimed to have caught a young Romani woman from a nearby 'nomad camp' trying to steal her baby from her apartment.[32] In response to this claim, and a frenzied flurry of media reports, groups of Italian men and boys attacked local 'nomad camps' and individuals who were ethnic Romanians as well as Roma. Despite the arrest of the young Romani woman and police patrols ostensibly attempting to stop the violence against Roma, on 13 May a group of between 300 and 400 Italians, led by women, attacked a 'nomad camp' causing great destruction.[33] On 13 and 14 May, police evacuated large and small Romani camps, leaving many to seek shelter in camps in other cities, but also establishing a new, larger camp for the evacuees. This new camp was designated by means of a police cordon and residents were afraid to leave, while their old homes and all their belongings were burnt down by Italian citizens, and then bulldozed by the local council. Surveys conducted after these events found that 75 per cent of the inhabitants had lived in a single camp for four years, and that the average length of time for living in one camp was 7.5 years.[34] The people who were so spectacularly segregated and cordoned off by the state as 'nomads' were not in fact nomadic.

The Italian parliament—chastised in part by media fascination with the women-led popular violence, portrayed as an act by 'the people' reduced to desperate measures—hastened the introduction of the 'security package'. It was necessary to wait until 21 May 2008 (for the approval of the Council of Ministers and publication of the law in the Official Gazette), yet the Mayor of Naples announced the appointment of a 'special commissioner' for the 'Roma emergency' on 14 May.[35] Police and the army were used to patrol the streets and, while this was explained later to international investigators as protection for Romani victims from Italian vigilante crime, the popular violence against Roma was in fact encouraged by politicians. The Interior Minister Roberto Maroni was quoted as saying: 'that [violence] is what happens when gypsies steal babies, or when Romanians commit sexual violence'.[36] In this way, politicians have constantly misrepresented racist violence—a problem of Italian society—as a 'Romani problem'. Umberto Bossi, the Lega Nord leader, stated that 'people do what the state can't manage', implying thereby that the state's role was to support the actions of 'the people' rather than to control violence and prejudice.[37]

These comments highlight a feature of the waves of physical and legislative violence in Italy in 2008 and 2009. Namely, that the racial stereotyping of Roma relied on gendered profiles: Romani men as primitive rapists and a sexual threat to Italian women; and Romani women as baby-snatchers. Both of these stereotypes embody the broader stereotype of Roma as ethnically primitive and uncivilized in terms of being unable to control supposedly biologically determined masculine (sex) and feminine (mother hood) traits. The new legislation concerning the expulsion of 'foreigners' would be implemented on the basis of a census, announced by the government on 26 May, that would fingerprint and register all Roma in camps.[38] In June 2008 Maroni declared that mayors would close down authorized camps without adequate water and electricity supplies, and that only ethnic Italian Roma and Sinti would be allowed to settle in authorized camps.[39] 'Foreign' Roma, including those born in Italy to Yugoslav-born parents, would only be allowed to use so-called 'transit' camps, and only for a period of up to three months. In this way, the new 'security package' went even further towards making nomadic non-citizens out of Roma who had been born in Italy or had lived there, sometimes for decades.

Only a newcomer to the field of Romani rights would be surprised by the few, and ineffective, international institutional responses to the gross violations of human rights that have occurred in Italy since May 2008. This is despite the best efforts of NGOs such as the European Roma Rights Centre (ERRC), the European Roma Information Office (ERIO) and OsservAzione. By the end of 2009, just three major reports on Italy had been produced, by the Organization for Security and Co-operation in Europe (OSCE), the EU's Fundamental Rights Agency (FRA) and the Open Society Institute (OSI).[40] In 2008 there was a single formal visit, and statement, from the Council of Europe's Commissioner for Human Rights.[41] The EU did not protest when Berlusconi's policy of fingerprinting Romani minors in 2008 began, even though it had not received the response to its objections that Italy had promised. Nor has the EU responded to NGO demands for a justification of this inaction.[42]

THE MOBILIZING POWER OF RAPE

On 14 February 2009, the rape of a fourteen-year-old Italian girl in the Caffarella Park in Rome became a prime example of how Italian society and Berlusconi's government use incidents of sexual violence to intensify both patriarchal control of women and racism as part of the same project of national identity formation. Following the incident, which the young victim claimed was perpetrated by men with 'Arab' accents, one with two fingers missing, local Italian youths attacked and hospitalized groups of innocent Romanian men in the area. By 18 February, the police had declared they had arrested the culprits.[43] The faces of two men were shown in all media outlets: two dark-skinned and poor-looking men who the viewers were told had been arrested in the 'nomad camps' in and just outside of Rome. Neither man was missing any fingers, and they were Romanian citizens with Hungarian Romani names. Romanian media and commentators eagerly highlighted the fact that the men were Hungarian Roma who just happened to be Romanian citizens.

There was no subsequent story in the mainstream press about the well-being of the rape victim. The Italian government leapt into action, however, to push through the final text of an emergency decree and, indeed, the 'security package', including authorization for the formation of community security patrols. Roberto Maroni described these as 'groups of unnamed citizens' working to 'assist the police by bringing to their attention events that might be damaging to urban security'.[44] On 23 February Berlusconi introduced the emergency decree that set a mandatory life sentence for the rape of minors or any attack in which the victim was killed.[45] (It is worth juxtaposing the speed with which this decree was enacted with the fact that it was only in 1996 that Italian law changed a Mussolini-era statute defining rape as a 'crime against the patrimony' to a 'crime against the person', highlighting just how recently the Italian courts recognized that a woman exists as an individual outside the patriarchal family.[46] It is also worth noting that, in Italy as in other European countries, national surveys show that victims primarily experience sexual violence at the hands of someone they know, mostly their intimate partner.[47])

Within a week, Italian police had bulldozed the camps where the two Romanians, aged 20 and 36, had previously lived. The right-wing Mayor of Rome, Gianni Alemanno, promised that all 'illegal nomad camps' in the city would be dismantled, making homeless 20,000 people, by his own estimate. Alemanno thereby managed to link Roma with stereotypical nomads and the camps with illegality when, in fact, they were government-sanctioned, controlled and policed spaces of segregation.

Three weeks later the police admitted, after pressure from the media and NGOs, that the men they had paraded as the captured rapists had in fact been cleared, not as a result of their unwavering protestations of innocence or statements that they had not been in Rome at the time of the crime, but because DNA tests showed no link between the men arrested and the perpetrators. The police still refused to release them on the grounds that they could jeopardize the ongoing investigation, yet their admission of false arrest raised questions in the media about racial profiling and the (im)possibility of a fair trial. Mainstream journalists reflected on whether Italy was indeed becoming *too* racist, but none wrote about how the rape had been used to provoke a reaction by the patriarchal state or to displace the violence, both sexual and otherwise, on to racialized men. In the week after the rape at Caffarella Park, the daily *La Repubblica* published 82 articles—and, in the month following the event, 176 articles—about foreign citizens and crime, causing a 'moral panic'.[48] But no one asked why it was 'rape' and not 'racism' that was constantly the focus of media reports, or indeed what that 'racism' meant for female victims of sexual violence.

The comments of Italian politicians regarding the incidence of rape in public spaces also became a focus of the media. Roberto Calderoli of the Lega Nord (Minister for Legislative Simplification) said that chemical castration was 'the only answer'.[49] Berlusconi himself famously defended the effectiveness of sending an extra 30,000 soldiers on to the streets to prevent rapes by stating that they would continue to occur unless there were 'as many soldiers as pretty girls'.[50] While Calderoli and Berlusconi are generally perceived as given to extreme and outlandish comments, their responses were widely reported. And the reactions of the media and the broader public are telling.

While Berlusconi's 'joke' was widely taken as yet another indication that his opinions are not typical of ordinary Italians, it nonetheless reflected and strengthened commonly held and heavily policed constructions of women as *naturally* vulnerable to men and thus needing their protection. Berlusconi perceives rape as a natural consequence of women being passive and feminine, and thereby provoking the masculine desire to rape, naturalized as an expression of heterosexual physical desire. In this way rape becomes an extension of the hetero-normative balance of the Italian state. This is an understanding that presumes that rape is an act of sexual desire, an understanding that has long been contested and indeed deconstructed by the argument that rape is not about sex but about power.[51] In Berlusconi's Italy, however, being a woman is (re)defined (with military support) as the very state of being a perpetually vulnerable, potential victim of rape. Within this paradigm, a 'real' Italian woman is attractive in order to gain the protection (against the potential of sexual violence) of her boyfriend, her countrymen, representatives of the Italian state. In order to be recognized as the Italian ideal of 'woman', Italian women need to understand themselves as requiring protection from assault. Cartoons in the press, like Livio Bonino's ..., played on this logic.

The focus on the rape of and sexual violence against white Italian women by racially 'other' strangers ('unknown', as well as 'foreign') in public space belies the fact that sexual violence most often occurs in the home at the hands of men known to the women.[52] There is scant discussion about how this dominant discourse reconfirms public space as the natural domain of men, and women as therefore consensually vulnerable in the street as objects of the masculine gaze, and, by extension, potential victims of sexual violence. Likewise, there is scant discussion of the fact that the private space to which women are relegated on threat of violence is the most violent space for them to be in. The patriarchy that owns the woman does not always protect her: in fact, the statistics highlight the opposite. Even as Italian law has redefined women as citizens in their own right, they remain sexual objects unless and until there are provisions for the prosecution of sexual violence in the home and in the family.

The posters put up throughout Rome in 2007 by a radical right-wing group called Forza Nuova both provide an insight into how the construction of Italian women as passive victims is vital to the racism of the New Right, and also shift the semiotic boundaries of the social debate. While the group that made them is on the extreme right, the posters were pasted throughout Rome and widely seen by everyday Romans regardless of their political persuasion. They were designed to bring people into the street, and to visualize the fear-mongering scenario hysterically repeated in the press at the time. These posters can serve as examples of the historically developed discourses invoked in common discursive and physical space: the images functioned behind and beyond their politically marginal creators. One poster ... depicts a white (implicitly Italian) woman screaming in terror, on the ground, while being assaulted by a brown-skinned long-haired man (implicitly an ethnic Rom).[53]

I am arguing here that we must pay attention to the fact that gender is vital to the functioning of racial stereotypes, that gender and race work together to mobilize contemporary anti-Romani racism in Italy. Not only is this crucial to understanding how the Romani man is stereotyped as sexually aggressive (hyper-masculine) but also to a recognition that this stereotypical repetition creates the ideal Italian woman as the object of masculine sexual aggression. Only white women of Italian ethnicity—as the mothers, wives and daughters of Italian men—are reported and imagined as objects to be raped.

WOMEN IN ITALY AND ANTI-ROMANI DISCOURSE

When Italian women displace the threat of sexual violence on to the racial Other, they are voicing their fear of and anger at violence, and simultaneously constructing themselves as Italian women requiring the protection of Italian men. This is a space from which women can demand, and receive, better legislative and medical protection from sexual violence. Women can also hold racist views and claim a speaking position of 'essential woman' as potential rape victim. One example is Stefi, who describes herself on her popular blog as a thirty-three-year-old of mixed English-Sicilian heritage who studied law in Italy and lives in East London. I am not claiming that Stefi's opinion is in any way representative of 'all women' or 'all white women', but simply that it is, like all positions, a singular one in which an individual is actively engaging with the available gendered and racialized discourse. Stefi argues—to a significant following on her blog—that race should be considered an aggravating feature in sexual assault, especially now (by her logic) that the Italian law recognizes gang rape and the age of the victim as aggravating features. She writes:

> For most white women being raped by a black man would be a worse ordeal than being raped by a white man. So if the victim identifies her rapists [sic] race or nationality as significant to her, this ought to be reflected in the sentence. If that leaves a rapist feeling racially discriminated against—tough—DON'T RAPE!!![54]

Displacing the threat of sexual violence against all Italian women on to racially 'other' men enables Italian women of all age-groups and classes to unite in demanding Italian patriarchal protection *as* Italian women. It also enables Italian women to displace anxiety about their own role in the oppression and abuse of non-Italian women. Many thousands of Romanian and Albanian women have migrated primarily to work as carers in Italian homes since 1990.[55] As discussed below, it is widely believed in Romania and Albania that these women face high levels of sexual harassment and violence with no practical recourse to the law.

To draw on another singular example, Silvana Pallotti is a sixty-five-year old woman in Rome who spoke to journalists about why she joined a mixed-sex community security patrol with the declared aim of protecting women after the February 2009 rape in Caffarella Park. Pallotti stated: 'I'm angry. I'm not racist, my maid is Romanian. But Romanian men are bad, they are all bandits'.[56] Pallotti mentions that she employs a Romanian woman as evidence of her lack of racism, and then continues to stereotype all Romanian men as 'bandits'. Participation in a neighbourhood committee that surveils *all* Romanian men enables Italian women to claim protection as Italian women, beyond class and age-group. These community security patrols also enable Italian men, across class and age-group, to perform masculine ownership and protection of public space and Italian women.

In contemporary Italy we can consider the relevance of Susan Brownmiller's classic conclusion that rape is the means by which all men intimidate all women.[57] I am not saying that individuals do not contest hegemonic discourses; individuals (and organizations) most certainly do contest them in everyday acts of resistance. My aim here rather is to trace the powerful state-sanctioned and historically developed discourses through which all people in Italy are constructed, regardless of whether they agree.[58] What does Berlusconi gain by implying that the government's role is to protect Italian women from the dangers of non-Italian masculinity in public space? These notions of both Italian masculinity and targeted ethnic groups shore up his and his government's own performances of control over public space, including the women therein.

Nonetheless, even if women are successfully constructed as requiring the protection of the Italian patriarchy, their brothers, their boyfriends, the Italian men and women in community security patrols, the media as well as the government and military, there is no guarantee that they will be safe or even supported. The displacement of sexual violence on to non-Italian racial groups makes it even harder to find a space to discuss the reality of sexual violence occurring primarily in the home, in private space, at the same time as it contributes to driving Italian women out of public space. The media have not reported on how those Italian women who have been raped have fared, and the government has not provided any additional support for rape victims. On the contrary, the Italian woman, whose claims that a Romani girl stole her baby began the May 2008 attacks on Roma in Naples and occasioned the government's 'security package', was subsequently derided in the press as hysterical and mentally ill. Likewise, the victim's description of the perpetrators of the February 2009 rape did not match the identity of the men police arrested after racial profiling. But the media were focussed on the sensational narrative of non-Italian rapists and not on the fact that the safety of the victim (and other potential victims) and the demands of justice required that the police find the real attacker.

Sexual violence against Italian women has *consistently* been used to mobilize and justify the increasingly violent anti-Romani actions and legislation in Italy in recent years. These incidents and the responses to them have reconfigured race and gender in new constellations. The process is intrinsically gendered. It cannot happen without the simultaneous gendering of racialized groups: of non-Italian men as hyper-masculine (violent rapists) and Italian women as vulnerable, requiring the protection of Italian patriarchy in the form of legislation, the military and the newly formed community security patrols. In the Italian case of anti-Romani racism, gender cannot be considered as a separate frame of analysis, as a term signifying solely what happens to women. Gender is an analytical category as intrinsic to the analysis of racism itself as it is to the formation and use of racialized discourse in post-colonial Europe.

NOTES

1. Nando Sigona, 'How can a "nomad" be a "refugee"? Kosovo Roma and labelling policy in Italy', *Sociology*, vol. 37, no. 1, 2003, 69–79.

2. In this paper, I take 'gender' to be an organizational concept and discursive construct rather than a reality experienced by individuals as a biological fact, together with the categories of 'race', 'ethnicity' and 'national identity'.

3. See Giovanni Picker, 'Welcome "in": Romani migrants and left-wing Tuscany 1988–2007', and Isabella Clough Marinaro, 'Life on the run: biopolitics and the Roma in Italy', both in Nando Sigona (ed.), *Romani Mobilities in Europe: Multidisciplinary Perspectives. Conference Proceedings* (conference held at the Refugee Studies Centre, University of Oxford, 14–15 January 2010), 152/65 and 36/40, respectively, available online at http://romanimobilities.wordpress.com/2010/01/29/romani-mobilities-in-europe-conference-proceedings-final-version (viewed 23 August 2010).

4. Cesare Lombroso, *L'Uomo delinquente* (Milan: Hoepli Press 1876).

5. For analyses of race, gender and Italy in Eritrea, see Ruth Iyob, 'Madamismo and beyond: the construction of Eritrean women', in Ruth Ben-Ghiat and Mia Fuller (eds), *Italian Colonialism* (New York: Palgrave Macmillan 2005), 233–44.

6. See Luca Bravi, 'La persecuzione e lo sterminio dei roma e dei sinti nel nazifascismo', and Paolo Finzi, 'A forza di essere vento. La persecuzione nazista contro roma e sinti: note storiche e considerazioni attuali', both in Roberto Cherchi and Gianni Loy (eds), *Rom e Sinti in Italia: Tra Stereotipi e Dritti Negati* (Rome: Ediesse 2009), 169–88 and 189–214, respectively.

7. Giovanna Campani, 'Immigration and racism in southern Europe: the Italian case', *Ethnic and Racial Studies*, vol. 16, no. 3, 1993, 507–35.

8. Nando Sigona and Nidhi Trehan, 'Introduction: Romani politics in neoliberal Europe', in Nando Sigona and Nidhi Trehan (eds), *Romani Politics in Contemporary Europe: Poverty, Ethnic Mobilization, and the Neoliberal Order* (Basingstoke and New York: Palgrave Macmillan 2009), 1–22 (10).

9. Laura Balbo and Luigi Manconi, *I razzismi reali* (Milan: Feltrinelli 1992). For a useful critique of the Italian case and preventative measures against 'multiculturalism', see Adrian Favell, 'Italy as a comparative case', in Ralph Grillo and Jeff Pratt (eds), *The Politics of Recognising Difference: Multiculturalism Italian Style* (Aldershot: Ashgate 2002), 237–44.

10. Anna Triandafyllidou, 'Nation and immigration: a study of the Italian press discourse', *Social Identities*, vol. 5, no. 1, 1999, 65–88. See also Asale Angel-Ajani, 'Diasporic conditions: mapping the discourses of race and criminality in Italy', *Transforming Anthropology*, vol. 11, 2002, 36–46.

11. See Annamaria Rivera and Paola Andrisani, 'Analytical study on discrimination and racist violence in Italy: 2000–2002', report compiled for Cooperazione per lo Sviluppo dei Paesi Emergenti (COSPE), National Focal Point of the EU Monitoring Centre on Racism and Xenophobia, September 2002, available on the COSPE website at www.cospe.it/uploads/documenti/allegati/rapporto_2002_su_violenza_razzista_en. pdf. Amnesty International reports can be found online at www.amnesty.org/en/region/italy, and Human Rights Watch reports at www.hrw.org/europecentral-asia/italy (all viewed 24 August 2010).

12. Nando Sigona, 'The "problema nomadi" vis-à-vis the political participation of Roma and Sinti at the local level in Italy', in Sigona and Trehan (eds), *Romani Politics in Contemporary Europe*, 272–92 (275).

13. About half of the officially estimated 150,000 Roma in Italy are said to be non-Italian. Those Roma who migrated from the former Yugoslav states during the wars now have their own children who were born in Italy but, as they have not been given documents or integrated into the system, they continue to be considered non-Italian. See the report by the European Roma Rights Centre (ERRC), *Campland: Racial Segregation of Roma in Italy*, Country Report Series no. 9 (Budapest: ERRC 2000).

14. Russell King and Nicola Mai, *Out of Albania: From Crisis Migration to Social Inclusion in Italy* (New York: Berghahn Books 2008), 84–7.

15. Sigona, 'How can a "nomad" be a "refugee"?'.

16. See Anne McClintock, '"No longer in a future heaven": women and nationalism in South Africa', *Transition*, no. 51, 1991, 104–23; Anne McClintock, 'Family feuds: gender, nationalism and the family', *Feminist Review*, no. 44, Summer 1993, 61–80; and Nira Yuval-Davis, 'Women, citizenship and difference', *Feminist Review*, no. 57, Autumn 1997, 4–27.

17. This point is elucidated at length in Elena del Giorgio and Emanuela Lombardo, 'Institutionalising intersectionality in Italy: gatekeepers and political dynamics', paper presented at the ECPR Joint Sessions Workshop 14 ('Instituting Intersectionality'), Lisbon, Portugal, 14–19 April 2009, available online at www.ucm.es/info/target/Art%20Chs%20EN/WHYIT_DelGiorgioLombardo_Jun09.pdf (viewed 25 August 2010).

18. Law Decree 181/2007 is available online at www.agesol.it/documenti_upload/dl_181_2007.pdf (viewed 25 August 2010).

19. Irina Angelescu, 'All new migration debates commence in Rome: new developments in the securitization of migration in the EU', in Part 1 of the EU Monitoring and Advocacy Program project, *Across Fading Borders: The Challenges of East/West Migration in the EU*, April 2008, available on the Open Society Foundation website at www.soros.org/initiatives/media/articles_publications/publications/across_ 20080429/angelescu.pdf (viewed 25 August 2010).

20. Ibid., 2.

21. The murderer was an ethnic Rom with Romanian citizenship, and as there are a large number of ethnically Romani Romanians, and a large number of Romanian migrants in Italy, it stands to reason that there are Romanian Roma among them. In addition, Romanians are perceived by Italians, along with Albanians, as the most significantly different European ethnic migrant group.

22. Angelescu, 'All new migration debates commence in Rome', 2.

23. For detailed evidence of increasing violence after the October murder, see EU Fundamental Rights Agency (FRA), *Incident Report: Violent Attacks against Roma in the Ponticelli District of Naples, Italy* (Vienna: FRA 2008), available on the FRA website athttp://fra.europa.eu/fraWebsite/material/pub/ROMA/Incid-Report-Italy 08_en.pdf (viewed 25 August 2010).

24. The media emphasis on the victim's status as the wife of an admiral in the Italian navy, and as a quiet Catholic woman, consistently constructed her as fulfilling the ideal of Italian femininity.

25. For an excellent analysis of Berlusconi's election campaign's reliance on unsubstantiated claims of security threats, see Elisabetta De Giorgi and Francesco Marangoni, 'The first year of Berlusconi's fourth government: formation, characteristics and activities', *Bulletin of Italian Politics*, vol. 1, no. 1, 2009, 87–109.

26. For an excellent overview of the 'security package' and its complex relation to Italy's international legal obligations, on which I will draw, see Massimo Merlino, *The Italian (In)Security Package: Security vs. Rule of Law and Fundamental Rights in the EU*, Challenge Paper

14 (Brussels: Centre for European Policy Studies 2009), available on the CEPS website at www.ceps.eu/book/italian-insecurity-package-security-vs-rulelaw-and-fundamental-rights-eu (viewed 25 August 2010).

27. Ibid., 6.

28. Ibid., 8. Note that Maroni also declared that in the future this legislation would be used to expel EU citizens who did not make a minimum income threshold, which would include many who live in the 'nomad camps'.

29. Ibid., 9. For a new study of the ways that 'begging' is gendered (with women beggars violating the stereotypical feminine role of caring for children), see Stefan Benedik, 'On the streets and in the bed: gendered and sexualised narratives in popular perceptions of Romani migrations within Central and Eastern Europe', in Sigona (ed.), *Romani Mobilities in Europe*, 11–19.

30. On 25 July 2008 the Italian Council of Ministers extended the state of emergency to the entire Italian territory in the face of a supposedly 'persistent and extraordinary influx of non-EU citizens' (Merlino, *The Italian (In)Security Package*, 11).

31. Ibid., 10–11.

32. For discussions of these events in relation to the centuries-old European stereotype of 'Romani women's criminality, see Gianfranco Faillaci, 'É vero che gli zingari rubano I bambini?', *Ucuntu* (online), 29 May 2008, available at www.ucuntu.org/I-ladri-dibambini.html (viewed 26 August 2010); and Sabrina Tosi Cambini, 'Lo stereotipo senza prove che perseguita i rom', *Il Manifesto*, 22 May 2008.

33. For the long list of Italian vigilante crimes against Romani camps during these days, see FRA, *Incident Report*. The camps had also been attacked by groups with Molotov cocktails in December 2007.

34. See FRA, *Incident Report*, 8, note 20.

35. The ministers used the widely accepted term 'Rom' in the emergency decrees, although the pejorative terms 'nomadi' and 'Zingari' continued to be used in the media and in statements by politicians. It is worth noting that pejorative meanings are discursively attached to the word 'Rom' as well.

36. Quoted (English translation) in Robert Owen, 'The politics of fear returns to Italy', *The Times*, 29 May 2008.

37. Quoted (English translation) in Tracy Wilkinson, 'Italian right targets Gypsies, migrants', *Los Angeles Times*, 24 May 2008.

38. The European Parliament resolution, 'Census of the Roma on the basis of ethnicity in Italy', P6_TA(2008)0361, Strasbourg, 10 July 2008, was critical of these measures as violating multiple European conventions, although there has as yet been no response to the Italian implementation of the census, despite pressure from a range of NGOs. The resolution is available on the European Parliament website at www.europarl.europa.eu/sides/getDoc.do?pubRef=-//EP//TEXT+TA+P6-TA-2008-0361+0+DOC+XML+V0//EN (viewed 27 August 2010).

39. FRA, *Incident Report*, 13.

40. OSCE Office for Democratic Institutions and Human Rights (ODIHR) and OSCE High Commissioner on National Minorities (HCNM), *Assessment of the Human Rights Situation of Roma and Sinti in Italy: Report of a Fact-Finding Mission to Milan, Naples and Rome on 20-26 July 2008* (ODIHR and HCNM: Warsaw and The Hague 2009), available on the OSCE website at www.osce.org/documents/odihr/2009/03/36620_en.pdf; FRA, *Incident Report*;

ERRC, Roma Centre for Social Intervention and Studies (Romani CRISS), Roma Civic Alliance (RCR), Centre for Housing Rights and Evictions (COHRE) and OSI, *Security a la Italiana: Fingerprinting, Extreme Violence and Harassment of Roma in Italy* (Budapest: ERRC 2008), available on the OSI website at www.soros.org/initiatives/brussels/articles_publications/ publications/ fingerprinting_20080715 (both websites viewed 27 August 2010).

41. Thomas Hammarberg, Commissioner for Human Rights, Council of Europe, 'Memorandum', CommDH(2008)18, Strasbourg, 28 July 2008, available on the Council of Europe website at https://wcd.coe.int/ViewDoc.jsp?RefCommDH(2008)18 (viewed 31 August 2010). See issues of the *ERIO Newsletter* for succinct summaries of statements by the Council of Europe, available on the ERIO website at http://erionet.org/site/index.html (viewed 31 August 2010).

42. See Lucia Kubosova, 'EU gives blessing for Italy's Roma fingerprint scheme', *euobserver. com* (online), 5 September 2008, available at http://euobserver.com/?aid 26691 (viewed 22 September 2010).

43. For the best overview of the whole sad story as well as of the media and police use of racialized scapegoats, see Amos Luzzatto, 'An excuse for a new wave of racism', *EveryOne* (online), 2 March 2009, available on the EveryOne Group website at www.everyonegroup.com/everyone/ MainPage/Entries/2009/3/2_A_case_of_rape_ in_Rome_is_exploited_by_politicians_and_ racist_patrols.html (viewed 27 August 2010).

44. Quoted (English translation) in Richard Owen, 'Italian minister calls for rapists to be castrated', *The Times*, 16 February 2009.

45. For the 'Decreto sicurezza', see the AltaLex website at www.altalex.com/ index.php?idnot45002 (viewed 22 September 2010). For recent rape legislation, see Merlino, *The Italian (In)Security Package*.

46. For the history of rape laws in Italy, see Kitty Calavita, 'Blue jeans, rape, and the "de-constitutive" power of law', *Law and Society Review*, vol. 35, no. 1, 2001, 89–116.

47. See Maria Giuseppina Muratore and Linda Laura Sabbadini, 'Italian survey on violence against women', *Statistical Journal of the United Nations Economic Commission for Europe*, vol. 22, no. 3, 2005, 265–78.

48. Marcello Maneri, 'Media and the war on migration', in Salvatore Palidda (ed.), *Criminalisation and Victimization of Migrants in Europe* (Genoa: Department of Anthropological Science, Genoa University 2008), 29–47, available online at www.reseau-terra.eu/IMG/pdf/ criminalisation.pdf (viewed 31 August 2010).

49. Quoted (English translation) in Owen, 'Italian minister calls for rapists to be castrated'.

50. Quoted (English translation), for example, in the Reuters report, 'Critics say Berlusconi's response to rape cases flippant', *ABC News* (online), 26 January 2009, available at www.abc. net.au/news/stories/2009/01/26/2474106.htm (viewed 22 September 2010).

51. Joanna Bourke, *Rape: A History from 1860 to the Present Day* (London: Virago 2007), 13.

52. Ibid., 16.

53. Note that the man in the picture also seems to be attacking the neck of the woman with his mouth, alluding, perhaps, to the legend of the (Romanian) vampire Dracula, and to the association of Roma with the occult and black magic.

54. 'Italian rape laws—viva l'italia', *Stefi's blog*, 5 March 2009, available at http://stephiblog. wordpress.com/2009/03/05/italian-rape-laws-viva-litalia (viewed 1 September 2010).

55. For a useful overview of Albanian and Romanian women workers in Italy, see Florentina Constantin, 'Migrating or commuting? The case of Romanian workers in Italy: niches for

labour commuting to the EU', OSI EU Monitoring and Advocacy Program paper, 1 January 2004, available on the Open Society website at www.soros.org/resources/articles_publications/articles/romanian-workers-italy20040101 (viewed 1 September 2010).

56. Quoted (English translation) in the Reuters report, Silvia Aloisi, 'Rape inquiry sheds light on racism in Italy', 13 March 2009, available on the Reuters website at http://uk.reuters.com/article/idUKTRE52C02S20090313 (viewed 1 September 2010).

57. Susan Brownmiller, *Against Our Will: Men, Women and Rape* (New York: Simon and Schuster 1975). Brownmiller also highlights the intersectionality of race and gender, and rape as vital to the policing of both.

58. For just one article discussing the agency of women in Italy acting against their construction in racialized and gendered discourse, see Heather Merrill, 'Space agents: anti-racist feminism and the politics of scale in Turin, Italy', *Gender, Place and Culture*, vol. 11, no. 2, 2004, 189–204.

*Shannon Woodcock is a lecturer in genocide studies at La Trobe University in Melbourne, Australia.

Shannon Woodcock, "Gender as a Catalyst for Violence Against Roma in Contemporary Italy," *Patterns of Prejudice* 44, no. 5 (December 2010).

Reprinted by permission of Taylor & Francis Ltd., http://www.tandfonline.com on behalf of *Patterns of Prejudice*.

Chapter 5: Locating "The Gypsy Problem." The Roma in Italy: Stereotyping, Labelling and "Nomad Camps"

*by Nando Sigona**

Romani camps are to be found all over Italy and host around 40,000 residents. They are known as 'nomad camps', implying that their inhabitants are vagrants who do not settle in one place. This article investigates how cultural concepts such as nomadism are employed in Italy to legitimise segregation policy. It also explores the role of space and place in the liaison between the Roma and the Italians. The focus, therefore, is not on the Roma themselves, but on how Italians interact with them and the degree to which Italian public policy and bureaucratic practice form, transform and manipulate their identity. By analysing the circularity of the relationship among stereotypes, labelling and policy, the paper deconstructs the so-called 'problema zingari' ('Gypsy problem'). Finally, it stresses the central role played by the camps as loci of the 'problem', both in preserving and reinforcing the status quo and in providing a refuge for people with minimal social and legal rights.

INTRODUCTION

A black ghetto is the place to study the defects of white society (Marchand 1979: 239).

Scampia is a deprived northern suburb of Naples (Italy) with over 41,000 residents. It is a recently developed district whose administrative borders were only established in 1987. A distinctive feature of the district is the near-absence of a private housing sector. Compared to the city's average, the population of Scampia is generally younger and the household size larger. There is a high incidence of unemployment, drug use and crime (Amato 1993; Morlicchio 2001). In June 1999 a squad of local inhabitants, armed with wooden clubs and petrol, reacted angrily to a car accident which involved a Romani car driver and two Italians on a motor scooter. For two days the Roma[1] living in Scampia were both verbally threatened and physically attacked by local residents who eventually set fire to several Romani huts. Commenting on the reactions of locals, a Neapolitan journalist noted:

Their invectives sound all the same way. No one seems to be ashamed or worried, no one seems to be sympathetic while watching Romani children and older people getting in the car and running away (Beneduce 1999).

Two out of the five Romani settlements in the area were burnt to the ground. Several overexcited residents watched the events from the windows of the apartment blocks surrounding the encampments, shouting and clapping their hands. By the end of the weekend, hundreds of Roma had packed their belongings in overloaded cars, vans and caravans and had left Naples. Only a small minority of the 1,600 Roma living in the area before the arson attacks stayed in the city. These remaining Roma were supported by a coalition of NGOs although, according to many camp residents, with little protection from the local police. In the immediate aftermath of the attacks, the Naples councillor in charge of social affairs visited the camps. Asked about the solution to the conflicts in Scampia, she replied that every effort would be made to guarantee the peaceful cohabitation of residents in the neighbourhood (reported in Marconi 1999). It appears that she already had a solution to 'the Gypsy problem': evict the remaining Roma and move them to a place where they would be rendered invisible to the other local residents. The new Roma camp was opened a year later in an isolated area behind the Secondigliano prison (Roma Rights 1999; Sigona 2002).

The aim of this paper is to examine the actors and dynamics involved in what is commonly called the 'problema zingari' or 'Gypsy problem'. These two words, it can be argued, encapsulate the ambiguity and ambivalence of Italian policy towards the Romani minority. What do politicians mean when they declare their will to solve the 'problema zingari'? Do they aim to address the problems that Roma face or, conversely, the problem that the Roma pose to 'us'? In reality, politicians probably mean both. This paper investigates this theme and aims to deconstruct the mechanism that allows the political system to achieve these ambivalent goals.

The label 'problema zingari', I argue, does not tell us a great deal regarding Roma; it rather sums up the way the majority and its political representatives see and represent them. Several actors take part, in various roles, in the definition of the 'Gypsy problem'. There are those who are in charge of ascribing and spreading definitions and those who use them. There are those who act in good faith and those who, instead, capitalise on the irrational and at times rational fears held by individuals. Finally, there are those who mediate between Roma and Italians and those who just speak for them.

As already mentioned, the focus of this paper, therefore, is not so much the Roma themselves as the ways in which 'we'—NGOs, bureaucrats, officials and society at large—interact with them, and the degree to which our public policy and bureaucratic practice form, transform and manipulate their identity (Zetter 1991). Paying attention to cultural concepts such as nomadism and sedentariness, the analysis shows how, in the Italian context, they are employed to legitimise segregation policy towards this particular minority.

Finally, emphasising the role played by camps in preserving and reinforcing the *status quo* and in providing a refuge for people without substantive legal rights, I propose an explanatory model of 'the Gypsy problem'.

METHODOLOGY

Based on research carried out between March 1998 and April 2001 in Romani settlements in Naples, Tuscany and Emilia Romagna, this paper builds upon previous work (Sigona 2002) by exploring the spatial dimensions of Roma marginalisation in the Italian context. My first contact with a Roma camp occurred in June 1998 when I began fieldwork for research on Italian policies concerning Roma and Sinti. In parallel with this I became actively involved with a community-based group in Naples called COMPARE (Committee for Non-Ghetto Housing for the Roma) which works in the areas of housing, Roma participation in decision-making and children's health and schooling. I was, to adopt Bernard's definition (1995: 138–9), an *observing participant*. In this context, it is important to acknowledge my dual role as political activist and researcher and the ways in which this role defined both the aims and the objectives of the research. The intertwining of diverse human, political and cultural factors directed my attention away from the Roma themselves to the interplay between them and the rest of the social fabric within the context set by regional laws and the Italian legal and bureaucratic system. From a 'traditional' anthropological approach I rapidly moved towards what Shore and Wright (1997) have termed *anthropology of policy*. The central argument is that policy shapes the way individuals construct themselves as subjects. 'Through policy', Shore and Wright (1997: 4) argue, 'the individual is categorized and given such statuses and roles as "subject", "citizen", "professional", "national", "criminal" and "deviant"' or, as in this paper, as 'gypsy'. Central government and regional policies in Italy concerning Roma have been explored, particularly relating to policy as a nodal point of intersection and articulation of ideologies, practices, power, and processes of contestation and accommodation. A comparative reading of Italian regional laws 'in defence of the Gypsies', together with an in-depth analysis of the political debate which led to the approval of the Tuscany and Emilia Romagna laws, set the context for my own fieldwork. *Nomad camps* and their *exceptionality* (Agamben 1998) are regarded here as the more visible achievements of these policies.

Given that the aim of the research was to examine the variegated world circulating inside and around camps, participant observation meant being involved in and observing how 'we' (politicians, aid-workers, scholars, *gadje*— non-Roma) interact with Roma. A particular focus is the ways in which the legal, social and cultural infrastructure that 'we', as a majority, are implicated in, affects and impacts on their lives. As a result, the *observing participant* status, which was not initially planned, became essential to the overall conduct of my research. Being actively involved with Roma in Naples allowed me to closely observe their relationships with civil servants, politicians, aid-workers and clergy and also to have access to and participate in informal discussions and official meetings. This type of access would scarcely have been possible to an academic researcher, working largely on the outside (Però 1999). This fact also helped me to build a network of contacts in Tuscany, Emilia Romagna and other regions of Italy that were extremely beneficial for my fieldwork. In order to test and develop insights and ideas emerging from the participant observation and the analysis of regional laws and their discourses (Fairclough 2003), semi-structured interviews with Roma, NGOs, volunteers, and civil servants were conducted in the three principle locations. The data which resulted were subsequently presented and discussed in a number of workshops and focus groups with both Roma and *gadje*.

ROMANI COMMUNITIES IN ITALY

Italy is the only country among the EU member-states where the number of Roma stemming from post-1945 immigrations virtually outnumbers the descendants of the important Romani communities who had established themselves there since the late Middle Ages. This brief overview aims to set the context for the analysis of 'the Gypsy problem'. The heteronym '*zingari*' incorporates a number of groups and subgroups, 'a world of worlds', according to the Italian anthropologist Piasere (1999). The three main components are Roma, Sinti and Camminanti. A further distinction, on legal grounds, has to be made between those with and those without Italian citizenship. Roma and Sinti began to settle in Italy in the fifteenth century: the Sinti reached the centre-north of Italy overland from the Balkan region, and the Roma crossed the Adriatic Sea from the south, settling in the southern part of the country (Karpati 1969,

1993). The origin of the Camminanti is unclear; their community is historically located in Sicily and travels throughout the whole of Italy for part of the year (Sidoti 2002; Soravia 1981). The Roma and Sinti are then divided into a plethora of other subgroups which often take their name from the province or region of main settlement or from their principle economic activity (e.g. Piedmont Sinti, Circensian Sinti, Abruzzo Roma, Napulengre Roma; see Viaggio 1997). In the absence of official statistics, figures on the overall Roma and Sinti population rely on generally accepted estimates, according to which there are approximately 120,000–150,000 Roma, Sinti and Camminanti currently living in Italy. A majority of them (about 60 per cent) are Italian citizens. Among the Sinti, about 15 per cent have an itinerant or semi-itinerant lifestyle connected to their economic activities, whilst the Roma tend to have a more sedentary one. The bulk of the remaining 40 per cent of Gypsies came to Italy in recent times, especially from the Balkans and Romania. They generally call themselves 'Roma' but the term assumes slightly different meanings within each community (Brunello 1996; Karpati 1969; Piasere 1988).

Many Roma who fled from war and persecution to Italy are *sans papiers* (undocumented). They have no legal permits to stay in the country or may simply have been granted short-term leave to remain on humanitarian grounds, an exemption from expulsion which is difficult to renew (Schiavone 1997). An increasing number of Roma children born in Italy to foreign parents are stateless, and face overwhelming obstacles in obtaining any passport at all.[2] About one-third of the Roma and Sinti population—including both Italian and an estimated 18,500 foreign citizens—currently live in authorised or unauthorised camps separated from the rest of Italian society (Brunello 1996; Monasta 2001). As reported by the European Commission against Racism and Intolerance (ECRI 2002), 'the situation of practical segregation of Roma/Gypsies in Italy appears to reflect a general approach of the Italian authorities which tend to consider Roma as nomads and wanting to live in camps'. Similar concerns were expressed in 1999 by the UN Committee on the Elimination of Racial Discrimination (CERD 1999) which declared that 'in addition to a frequent lack of basic facilities, the housing of Roma in such camps leads not only to a physical segregation of the Roma community from Italian society, but a political, economic and cultural isolation as well'. The label 'nomads' is applied indifferently to the whole Roma and Sinti population, regardless of whether they are Italian citizens or foreigners, travellers or sedentary people, war refugees or economic migrants. The conflict over the term is a key issue in the ongoing debate in Italy and Europe over the recognition of the Romani minority and its rights, a debate whose effects can also be detected in camps, as the following quote from my fieldwork shows:

Several motivations drove me to change my life: first, the fact of being 'nomad', that is from Rom to become 'nomad', to become 'zingaro' with many prejudices, mainly negative. I never thought of myself as a nomad in my home country, I didn't think of me as a 'zingaro': dirty, tattered, thief. That is why I decided to be actively involved for Romani rights here in Italy. I want to show to Italians that no 'zingaro' would call another Rom: 'zingaro' (BH, Macedonian Rom).

Analysing the relationship which binds labelling to policy and practice, the following section examines in detail the wanted and unwanted outcomes of the political use of the term 'nomadism', specifically as this is applied in the legal framework set by regional laws 'in defence of nomadic people'.

CAMPS AND LABELLING

The camp neither improves the situation nor changes it. It doesn't help the Roma participation in the social fabric, it rather hinders this process. The camp surrounds and excludes its inmates to the point that later people can affirm that these are the Roma and they will be always the same, they will never change (DM, Macedonian Rom in Florence).

Labels, it has been suggested (Sigona 2002), can be regarded as an expression of the Foucauldian *régime of truth*. 'The truth', in Foucault's words (1998: 133), 'is linked in a circular relation with systems of power which produce and sustain it and to effects of power which induce and which extend it'. The circular relation linking systems of power and the effects of power in the definition of the truth, which is always 'official', also affects legislation. Liégeois' remark (1980: 28) illustrates this well:

Legislation, for its effects, contributes to feed and reinforce those aspects of the image, which are indispensable to itself. ... The law feeds itself with the image. The image helps to rationalise it. The image is, hence, re-strengthened by it.

In the 1980s and early 1990s, 10 out of the 20 regions in Italy adopted laws aimed at the 'protection of Gypsies' and 'their nomadic culture'. Each regional law defines its target group in a slightly different way. They may refer, for example, to nomads, Roma, Roma and Sinti or *zingari*. This variety has to be acknowledged because, as suggested by Marta (1994: 249), 'heteronyms constitute a key element of policy making for those regional and local authorities that develop a strategy of intervention towards Roma'. In order to achieve the goal of protecting 'nomadic culture', regional laws enlist a number of tools. By far the most significant of them is the building of camps (see, for example, Law 32/90 Regione Umbria; Law 11/88 Regione Friuli-Venezia Giulia; Law 299/90 Regione Lombardia). By this means the perception that all Roma and Sinti are nomads and therefore should live in camps, isolated from mainstream Italian society, is given the official stamp of approval. As a result, many Roma have effectively been forced to live out the romantic but nonetheless repressive projections of Italians.

The description of Roma as 'nomads' is not only used in the service of segregating Roma, but also in order to reinforce the popular idea that Roma are not Italians and do not 'belong' to Italy. As such, the existence of local administrative offices for 'Nomads and Non-Europeans' indicates that Roma are commonly perceived as foreigners in the eyes of the Italian authorities (Piasere 1991). Prejudices and stereotypes concerning Roma are to be found across the entire political spectrum. As Clough Marinaro's work on the Roma in Rome shows, despite a well-intentioned initial approach, the policy of the city council was largely based on a set of assumptions which viewed the Roma as 'inherently nomadic, dishonest and incapable of functioning in a modern society' (Clough Marinaro 2003: 203–4). In practice, the 'nomad theory' is often used to provide a form of cultural legitimation for marginalising the Roma. In regional laws, the link between the protection of nomadism and the building of camps is blatant. It is as if a cause-and-effect relationship exists between the solemn aim of protecting nomadic culture, and the efforts made by local authorities—with the support of regional governments—to build camps. Another element emerging from the regional laws is a very little information on their actual target group and its needs; conversely, there is a greater emphasis on the 'real gypsy' myth and on the measures needed to preserve 'gypsy culture'. According to Sibley (1995), 'while they [the Roma] may be considered exotic and interesting at a distance, they become deviant when enmeshed in the social mainstream'. However, as I will argue later, camps also suit a range of other purposes.

Enforcing the separation of Roma from mainstream society through the use of camps is a key factor in the perpetuation of their status as 'enemies' rather than 'strangers' (Bauman 1990, 1992). The 'stranger', because of his proximity to the known and familiar, suggests tangible difficulties for the building and renegotiation of relationships and identities, whereas the 'enemy' can be more readily manipulated because of his status as an outsider. The 'Gypsy' stands in between these two cases. Despite living in 'our' cities, s/he rarely intermingles with 'us'. Besides, Gypsies are so politically weak that they can hardly dispute the official image of them that we may construct. The 'Gypsy', as I have suggested elsewhere, is the 'inner enemy' (Sigona 2003). As a consequence of their isolation, Roma do not exist as *personae* for the majority of Italians but only as stereotypes. This is a more general phenomenon which does not affect only Italy, as Fonseca argues:

> The more exotic Gypsies appear to be, the more 'genuine' they are considered and, paradoxically, the more acceptable they become (in the local imagination, if not in the local pub). Whoever best fits the stereotypes wins (Fonseca 1995: 238).

A key question arises: Can first-hand experience break down this self-perpetuating circle? According to Sibley (1981: 6):

> Where outsiders come into close physical association with the larger society, particularly in cities, the romantic image, the pervasive myth about minority culture, is retained as a yardstick against which they are measured. Experience of the minority at first hand contradicts the myth but it does not explode it. The myth can be retained because failure to meet mythical expectations is attributed to deviancy or to social pathologies that are somehow a product of urban living.

The explosion of the 'Gypsy myth' is a nodal point which, as I will argue in the final section, cannot be resolved merely by moving Roma out of the camps. The gatedness of Roma camps is not just a matter of housing. There is a need for a more holistic approach that makes the Roma themselves key actors in policy development and implementation. Calling for an integrated approach which has the Roma, but also civil society, and in particular local inhabitants, as foci, is a way of reminding us of what the promoters of the 'real Gypsy' myth tend to forget—that most camps are planned, designed and built by architects, engineers and planners. They are not in this sense a *naturally occurring* feature of Roma culture but rather an architectonic projection of how Italians view them (Eco 1980). It is a projection which has some very real and dramatic consequences. The vicious circle which results in the building of camps not only affects the daily lives of thousands of individuals but also their expectations, demands and chances of social enhancement (Sigona 2003).

TEMPORARY SOLUTIONS

In Italy, Roma settlements are built, or allowed to exist, in areas close to prisons, dog pounds and rubbish dumps—land with a very low economic value (Brunello 1996; Karpati 1999; Però 1999; Revelli 1999; Tabucchi 1999). Roma are 'a residual population in a residual space' (Sibley 1995: 68). The choice of location reveals, according to Solimano and Mori (2000: 40), a widespread attitude: 'Gypsies must be kept apart from the general population, and the general population would do [its] best to keep their distance from them'. Illegal settlements, whose forms remind us of the slums of many third-world cities, are often without running water, toilets and electricity. Their size may vary considerably: in Rome in the 1990s the Casilino 700 camp had more than 1,300 inhabitants, whereas in Scampia the smallest camp had no more than 40 inhabitants before it was burnt down in 1999. Legal settlements are either built *ex novo* by local authorities or started off as illegal camps which are later given the 'official' label. They are all commonly called '*campi nomadi*' (camps for nomads), even though in the last few years some local authorities (for example in Naples), conscious of increasing concern about the use of the nomad-camp label, began to introduce a series of new definitions, including *villaggio di accoglienza per Rom* (reception village for Roma). It has to be noted that changing names has only in a few cases resulted in a consistent change of practice.[3] As far as the structure of the legal camps built *ex novo* by local authorities is concerned, they are being presented as temporary solutions which allow local authorities to build according to different (and lower) standards than would usually be the case. Their plan is generally geometric, following the military camp model, with residents allotted a numbered place with a caravan or, sometimes, a prefabricated container. It is an imposed structure with very little attention given to residents' social networks and family connections. Former illegal settlements, on the other hand, normally maintain their apparently chaotic structure.[4] Public intervention is often limited to installing a few hygiene-related services and, where possible, installing running water or periodically refilling water tanks.[5] A common feature of the two types of legal camp is that they are enclosed: their entrances are under surveillance and the movements of Roma and non-Roma alike are monitored.

Regional laws concerning Roma and Sinti typically enlist principles such as the protection of Gypsy culture, traditional jobs and nomadism. They may also include guidelines for building camps and allocating funding. In reality, however, the actual power to decide whether or not to intervene is the responsibility of local government. City councillors, in the last two decades, have not proven particularly responsive to the cultural arguments presented in the regional laws. They have, in most cases, only intervened when health and security problems in the illegal settlements have come to the attention of the local and national media. In these circumstances, local authorities have found in the camps, not so much a perennial feature of Roma culture, as a ready-made housing solution (at relatively low cost) to what is perceived as a constant state of 'emergency'. Concerning the involvement of local authorities and their underlying political rationale, two aspects are rarely taken into account. Firstly, the concept of 'emergency' is never questioned. Rather, it tends to be presented as an unavoidable situation whose precise causes remain vague. Secondly camps, although presented as transitory solutions, have become, *de facto*, the permanent home of thousands of Roma. The notion of emergency can be seen as a central category in the contemporary political struggle. 'It is not', Tosi (1993: 32) argues, 'a rational definition of urgencies and priorities, but rather a permanent construction aimed at defining the boundaries of negotiability of a given issue'. Emergency as a political category allows the complex causes of migration flows and the structural causes of poverty to be largely sidelined in public debate. As a result, political intervention, if and when it occurs, is limited to meeting the most basic of housing needs (Rahola 2003).

The Spatial Dimensions of the 'Gypsy Problem'

The definition '*problema zingari* ' expresses in its very wording the ambiguity which permeates Italian policy towards Roma. Such ambiguity expresses itself fully, and is effectively reified in the structure of camps. The interconnection between labels and policy has emerged as one of the key aspects affecting the relationship between Roma and Italians. Nomadism, recognised—by 'us'—as a feature of the Roma people, is objectified through the law, turning the stereotype into a label. The main consequence of this process is that nomadism, once inscribed in official discourse, becomes one of the two compelling arguments supporting the camp policy. As I have shown, the second argument is based upon a perceived state of permanent emergency.

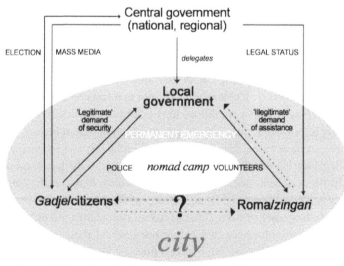

Figure 1: The multidimensional relationships of the 'problema zingari'.

The model outlined in Figure 1 portrays the actors involved in the '*problema zingari*' and their mutual relationships. Two different, and opposing, structural principles regulate the territory where Roma settle. On the one side, there is the emergency principle, the driving force of most initiatives targeted at Roma, the main attribute of which is precariousness; on the other, there is the stability principle, which represents the world of secure and enduring relationships, of legal rights and entitlements. The interplay between these two regulative principles, and their strict interdependence, has been summed up in the model with the words: 'permanent emergency'. The outcomes of their interactions materialise in various aspects of life in camps. Looking, for example, at those who intervene and mediate between Roma and *gadje* (the non-Roma), it is possible to identify two main groups: the first is made up of volunteers, aid-workers and NGOs, the second by the police and bureaucratic apparatus. In the first case, we encounter people who are normally linked to relief operations in emergency situations. Due to the fact that many of these individuals are on short-term contracts, they, too, may be said to fall into the sphere of precariousness. The second group, instead, are more generally related to the sphere of social stability.

The urban margins are the arena in which the relationship between Roma and Italians takes place, shaped by the condition of 'permanent emergency'. The urban level is where the 'problem' is localised and where the space for dialogue and/or conflict can be found. In such a context, the camp becomes a limitation, if not an obstacle, to the relational space, making contact more difficult between groups living in the same community. As shown in Figure 1, there are three main actors involved, even though their names may vary: the Roma/*zingari* (or the politically correct 'nomads'), the local authority and the citizens/*gadje*.

The interplay between these groups is strongly asymmetrical. Local authorities, through drastically sectorialised policy, manage the social fabric. One outcome of this *divide-et-impera* process is the compartmentalisation of the population into smaller and smaller subgroups. As far as Roma and their needs are concerned, the consequence of this phenomenon is their artificial separation from those living in the same neighbourhood and city. Roma are treated as a *special* subgroup, occupying a spatial and temporal enclave, thus denying the immediacy of their existence. Their perceived distinctiveness is not based upon the acknowledgement of their specific conditions and needs, but is rather rooted in a lack of knowledge and on fixed stereotypes. Graphically, the split of the local community along ethnic boundaries can been represented through a triangle whose base is constituted by the Roma and the other citizens, polarised in the two corners, and whose vertex is occupied by the local authority. However, the fragmentation of the base is not only the result of local policies. The separation between Roma and other citizens is founded on deep-seated and interiorised disparities in legal and social status. The Italian system makes them legally different and treats them as distinct entities. The Roma represent the weakest corner of the triangle, those with the least power of negotiation. They are relegated to a condition of juridical limbo which, in the case of most foreign Roma, means having more than one expulsion decree pending on their shoulders. The main cause of this condition can be found in the national policy of giving temporary permits-to-stay to displaced people from the Balkans, rather than allowing them to claim asylum according to the Geneva Convention (Schiavone 1999; Vincenzi 2000; Zetter *et al.* 2002). These temporary permits-to-stay, despite being renewable, are a source of great anxiety and insecurity for their owners—and especially for foreign Roma—who may live for several years under the continuous threat of expulsion.[6] Thus, in practice, their juridical precariousness is often transformed into a state of existential precariousness.

Camps, in such a context, become a refuge, a place to find protection, where alliances and social networks may help to overcome the Roma deficiency in relation to citizenship and social entitlements. Any camp, Giorgio Agamben (2000: 42) argues, 'is an apparently anodyne place … in which, for all intents and purposes, the normal rule of law is suspended'. The very precariousness of their legal status makes any Roma demand appear 'illegitimate'. The central point here is that the main cause of Roma precariousness cannot be found at the local level but is rather a consequence of a national strategy whose impact is felt at local level. The '*problema zingari*', therefore, is multi-dimensional, with national strategies affecting local actors and social dynamics.

As far as the national level is concerned, it is important to note the general absence of communication between Roma and the national authorities. While citizens have various tools with which to make their voice heard in the national arena—for example the political election—Roma, like many immigrants, do not have any tools with which to respond to national government. Meanwhile, local authorities are more or less obliged to cope with the Roma and their living conditions because of their visibility and the scale of outcry from the rest of the population. They cannot simply ignore the Roma's demands for assistance, however 'illegitimate' they may be. Turning attention now to how local authorities manage this 'Gypsy problem', a crucial feature is the exclusion of the third actor. Reviewing policy and practice in most Italian municipalities that have dealt with Roma, it appears that there is a tendency to systematically exclude either the Roma or the Italians from the decision-making process. Consequently, if local authorities are forced to take action to address Roma requests for assistance, they turn to emergency plans, characterised by low, short-term costs, poor quality of provision and virtually no participation from the local community and the Roma themselves (Tosi 1993).

Camps are therefore the solution to what is constructed as a humanitarian emergency. From an organisational perspective they allow better management of the target group. In camps, service provision and assistance maintain their attribute of exceptionality, stressing implicitly that it is not rights which are being referred to here but basic needs, which have to be addressed. If citizens ask for more security and protection from the 'dangerous Gypsies', the response of local authorities will typically be for more policing in the area. Encouraging public debate or making any attempt to identify the reasons for protest at a local level tends to be scrupulously avoided. Hence, *the Gypsy problem* viewed from the local authorities' or citizens' perspective is mainly an issue of public order and security. As highlighted in the model, the citizens' demand for security can be seen as 'legitimate' because citizens, being full members of the social fabric, are bearers of rights and entitlements. Their demand finds its answer in two types of measure: policing and camps. From this perspective, camps lose their humanitarian veil and appear as places of control, surrounded by material—and immaterial—fences.

As implied earlier, the implementation of local strategies is mainly delegated to the voluntary sector, which has the fundamental task of mediating between local government and the Roma. However, as many failed projects which aimed to improve living conditions and to promote Roma participation have shown, there are two main risks which volunteers and NGOs may incur: firstly, confusing their role of mediator with that of representative; therefore, rather than facilitating the communication of Roma needs, they change roles and begin to speak 'for' them; secondly, institutionalising Roma and making them dependent upon the mercy of the host society instead of promoting their participation and mobilisation (see Goffman 1968 and Harrell-Bond 1986 for further exploration of this phenomenon).

In most Italian nomad camps these two processes are clearly visible (Brunello 1996; Sigona 2002). As shown in the model, the missing link is the relationship between the two groups occupying the base of the triangle. The geographical separateness is just one of the factors to be taken into account. Another crucial factor refers to labelling and is stressed in the model by the double definitions: Roma/*zingari* and *gadje*/citizens. Are we talking of the Roma/*gadje* relationship or the *zingari*/citizens one? 'Roma' is an autonym: an ethnic self-definition given by the group itself. The '*gadje*' label is attributed to those who are not Roma by the Roma. Therefore, referring to the Roma/*gadje* relationship means approaching the interplay between the two groups from the perspective of Roma. On the contrary, if we approach the two groups from the other perspective, the labels change. On one side, there are the 'citizens' or the 'Italians', those with full rights; on the other, the '*zingari*' or 'nomads'. '*Zingari*' and 'nomads' are heteronyms: ethnic definitions imposed upon a group by someone else. Of course, the actual relationships in the field contain both perspectives. They can in fact be regarded as the result of the competition of the two sets of definitions. Nevertheless, it seems useful to stress the duality of the conjunction based upon the essential incommunicability between the two sides. Their reciprocal knowledge, in the absence of first-hand contact (with the exception of the Roma beggars who are much more visible than statistically representative), is largely mediated by the national and local media, which create and reproduce stereotypes. Volunteers and aid-workers who work on the edge between the two worlds are also active in this process, sometimes facilitating the exchange of information, sometimes obstructing it.

CONCLUSIONS

> Policies are most obviously political phenomena, yet it is a feature of policies that their political nature is disguised by the objective, neutral, legal–rational idioms in which they are portrayed (Shore and Wright 1997: 8).

The analysis of Italian policy and practice reveals a lack of political will to develop and implement projects aimed at bridging the gap between the Roma and their neighbours. Furthermore, there is also a failure of will to recognise the Roma as full inhabitants of their community and, therefore, to recognise their right to participate in the public life of their territory and in the distribution of resources and benefits allocated to the local community. In deprived areas, such as those where most camps are located, these resources are normally very poor. Local conflicts may arise connected to the battle for the allocation of resources. Nevertheless, considering the already existing tensions between the two groups, the recognition of Roma citizenship would transform rather than increase the potential for conflict. The Roma, from being an irrational and unaccountable threat, would become party to a more accountable and transparent conflict between equal contenders. The ghettoisation of Roma in camps, I suggest, blocks contact between them and the rest of the local inhabitants, thus denying a space for conflict and also for its possible solution to emerge:

'The space' is the battlefield on which an increasing number of issues is born; it is where segments of population meet and aggregate around an occasional common interest. The gradual and progressive decrease of collective-based conflicts is contrasted by the proliferation of locally-based micro-conflicts, whose rationale becomes more and more local and sectional, questioning well-established social identities (Solimano 1999: 136).

The polity tends to deal with the spatial dimension of conflict only reactively: guarding the distance between Gypsies and Italians, recognising and representing in public discourse the fear of 'the other' in 'our' backyard, without attempting to acknowledge it. Choosing the spatial dimension as a starting point permits an expansion rather than a reduction of the semantic and political territory of 'the Gypsy problem', which is then not merely a housing issue (the building of camps) but a question of creating a shared space and of providing the grounds for peaceful coexistence. The camp, with its multi-functionality, incorporates and appears to resolve the ambiguity of the 'Gypsy problem'. It becomes the stage where contradictory policies are played out. The exercise of local polity, by concealing one of the actors, prevents the clash between them. By doing this, it may manage to avoid conflict but it does so without solving it. The end result of this strategy is to postpone the conflict without addressing its root causes, thereby opening up the potential for future conflicts to be played out in other social spheres and at a more irrational level.

ACKNOWLEDGEMENTS

The author wishes to thank the Brookes Contemporary Ideology Forum and the London Romani Studies Seminar Group, where an earlier version of this paper was presented and discussed, as well as David Griffiths and Paul Allender for their comments and support.

NOTES

1. In acknowledgement of the preference of many Roma who are active in the international and national movements on behalf of Roma rights, and following a widely recognised practice, the ethnonym 'Roma' is also used sometimes in this article to refer to the overall Roma, Sinti and Camminanti population, as a synonym of 'zingari ', which is regarded as derogatory. However, the generic use of 'Roma' should not be regarded as an implicit taking of sides in the ongoing international and European debate concerning the making of the Roma nation (see Gheorghe and Mirga 1997; Hancock 1987; Kovats 2001; Liégeois 1994).

2. This issue was raised in the conference 'Personal Documents and Threats to the Exercise of Fundamental Rights among Roma in the Former Yugoslavia' organised by the European Roma Rights Center in September 2002 in Igalo (Montenegro).

3. Among the few exceptions is the Tuscany region which, in the last two decades, issued three laws concerning Roma and Sinti. In the latest law, the word 'camp' is banned. The regional government is also trying to develop and implement a new housing policy, but often encounters the opposition of municipalities.

4. Piasere (1991, 1999) has extensively discussed the proxemics of Roma encampments, emphasising the crucial role played by the disposition of caravans, shanks and huts and the management of space and place both in representing social networks and relationships and balancing and softening tensions.

5. In Florence, the Poderaccio camp has just 16 toilets and eight showers for a population of 250 persons (see Hasani and Monasta 2003; Szente 1997).

6. Despite being citizens, Italian Roma and Sinti often face similar problems, finding it much more difficult to benefit from rights and entitlements of which they are formal holders (see ERRC 2000).

REFERENCES

Agamben, G. (1998) *Homo Sacer. Sovereign Power and Bare Life.* Stanford: Stanford University Press.

Agamben, G. (2000) *Means Without End: Notes on Politics.* Minneapolis: University of Minnesota Press.

Amato, F. (1993) 'La città del disagio: le periferie settentrionali di Napoli', *Spazi Urbani e Quadri Sociali, 11–12*: 10–51.

Bauman, Z. (1990) 'Modernity and ambivalence', *Theory, Culture and Society,* 7(2–3): 143–69.

Bauman, Z. (1992) 'Soil, blood and identity', *The Sociological Review,* 40(4): 675–701.

Beneduce, T. (1999) 'L'odio degli aggressori: "Sono delinquenti, avremmo dovuto bruciarli vivi"', *Corriere del Mezzogiorno,* 20 June 1999.

Bernard, H.R. (1995) *Research Methods in Anthropology.* Thousand Oaks, London and New Delhi: Sage.

Brunello, P. (ed.) (1996) *L'Urbanistica del Disprezzo.* Rome: Manifesto Libri.

CERD (1999) *Concluding Observations on Italy.* Geneva: United Nations.

Clough Marinaro, I. (2003) 'Integration or marginalization? The failures of social policy for the Roma in Rome', *Modern Italy,* 8(2): 203–18.

Eco, U. (1980) *La Struttura Assente.* Bologna: Bompiani.

ECRI (2002) *2nd Report on Italy Adopted the 22nd June 2001.* Strasbourg: European Commission against Racial Intolerance.

ERRC (2000) *Campland. Racial Segregation of Roma in Italy.* Budapest: European Roma Rights Center.

Fairclough, N. (2003) *Analysing Discourse.* London and New York: Routledge.

Fonseca, I. (1995) *Bury Me Standing. The Gypsies and their Journey.* New York: Vintage Books.

Foucault, M. (1998) *The History of Sexuality. Vol. 1: The Will to Knowledge.* London: Penguin Books.

Gheorghe, N. and Mirga, A. (1997) *The Roma in the Twenty-First Century: A Policy Paper.* Princeton: Project of Ethnic Relations.

Goffman, E. (1968) *Asylum: Essays on the Social Situation of Mental Patients and Other Inmates.* London: Penguin Books.

Hancock, I. (1987) *The Pariah Syndrome.* Michigan: Karoma Publishers.

Harrell-Bond, B.E. (1986) *Imposing Aid: Emergency Assistance to Refugees.* Oxford: Oxford University Press.

Hasani, B. and Monasta, L. (2003) *Vite Costrette. Un viaggio fotografico nel campo Rom del Poderaccio.* Verona: Ombre Corte.

Karpati, M. (1969) 'La situazione attuale degli zingari in Italia', *Lacio Drom*, 3–5 :77–83.

Karpati, M. (ed.) (1993) *Zingari Ieri e Oggi*, Rome: Edizioni Lacio Drom.

Karpati, M. (1999) 'Le politiche attuali nei confronti degli zingari', *Atti del Seminario: Rom e Sinti Oggi*. Regione Emilia Romagna.

Kovats, M. (2001) *Opportunities and Challenges: EU Enlargement and the Roma/Gypsy Diaspora*. Budapest: Open Society Institute, EUMAP (www.eumap.org).

Liégeois, J.P. (1980) 'Il discorso dell'ordine. Pubblici poteri e minoranze culturali', *Lacio Drom*, 5: 9–29.

Liégeois, J.P. (1994) *Roma, Tsiganes, Voyageurs*. Strasbourg: Council of Europe.

Marchand, B. (1979) 'Dialectics and geography', in Gale, S. and Olson, G. (eds) *Philosophy in Geography*. Dordrecht: D. Reidel, 237–67.

Marconi, L. (1999) 'La incostante: il problema sarà risolto con la costruzione dei nuovi campi', *Corriere del Mezzogiorno*, 20 June 1999.

Marta, C. (1994) 'Zingari, Rom e nomadi: una minoranza di difficile definizione', in Vallini, C. (ed.) *Minoranze e Lingue Minoritarie*. Naples: IUO, 245–60.

Monasta, L. (2001) 'Nota sulla mappatura degli insediamenti di Rom stranieri presenti in Italia'. Unpublished paper presented at the University of Florence, 17 December 2001.

Morlicchio, E. (2001) *Spatial Dimensions of Urban Social Exclusion and Integration: The Case of Naples*. Online at: http://gp.fmg.uva.nl/urbex/resrep/r17_naples.pdf

Però, D. (1999) 'Next to the dog pound: institutional discourses and practices about Roma refugees in left-wing Bologna', *Modern Italy*, 4(2): 207–24.

Piasere, L. (1988) *Il Fenomeno della Migrazione in Riferimento alle Difficoltà di Adattamento Sociale delle Componenti Nomadi*. Rome: Istituto Internazionale di Studi Giuridici.

Piasere, L. (1991) *Popoli delle Discariche. Saggi di antropologia zingari*. Rome: CISU.

Piasere, L. (1999) *Un Mondo di Mondi. Antropologia delle culture rom*. Naples: l'Ancora.

Rahola, F. (2003) *Zone Definitivamente Temporanee*. Verona: Ombre Corte.

Revelli, M. (1999) *Fuori Luogo. Cronaca da un campo rom*. Turin: Bollati Boringhieri.

Roma Rights (1999) 'Pogrom in Italy', *Roma Rights*, 2: 9.

Schiavone, G. (1997) 'I Rom rifugiati', in Osella, C. (ed.) *Zingari Profughi: il popolo invisibile*. Turin: Edizioni Gruppo Abele, 63–81.

Schiavone, G. (1999) 'Il diritto d'asilo nell'Italia di oggi', *Lo Straniero*, 8 (Autumn): 158–74.

Shore, C. and Wright, S. (1997) *Anthropology of Policy*. London: Routledge.

Sibley, D. (1981) *Outsiders in Urban Societies*. Oxford: Blackwell.

Sibley, D. (1995) *Geographies of Exclusion*. London and New York: Routledge.

Sidoti, S. (2002) *Pratiche d'Erranza Quotidiana in una Comunità di Camminanti Siciliani*. Rome: Progetto OPRE, The Education of Gypsy Childhood in Europe.

Sigona, N. (2002) *Figli del Ghetto. Gli italiani, i Campi Nomadi e l'Invenzione degli Zingari*. Civezzano: Nonluoghi.

Sigona, N. (2003) 'How can a "nomad" be a "refugee"? Kosovo Roma and labelling policy in Italy', *Sociology*, 37(1): 69–79.

Solimano, N. (1999) 'Immigrazione, convivenza urbana e conflitti locali', *La Nuova Città*, 2(4): 135–40.

Solimano, N. and Mori, T. (2000) 'A Roma ghetto in Florence', *The UNESCO Courier*, June 2000, online at http://www.unesco.org/courier/2000_06/uk/ethique2.htm

Soravia, G. (1981) 'Zingari in Sicilia', *Lacio Drom*, 2:31–3.

Szente, V.L. (1997) 'Field report: Italy', *Roma Rights*, Autumn 1997: 51–3.

Tabucchi, A. (1999) *Gli Zingari e il Rinascimento*. Bologna: Feltrinelli.

Tosi, A. (1993) *Immigrati e Senza Casa*. Milan: Franco Angeli.

Viaggio, G. (1997) *Storia degli Zingari in Italia*. Rome: Anicia.

Vincenzi, S. (2000) 'Italy: a newcomer with a positive attitude', *Journal of Refugee Studies*, 13(1): 91–104.

Zetter, R.W. (1991) 'Labelling refugees: forming and transforming a bureaucratic identity', *Journal of Refugee Studies*, 4(1): 39–61.

Zetter, R.W., Griffiths, D. and Sigona, N. (2002) *Survey of Policy and Practice Related to Refugee Integration in the EU*. Oxford: Oxford Brookes University, online at http://www.brookes. ac.uk/ schools/planning/dfm/RefInt/index.htm

***Nando Sigona** is senior research officer at the Refugees Studies Centre at the University of Oxford.

Nando Sigona, "Locating 'The Gypsy Problem.' The Roma in Italy: Stereotyping, Labelling and 'Nomad Camps,'" *Journal of Ethnic and Migration Studies* 31, no. 4 (July 2005).

Section II:
Roma School Segregation: The Case of *D.H. and Others vs. the Czech Republic*

In 2007, the European Court of Human Rights declared the Czech Republic's two-track system of schooling—which effectively saw Roma children segregated in technical high schools and denied access to precollegiate gymnasiums—to be a violation of the Convention for the Protection of Human Rights and Fundamental Freedoms. Celebrated as a cornerstone in legal recognition of discrimination against Roma in Europe, the ruling, however, had limited effects on the actual education practices in the Czech Republic. While local legislation has been adjusted to reflect the Court's ruling, school practices involving Roma children throughout the Czech Republic and much of Europe remain highly discriminatory. This section debates the impact of the 2007 ruling in the *D.H. and Others vs. the Czech Republic* lawsuit not only on education, but also on discrimination against Roma and the law in general. The articles in this section seek to better our understanding of the underlying causes of unequal access to education—largely blamed on Roma parents' lack of necessary social and cultural capital when negotiating with schools on behalf of their children. It also discusses the extent to which the 2007 ruling could be used as legal precedent for further rulings about school segregation and other forms of discrimination against Roma. Signs are encouraging. Courts in Hungary, Bulgaria, and Greece have awarded punitive damages to Roma plaintiffs who were denied access to primary education, while; new legislation in Romania, Bulgaria, and Hungary has allowed NGOs to bring *actio popularis* claims in front of national courts.

Chapter 6: Solving the "Gypsy Problem": D.H. and Others v. the Czech Republic

*by William S. New and Michael S. Merry**

The history of Roma participation in European education is dismal, a history of violence and erasure. As the European Union (EU) expands, garnering to itself Europe's 8–10 million Roma, the "Gypsy problem" becomes increasingly important, bearing symbolically, and in real social and economic terms, on EU promises of democratic governance and equal opportunity. Until the Soviet period, the formal schooling of Roma children was rarely part of anyone's conversation (Crowe 1996), but in the "New Europe," bound by a commitment to inclusion, this historical state of affairs is ending, however slowly and however unwelcome. Since the end of Soviet-style socialism, eliminating discrimination against Roma students has been the goal of the European Roma Rights Center (ERRC), a transnational nongovernmental organization (NGO) based in Budapest, Hungary. The ERRC (1999) has targeted the two-track schooling system created during the communist era, in which Roma children were typically assigned from an early age to segregated "remedial schools." Enrollment in these schools effectively precluded the possibility of high school graduation, let alone attendance at university, and participation in the "knowledge society."[1]

In a 2007, the European Court of Human Rights (ECHR) declared this two-track system of schooling to be a violation of the Convention for the Protection of Human Rights and Fundamental Freedoms (hereafter, the European Convention on Human Rights; Council of Europe 1950).[2] Yet court rulings by themselves do not produce social conditions in which the rights of historically marginalized groups are enjoyed or respected, especially in schools. Roma students are entering an educational space in which long- standing resistance to their full inclusion remains, but where legal and other formal mechanisms for inclusion are in effect. While dismantling systems of de jure segregation is important, the process may reveal a new set of structural problems with respect to de facto segregation and inequality that do not lend themselves easily to legal remedies.

This article examines how the "discourse moment" constituted by *D.H. and Others* might affect the future of schooling for Roma youth. We revisit the questions posed by Douglas Ray and Dee Poonwassie (1992, 533–34) with respect to education and ethnic differences:

1. What steps can be taken in school policy, the curriculum, and evaluation
. . . to support the required level of autonomy of the minority group?
2. How can minority populations interact successfully with the host
populations—especially if the latter are blind to minority rights?
3. What schooling is appropriate for minorities to preserve their identity
but not isolate them from the majority populations of their nation?

Answers to these questions depend in this case on how discrimination is understood. It is only through some notion of proscribed discrimination that minority rights and state obligations can be rendered as policy. There exists no doubt that Roma students are subject to discrimination in the basic sense of being treated differently, but what rights does this minority have with respect to discrimination?

Former director of the ERRC Dmitrina Petrová (2001) reminds us that minority rights can be conceived in multiple ways, starting from the traditional liberal position that no individual should suffer discrimination on the basis of his or her membership in a minority group, however constituted. The stronger position with respect to minority rights, however, is that members of vulnerable minorities be afforded special protection and even "positive discrimination," that is, affirmative action (Petrová 2001; Hancock 2002). The EU Race Directive—with which the Czech Republic became aligned after the 2009 passage of an antidiscrimination law—takes the stronger position by adopting an active stance toward "indirect discrimination," defined as a situation where "an apparently neutral provision, criterion or practice would put persons of a racial or ethnic origin at a particular disadvantage compared with other persons, unless that provision, criterion or practice is objectively justified by a legitimate aim and the means of achieving that aim are appropriate and necessary."[3] While the Czech educational system seems accepting of the principles of individual equality and freedom from direct discrimination, there has been little enthusiasm for recognition of group rights, which tend to be decided on grounds of indirect discrimination. The processes by which the ECHR came to its decision in *D.H. and Others* and how the Czech government put the court's mandate into practice bear on the central problems of governance and mapping of ethnic identities in transnational spaces (Popkewitz 2000).

METHODOLOGY

In the Czech Republic—where Roma tend to fall off the statistical map—Jiří Večerník (2004) notes the value of qualitative methods for understanding the perceptions and coping strategies of people "down below." In that spirit, Francis

Vavrus and Leslie Bartlett (2006) propose the vertical case study "as a means of comparing knowledge claims among actors with different social locations." This postpositivist orientation resonates with recent trends in policy analysis. For instance, Frank Fischer (2003) maintains that traditional policy analysis proceeded from the premise that policy makers (as agents of the state) and their consultants make policy, both in discursive and practical terms, and that others (those at the bottom) mostly respond to policy. He insists, however, that policy is better seen as a shared negotiation, even if the sharing is neither equal nor equitable.

A framework of shared negotiation is essential to an understanding of cases involving Roma actors because analyses of legal decisions in education tend to assume that the positions of the actors "represented" in the case correspond to what is said about them. Roma parents, for instance, are distinct, but not independent, from their discursive proxies, such as NGO counsel for their children. Critical discourse analysis is sensitive to such concerns. It is oriented to structure, interaction, and the social resources—such as social and cultural capital—that enable and constrain interaction. Moreover, critical discourse analysis focuses on how these resources appear in discourse and are realized in social practices.[4] The discourse moment (here, the court decisions in *D.H. and Others*) is only one aspect of a historical social process. Other moments include social relations; power; material practices; beliefs, values, and desires; and institutions and rituals. Each moment incorporates the others without being reducible to any of them (Harvey 1996).

In this article, we follow the scheme proposed by Lilie Chouliaraki and Norman Fairclough (1999), who suggest a five-part framework for critical discourse analysis: statement of the problem, discussion of the obstacles to the problem's solution, function of the problem in the practice, possible ways past the obstacles, and reflection on the analysis itself. We have identified the problem—that is, the Gypsy problem—and through a discussion of social exclusion, the interplay between ethnic animus and social deviancy, and parental involvement in schools, we examine obstacles to its solution. We then take up the analysis of three discourse strands related to the problem in practice, the court decision. Finally, we consider possible solutions to the problem and conclude with reflective remarks on underlying, unresolved conflicts in the project of improving education for Roma students.

OBSTACLES TO SOLVING THE "GYPSY PROBLEM" IN EDUCATION

Social exclusion is intimately related in the Czech Republic to nation building and its functional correlate, the assimilation of "foreign elements" (i.e., the

Roma), through education. The historical "excellence" of the Czech school system is both context and stake in this struggle between the national pursuit of success and the less enthusiastic pursuit of equity: inclusion of "foreign elements" on anything approaching equal terms is represented in populist discourse as a threat to the educational health of the nation. While the standardized and relatively transparent structure of the Czech educational system might be expected to facilitate the integration of minority students (Park 2008), that outcome is possible only when parents are empowered to choose options other than the inevitable trajectories of their children's class- and race-based educational histories, trajectories to which their communities have been subjected throughout history. For Roma parents, the choice points in the Czech system are at the preschool (mateřske školy) and primary levels (základní školy), because advancement beyond these levels has been atypical.[5]

To understand these choices, we explore the theoretical category of social exclusion. We pay particular attention to the distribution of social and cultural capital in Czech social space and to the "placement" of Roma parents and children in that space. We then turn our attention to the exclusion and assimilation of Roma parents, specifically because it is here that parents' struggle for agency is represented by policy makers.

Social Exclusion and Social and Cultural Capital

Social exclusion refers to a complex set of institutional processes whereby persons are barred from economic opportunity, political voice, and social and cultural recognition (Portes 1998; Hick et al. 2007). Social exclusion is usually associated with unfavorable attitudes and (in)actions of majority groups toward minority groups, who are perceived as embodying differences that threaten the social, political, and moral fabric of the mainstream culture (Ray and Poonwassie 1992; Petrová 2001). As John Ogbu (2008) asserts, social exclusion is also associated with marginalized groups' resistance to efforts by the dominant class to include the less powerful on terms that favor the more powerful. Finally, social exclusion carries a spatial sense of displacement, marginalization, and isolation. For instance, the physical and topographical isolation of Roma students, in relation to their Czech peers, is the central question of *D.H. and Others*.

The relational character of social exclusion in the Czech Republic can be described in terms of *social capital* (Coleman 1988; Bourdieu et al. 2000). Tomáš Sirovátka and Petr Mareš (2008) delineate three types of social capital: *bonding* (between members of relatively homogenous groups), *bridging* (with people different than oneself or outside one's group), and *linking* (among members of different social classes). These forms of social capital can be distinguished along axes of intra-and intercommunity integration and linkage. This configuration yields four possible scenarios, the last of which—high integration and low linkage—is most relevant to the social exclusion of the Roma. This scenario points out that informal networks, correlated highly with intragroup cohesion, tend to have great importance in postcommunist societies, but that these bonds are not effective in overcoming material deprivation, particularly when connected with lack of trust in institutions and members of other groups. Given the high level of stratification of educational opportunities in the Czech Republic (Mateju and Smith 2008) and the lack of positive connection between Roma families and the individuals and institutions responsible for schooling, it is not surprising that the Roma lack the social capital to secure access to educational opportunities.

Pierre Bourdieu (2001, 98) links social capital to *cultural capital*, which can exist in three forms: "[in] the embodied state, that is in the form of long-lasting dispositions of the mind and body; in the objectified state, in the form of cultural goods (pictures, books, dictionaries, instruments, machines, etc.) . . . ; and in the institutionalized state, in the form of . . . legally guaranteed academic qualifications." The relationship between social and cultural capital is dialectic, operating historically: one may not accumulate cultural capital without the right kinds of connections, and one cannot make the right kinds of connections without the right dispositions, cultural goods, and qualifications.

Given that upward social class mobility in the Czech Republic is highly constrained—dependent on passing through the narrow gate to precollegiate gymnasiums rather than technical high schools—the educational prospects of Roma children would be severely compromised even if their Roma identify were not a factor, that is, just by virtue of their poverty (Mateju and Strakov 2005). This set of constraints on social mobility involves both social and cultural capital and compromises opportunity at every juncture. Roma parents without useful cultural capital—that is, for example, command of a mode of speech that would allow them to communicate as equals with school authorities— are not recognized as deserving of the respect of those with the power to advance the cause of their children, a respect that would be foundational for "bridging" or "linking" forms of social capital. Roma children without bridging or linking social capital may be prejudged by school personnel as lacking the dispositions and qualifications—cultural capital—necessary for academic advancement (Bourdieu and Wacquant 1992; Bourdieu 1996).

Ethnic Identity and Social Deviance

Modern popular attitudes toward the Roma are grounded in the Slavic majority's history and racial identification. A late eighteenth-century historian describes the Roma as "black horrid men. . . . The dark brown or olive- colored skin of the Gipsies, with their white teeth protruding between red lips, may be a disgusting site to Europeans, unaccustomed to such objects" (Grellman 1783, quoted in Hancock [2002, 56]). Anti-Gypsy regulations appeared in the Czech lands as early as 1538, when expulsion was ordered, and the killing of Roma was decriminalized. Racial persecution is a continuous feature of European Roma history, culminating in the *Porajmos*, the "devouring" of approximately half a million Roma in Nazi death camps (Crowe 1996).

Present-day Czech attitudes and policies toward the Roma originate in the events and discourse of the immediate post–World War II period. First, nearly all Czech Roma perished in the Holocaust, making it easier for Czechs to regard the postwar Roma population in the Czech lands—migrants from the Slovak half of the country and from Romania—to be even more foreign than they had previously regarded "their own" Roma. Second, having been abandoned by the West and overrun and brutally occupied by the Nazis, the Czech people in the postwar period exhibited extreme nationalism, exhibited by the "ethnic cleansing" of the large German minority in the Sudetenland. The Roma were caught up in this xenophobic sentiment, through which most Czechs' and Slovaks' historical distaste toward the Roma was magnified.

This anti-Roma resentment was wedded to a strong animosity toward "Gypsy wandering." Nomadism, though hardly universal among the Roma, was a cultural practice taken up at least in part in response to being barred from many localities. Non-Roma, however, tended to apply an ahistorical, racial interpretation to this social practice, seeing it as a violation of Czech cultural conventions about "the proper way to live." The high integration and low linkage social pattern of the nomad served both as an ethnic marker, distinguishing the Roma from their Slavic "hosts," and as a threatening kind of social behavior. Metaphors that associated disease and lawlessness with "wandering" were common in the popular press and official documents (Sokolova 2008).

Despite the predilection of the Czech public toward prejudice and discrimination against the Roma (Fawn 2001; Gabal et al. 2008), the "socialist" government that came to power in 1948 prohibited all forms of ethnic discrimination and did not officially recognize ethnicity (versus social class) as a salient category in making, or at least articulating, Roma-related policies. In a decree issued in 1952, the government charged its national committees to "keep the same principles of socialist lawfulness toward the gypsies as they do toward other citizens, because the laws . . . are equally binding for all citizens regardless of their nationality of race." This was not to say that the Gypsy problem was solved from the government's perspective: on the contrary, continuing educational reform sought to teach the Roma to realize the "kinds of [standard of life] proper living brings" (Sokolova 2008, 87). Whether couched in terms of ethnic inferiority or social backwardness, the state's role was to use schooling to civilize and assist, to transform the Roma from beggars to workers and from criminals to law-abiding citizens, and to mitigate poor parenting practices.

The shift from portraying the Roma as ethnic outcasts to social deviants was completed symbolically in 1958 with the passage of a law titled "On the Permanent Settlement of Wandering Persons." While the Roma are mentioned by name nowhere in the law, documentary evidence from its production and implementation indicates that they were precisely its subject.[6] The "nomads" to which the law refers are characterized as prone to disrupting the social order and to avoiding work or working dishonestly. For instance, this law prohibited "any conduct whose purpose is to gain ways of support without any endeavor, meaning without work . . . or . . . such actions or forms of conduct that is in conflict with laws or the moral attitudes of our society" (Zákon č.74/1958 Sb., quoted in Sokolova [2008, 96]). The regulation served in practice as a way for authorities to criminalize everyday Roma behavior and to intervene forcibly—with arrest and jailing—in the social and economic life of the Roma. Vera Sokolova (2008, 96) claims that the proscription of a mobile lifestyle "relegated the Romani population into a subordinate status of childhood and otherness—to the level of objects, rather than subjects—who needed to be constantly looked after, educated and cared for. [It] . . . was only the first step in a long-term policy of assimilation." For a social and ethnic group such as the Roma, which had little to no usable social capital and was perceived as lacking the requisite (or proper) cultural capital, the ascription of culture that matters most to everyday life tends to come from without. That is not to say that *romipen*, the core identities shared by most Romani children and adults, is illusory or nonmeaningful, but simply that it has not been meaningful to—or at least not positively evaluated by—members of the dominant culture (Hübschmannová 1998). And external markers of the Roma, most notably poverty and illiteracy, become salient in ascribing ethnic Roma identity by non-Roma and Roma alike (see, e.g., Ringold et al. 2005; Ahmed et al. 2007).

Marginalization, especially when it becomes a long-term historical feature of life, as it has for the Roma, carries cultural consequences. Jaromil Skupnik (2007) suggests that the attention-as-violence and misrecognition afforded the

Roma by majority social groups (in Slovakia, in this case) results in the formation of counterworlds or countersocieties with value systems that differ from the
"original" culture and from the unwelcoming host culture. Within these counterworlds, inhabitants receive positive attention, recognition, and confirmation
of the legitimacy of their values. That is, their historically conditioned *romipen*
is meaningful. The historical rule in the Czech Republic and all other European
countries, however, has been that this *romipen* has been racialized and demon-
ized, with the effect of intensifying the animus against the Roma, animus that
has been expressed potently against Roma children in schools (Lacková 2000).

Parental Capital, Parental Involvement, and Stigma

Although parents' engagement with their children's schoolwork generally
boosts confidence and enhances academic outcomes for children, this axiom
seems not to apply to parents and students whose social and cultural capital
is undervalued in the school environment (see Lareau 2002, 2003; Horvat et
al. 2003). Many studies suggest that parents' level of schooling strongly influ-
ences the success of their children, as does their socioeconomic class, nationality, country of birth, and language used in the home. But the social and cultural
capital of parents from different social classes and ethnic groups has differing
utility with respect to facilitating (or decreasing) the success of their children
(Bourdieu et al. 2000; Bourdieu 2001). Social capital is a good predictor of parental involvement, but it also predicts the educational value that different
kinds of involvement are likely to produce.[7] The value of parents' social capital
also varies with the type of school system in which it is used: poor parents are
able to get more educational value from the capital they do have when school
structures are more transparent and choice or differentiation is limited (Park
2008). Parental social capital can also be conceptualized as a form of community wealth, where the most pressing questions concern the extent to which this
wealth is "redeemable" in public schools and what mechanisms exist to sustain
and/or improve that situation (Yosso 2005).

Roma parents' social capital—however rich in sustaining internal cohesion
and support for their community's members—has often not been "educationally
relevant" (Horvat et al. 2003), partly because these parents have weak ties to
institutions and to the people who control them. Roma parents' social capital,
based mostly on intragroup connections, also may work against them in school
settings because school personnel perceive the group to which they belong as
ethnically uneducable and socially deviant. The conventional wisdom of dominant groups across Europe is that Roma parents just do not value education

(Hancock 2002). But belying the stereotype of disinterest in education or social integration, Roma parents consistently express determination that their children receive the best educational opportunities, despite the obstacles in their paths.[8]

Roma parents have a history of ambivalence toward school authorities. Not unlike other Czech citizens, Roma parents expect the state to provide services, and in cases where rates of unemployment are extremely high, there is a high degree of dependence on the state to meet other basic needs. However, Roma parents also have lifetimes of experience with discrimination by public institutions and tend to distrust the intentions of officials and be skeptical of their promises (Barány 2002; Pogány 2004).

The Rolling Pin, a short story by Roma author Ilona Ferková (discussed in Vaughan [2004] and Vaughan and Evans [2005]), gives a dramatic sense of the conundrum that Roma parents face when dealing with state authorities about the welfare of their children. In the story, Julka has just given birth to a child, and a nurse tells her that the baby's leg is dislocated and requires an operation. The mother is distraught, but the doctor says, "'Look what a fine boy you have. . . . Everything will be alright, we just have to operate as soon as possible.' . . . Julka began to kiss his hands with tears running down her face" (Vaughan 2004). But when Julka and her husband come to pick up their baby, now recovered, 3 months later, the doctor suggests putting the child in a children's home. The parents refuse the suggestion. Several weeks later, a social worker comes to their door and says, "You know the child would be better off in a children's home. Don't be afraid, they'll look after him properly there, better than you can." Julka is furious: "So you've come to steal my Julecek?" she shouts, and points to the door with the rolling pin that was in her hand. The social worker retreats in a rush. A few days later, Julka receives a summons to the police station on charges of threatening a state official. Ferková reverses the folk story of the Gypsy coming at night to steal children and asserts the intense attachment of Roma parents to their children. This attachment is always vulnerable, however, to their dependence on the state to provide services to their children, the state's belief that Roma parents are not fit to take care of their children, the power wielded by the authorities, and the lack of redress for Roma parents.

D.H. and Others v. the Czech Republic

In 1999 the ERRC published a report on school conditions in the Czech Republic that included a case study of schooling in Ostrava, where a large percentage of Roma students were placed in special schools for the mentally handicapped, from which they were very unlikely to progress to high school or higher education (ERRC 1999). According to the ERRC report, Roma students were more than 27 times as likely to be placed in special education as Czech students were, a claim not disputed by the government. With support from the ERRC and the Open Society Justice Initiative, which provided legal counsel, 18 Roma students claimed that placement policies and practices in the Czech Republic constituted a form of racial discrimination under Article 14 of the European Convention on Human Rights (Council of Europe 1950). After defeat in the Czech courts, the case was accepted for hearing by the ECHR in 2005. The case was decided against the Roma students by Section II of the court in 2006, but this decision was overturned a year later by the Grand Chamber, which included all the justices of the court.[9] During the 6 years that the case languished on the docket of the ECHR, the Czech Republic joined the EU and propagated a new national education law.

The Case for the Czech Roma Students

Counsel for the plaintiffs, D.H. and Others, offer two perhaps contradictory arguments about how and why Czech officials in Ostrava placed the Roma children in special schools.[10] The plaintiffs argue that parents were without choices and that parents were making the "wrong" choices. That is, the discriminatory effects of institutional racism and personal discrimination left Roma parents and children without power to make positive decisions in support of their children's education. They maintain that the Czech state had established a stratified system of special and regular schools, had implemented biased testing instruments and procedures to determine placement, and had entrusted decisions about placements to psychologists who believed that Roma children are deficient by nature. Parents thus encountered a system that manifestly discriminated on racial/ethnic grounds, though "legitimate" authorities refused to acknowledge this bias. Roma parents could either accept the placements and test results as offered, even when they knew that the tests were biased and the placements led to dead ends, or they could refuse, which deprived their children of educational and social opportunities and reinforced negative stereotypes about the Roma's attitude toward education. This cycle, according the plaintiffs, amounts to racial discrimination without legal recourse.

Since the Czech state could demonstrate that parents did, in fact, sign off on the placements in almost every case, the plaintiffs must acknowledge that the parents did have a choice, but they also emphasize that it was a choice between two negatives. That is, the available choices were illusory, and parents did not have agency to act in the best interests of their children. Later, the appeal describes parents who made the more difficult choice of refusing or appealing placements. Though such appeals faced great resistance, parents' actions demonstrated that an appeal process was, in fact, available. Since most parents did not pursue this more challenging, perhaps more heroic, option, the plaintiff's legal counsel insists that the parents erred and that, in the best interests of the child, the state had responsibility to correct the parents' mistake.[11]

These two narratives of Roma parenting cohere only insofar as Roma parents are identified as powerless and/or incompetent. This kind of representation is not the likely intention of the plaintiff's counsel, since they are engaged in what appears as precisely the opposite struggle, but it is quite possible that the constraints of the context—the policy discourse community in which they have placed their words for strategic purposes—allows nothing better. It is also notable here that the plaintiff's counsel makes no argument for a particular kind of education apart from one that (a) is not segregated and (b) does not permit discrimination by school authorities. Parents are told that they can accept this alternative or else be held negligent of the protection of their children's rights: they may and ought to refuse an educational alternative that separates their children from other Czech children but must accept placement in which inclusion beyond physical copresence is not imagined.

The Official Czech Account

The Czech government did not deny that school conditions and outcomes for Roma students were poor or that very high levels of de facto segregation existed. The Czech defense of this education policy consists mostly of saying that while these results are unfortunate, they are not the intention of the policy or of individuals carrying out that policy. While the school placement and special school policy in place in 1999 was barely defensible on the grounds of intent, it could be presented as a flawed "communist" policy in the process of reform. By 2004 a new education law was in effect, based on EU principles and rationalized fully in a white paper (MEYS 2001). The white paper argues that the state has a legitimate interest in the best education system possible, where the creation of special education programs for those who cannot succeed in normal classrooms is essential, in which the system is grounded in principles of fairness and cultural tolerance, and where any racial or ethnic segregation is an unfortunate and unintended by-product of these legitimate aims. The policy notes the importance of participation by parents as partners with school officials in administration and instruction and as the final arbiters in decisions affecting their children. In stressing the interdependence of parents and school officials in policy implementation, the white paper (MEYS 2001, 63) also stresses the rights and freedoms of parents with respect to the education of their children: "The state's task is to ensure the maximum autonomy of the parents of all these children in deciding on the form of their education, while the quality of all existing forms of education must be preserved."

Roma children are mentioned almost tangentially on the same page as belonging to the "increasing number of . . . children at risk in their development as a result of a disadvantageous socio-economic environment" and are discussed in the section devoted to special education. The other categories of disability listed alongside socioeconomic disadvantage are learning difficulties, neurological or psychiatric disorders, and emotional disorders. A careful reading suggests that socioeconomic disadvantage is interpreted to have similar sequelae to neurological and psychiatric disorders. Putatively, Roma parents have the same rights as other Czech parents to refuse the judgment of school personnel as to the appropriate placement of their children, but their children are de facto candidates for special education placement unless they have been able to overcome the barriers of inadequate preschool socialization. The dissolution of special schools, as such, is promised, but integration remains quite distant because of the intractability of the social disadvantages that impair the learning abilities of Roma children and the lack of qualified teachers to manage integrated classrooms. Parents are given choices and due process in placement decisions, but the choices are limited, as are the capacities of the parents themselves to make well-informed decisions about their children. In the best case, a Roma parent could choose to place his or her child in a regular Czech classroom. However, insofar as the Roma are not identified as an ethnic minority but as a socially disadvantaged group, there is no guarantee of a Roma child being recognized in the classroom as anything more or less than a Czech student. For example, there is no guarantee of receiving instruction that addresses cultural difference or special needs with respect to developing literacy.

Representation of Roma Parents by the Court

The ECHR is the judicial organ of the Council of Europe, an organization founded in 1949 with 45 member countries, including all 25 EU nations and all former Soviet states (except Belarus). Since the breakup of the Soviet bloc, the Council of Europe has been a key facilitator for the transition from dictatorship to democracy. Boasting a mission to defend human rights, parliamentary democracy, and the rule of law, the council developed the European Convention on Human Rights in 1950. The convention spells out civil, political, and economic rights and freedoms that member countries must respect. The primary role of the ECHR is to interpret and aid in the enforcement of the convention, and though its enforcement powers are limited, member states typically take ECHR decisions seriously and change national and local laws to conform to its rulings (Leach 2005).

In light of precedent and the "facts" of the case, it is easy to see why, on first reading, the Second Section of the ECHR would conclude that there was no actionable discrimination or denial of the right to education:

> The Court observes that the rules governing children's placement in special schools do not refer to the pupils' ethnic origin, but pursue the legitimate aim of adapting the education system to the needs and aptitudes or disabilities of the children. . . . It was the parents' responsibility, as part of their natural duty to ensure that their children receive an education, to find out about the educational opportunities offered by the State . . . and, if necessary, to make an appropriate challenge to the decision ordering the placement if it was issued without their consent. . . . While acknowledging that these statistics disclose figures that are worrying . . . the Court cannot in the circumstances find that the measures taken against the applicants were discriminatory.[12]

Juxtaposed against the court's begrudging sympathy for individual Roma parents and children are (a) its obligation to defer to the legitimate aims of the state, sanctioned by the testimony and actions of experts, and (b) a reluctance to ascribe motivation to discriminate without direct evidence of policy intent. The Second Section of the court observes that because the rules governing children's placement in special schools do not refer to the pupils' ethnic origin, and because there is a justification for treating children determined to have learning disabilities differently than their nondisabled peers, the fact that Roma children are treated differently does not amount to discrimination. This absence of nationality or culture is part of the general meaning of the court's narrative. Yet a so-called Roma parent is no different from any other Czech parent with respect to the protection of the rights of his or her children to education, except insofar as being Roma can be equated with being socially and/or economically disadvantaged.

The Grand Chamber overturned the initial ruling by moving the burden of proof from the plaintiffs to the Czech state, admitting statistics of disproportionate placement of Roma students in special schools as evidence, and affirming the special obligation of the court to extend special protection to disadvantaged and vulnerable minorities, particularly the Roma. The Grand Chamber substantially lowers the bar for demonstrating discrimination in asserting that "all that has to be established is that, without objective and reasonable justification, [Roma children] were treated less favorably than non-Roma children in a comparable situation and that this amounted in their case to indirect discrimination."[13]

With regard to the Roma parents' role in their children's school placements, the Grand Chamber begins by stating the conditions under which one might waive one's rights or those of one's dependents. As the court had already determined that differences in treatment qualify as discriminatory, consent to special placement constituted a waiver of the right not to be discriminated against. The argument also takes into consideration the failure of the state and local authorities to provide information about alternatives or to ensure that parents knew what they were signing up for or signing away. The court also expresses sympathy regarding the dilemma faced by Roma parents in making this decision for their children: they were offered only a "choice between ordinary schools that were ill-equipped to cater for their children's social and cultural differences and in which their children risked isolation and ostracism, and special schools where the majority of the pupils were Roma." Placing these parental decisions in the context of social discrimination generally, the court concludes that "no waiver of the right not to be subjected to racial discrimination can be accepted, as it would be counter to an important public interest."[14] The public interest that the court seems to have in mind is a tolerant, civil society—that is, a society where de jure racial discrimination is not permitted.

By concluding that the Czech regulatory strategy for the education of Roma students operates in violation of Article 14 of the convention and Article 2 of Protocol 1 (regarding the right to education), the court acknowledges the challenge of creating curricula and school structures that meet the demands at both ends of the spectrum of needs but offers no remedies for this potentially intractable problem. The court affirms that, no matter what institutional solutions the state eventually adopts, the state is obligated to take into full account the special needs of members of disadvantaged classes. The court also noted that in the special schools, students received an education that "compromised their subsequent personal development instead of tackling their real problems or helping them to integrate into the ordinary schools and develop the skills that would facilitate life among the majority population."[15] While the court employs the nonspecific classificatory scheme of "disadvantaged classes" in articulating the violation of Article 14—a scheme that has served since the socialist era in the Czech lands to conceal the racial/ ethnic character of education policy—its decision in *D.H. and Others* also clearly marks the discrimination against Roma students and parents as cultural and racial.

UTOPIAN AND DYSTOPIAN FUTURES

At the outset, we asked: what steps might be taken in school policy, curriculum, and evaluation to support the required level of autonomy of the Roma in the Czech Republic? The court (quoted above) interprets autonomy as freedom from forms of illicit discrimination—that is, school segregation and procedural obstacles—that diminish parents' ability to make the same choices about their children's futures as those available to other Czech parents and reduce students' access to opportunity. In other words, the court sees discrimination as a guarantor of continued dependence on the state, the opposite of social autonomy. The Grand Chamber extends the reach of the meaning of discrimination beyond individual intention—where the Second Section had taken its position—averring that the systemic consequences of the special school apparatus count as a violation of individual rights.

In its own terms, the court comprehends the intimate relationship between exclusion, stigma, and social and cultural capital. Offering Roma parents and children equal access to an integrated educational environment could potentially undo the historical effects of ethnic stigma that depends for its sustenance on this "artificial" separation. Stigma underwrites the mechanisms by which the Roma are deprived of the cultural capital necessary to be seen by members of the dominant group as persons of worth, capital that they might exchange for the bridging and linking forms of social capital necessary for access to high-quality social prospects (Bourdieu and Wacquant 1992; Sirovátka and Mareš 2008).

The Czech Ministry of Education preempted the court's decree in 2005 by officially discontinuing the system of special schools and making other concessions for inclusion. The accompanying report promised eventual "full respect" for Roma culture—including education in the Romany language (*Romanes*), multicultural curricular materials, increased numbers of Roma teachers and assistants, and increased participation by Roma parents in educational decisions. The document also admits, however, that the resources for full implementation are neither available now nor likely to be in the near future (Government of the Czech Republic 2005). Thus, the ERRC (2007) states that the official dismantling of the special school system has not significantly reduced de facto school segregation in the Czech Republic. And Kumar Vishwanathan, founder of the local NGO that first attracted international interest to Ostrava, reported that while some improvements had been achieved, "in its essence hardly anything has changed. The segregation is still continuing, the sub-standard education is still continuing, the teachers are not prepared to meet the individual needs of these children" (Lazarová 2006).

The disappointment expressed by Vishwanathan (Lazarová 2006) originates in part from a misapprehension about the presumptions underlying the problematics of equity in the practice of transnational governance—that is, when international bodies like the ECHR seek to regulate the behavior of a national and municipal structure like a school system. Governance in this context may not be a matter of the state implementing policies of reform that coincide with extranational notions of equality but rather "the ways in which systematic forms of pragmatic knowledge—the practical rationalities of daily life, know-how, expertise and means of calculation—structure the field of possible actions and participation" (Popkewitz 2000, 186). In other words, the decrees of the court and the changes in the Czech education law may have little effect on how historical ethnic praxis structures the life chances of all its participants, at all levels of the social structure.

This brings us to our second question: How might the Roma interact successfully with the culturally dominant Czech population, especially if the latter are blind to minority rights—and, we add, even after a powerful international body and the national Ministry of Education has required recognition of minority rights? Michael Kocáb, Czech minister for human rights and ethnic minorities, maintains that even as progress has been achieved toward a broader acceptance of tolerance as a necessary principle for a multicultural society, the public remains xenophobic: "These problems have been with us for 700 years. These prejudices have deep roots. It will take a long time to overcome them. We are trying in small ways but it is a work for a hundred years to come" (quoted in Johnstone [2009]). Substantive reform in the areas of residential housing, segregation, terrible employment prospects, health care, nutrition, and so on has been even slower to come than educational reform has, undermining the potential benefits of improved opportunities in schools and conspiring to keep the structures of stigmatization in place.

The reformed Czech system today offers three possibilities to Roma parents for their children: (a) placement in "practical schools" that are not distinguishable from the now-banned "special schools," (b) placement in school settings with a predominant Roma population and a Roma-centric approach, or (c) placement in regular Czech classrooms where Roma children are not officially recognized as culturally different. The potential consequences for Roma children are bleak. For example, Kazuyo Igarashi's (2005) investigation describes a "Roma" school that had strong ties to the community and offered instruction in Roma culture and language and a "Czech" school that offered the standard Czech curriculum with minimal adaptation to its Roma students. Roma students in predominantly Czech schools were not recognized as different. In the words of one teacher (Igarashi 2005, 448), whose integrated school had more than 20 percent Roma enrollment, "there are absolutely no Roma at this school."

Few Roma-centric schools exist, however, and there are pressures to enroll Roma children in practical schools rather than in regular Czech classrooms. It is estimated that at least one-quarter of Roma elementary students attend these practical schools (Together to School Coalition 2009), notwithstanding the public commitment on the part of the Ministry of Education for full integration. Neither community-based Roma schools nor the "practical" Roma schools are producing academic results that begin to approach those of Czech students in regular schools. Advancement to secondary schools and beyond, for Roma students in particular, depends much more on their academic achievement in the prescribed disciplines than on cultural or political understandings (Igarashi 2005). The court and the NGOs, which supported the Roma children's cause, reject out of hand the first option as a continuation of the policy declared illegitimate, while remaining silent about the second Roma-centric option. In their view, the best hope for social inclusion is the dismantling of segregated schooling once and for all.

Thus, in terms of social and cultural capital, and in thinking about the well-being of Roma children in the present and future, the choices offered Roma parents after the ECHR decision are difficult. If they place their children in predominantly Roma classrooms, they might reproduce the important intracommunal capital (i.e., cultural capital that is important to them, even if devalued by others) while also protecting their children from the anti- Roma hostility that endures in regular Czech classrooms (Lacková 2000). If they do not secure placements for their children in regular schools, however, they may well sacrifice their children's best chance to acquire the connections (i.e., social capital) and the ideas and practices (i.e., cultural capital) that can be converted into economic and social benefits.

It is in this context of limited and uncertain choices that we ask the question: what schooling is appropriate for minorities to preserve their identity but not isolate them from the majority populations of their nation? The choices appear stark. A Roma parent of the previous generation, and grandparent of this one, comments on the dilemma facing Roma parents when inclusive, but assimilationist, schooling is offered:

[When I was raising children,] everyone said to us, "Speak Czech with your children, so they can get on in life. If they speak Czech, they'll do well at school." They hammered this into our heads. We felt that we hadn't had a chance, but at least our children would. We thought—if our children are going to school, the teacher won't speak Romany—he won't understand what she wants, so we started to speak Czech at home with our kids—including myself. Because we started speaking Czech, our parents learned Czech from us. Otherwise they wouldn't understand their own grandchildren. This was a big problem for my father and mother. (Vaughan 2004)

Assimilation does offer the usual inventory of liberal benefits, but with conditions that Roma children will be challenged to meet while still being Roma, at least in an overt way recognized by other Czechs—teachers, principals, classmates. Whether Roma children, if they are able to conform to school expectations, will find themselves eligible for full membership in the "knowledge society" or will enjoy a reasonable standard of living is an open question, although pressures from the EU to enforce affirmative action policies in hiring practices seem to enhance prospects for formally educated Roma. As this mother and grandmother suggests, though, the cost of successful education in the Czech system for Roma families and communities, in terms of intergenerational alienation and the decreased use of *Romanes*, is potentially very high and is generally experienced as "culture loss."

CONCLUSION

The *D.H. and Others* decision and school reforms implemented by the Czech government signify enormous improvement over the status quo ante, when it was not possible for Roma even to appear in the public sphere, let alone exercise the limited agency to which they now have access. While the majority of Czechs may be unenthusiastic about multicultural reform, many Czechs now reject intolerance and ethnic violence. The public discourse does feature extremism and recalcitrance, but it also features resistance to perpetuating the Czech, and European, traditions of ethnic hatred. Before, Roma parents had little say in the segregated education of their children; now such exclusion from equal opportunity is officially banned (though mostly just displaced). Before, the answer to the question, "Who speaks for the Roma?" was "no one"; now, the Roma have powerful friends in high places who speak for them.

On the other hand, the high-status players in the legal drama of *D.H. and Others*, whose social practice is almost exclusively discursive, seem to have internalized in their arguments the logic that historically constituted the discriminatory material practices of Roma education. From the antiwandering policies of the 1950s (Sokolova 2008) to well-funded contemporary studies of social marginalization and displacement (Gabal et al. 2008), the discursive logic of Roma policy has demanded their absence, physical and symbolic, and their (mis)representation by proxy in the speech of non-Roma policy makers, experts, and helpers. In absentia, Roma parents and children continue to be represented either as victims of violence and domination that they are powerless to resist or even understand or as witless perpetrators of ethnic parochialism who prefer their children to grow up like them, as Roma, rather than to enjoy the (promised) benefits of mainstream Czech society. This situation constitutes an unresolved conflict at the heart of efforts to secure the rights of Roma parents and children. The autonomy of the Roma that the ECHR seeks to secure is threatened by their exclusion from the conversation in which their interests and identity are determined.

In short, the process itself is manifestly undemocratic with respect to participation in policy development. The process of implementation—that is, the creation of integrated classrooms in which "there are absolutely no Roma" (Igarashi 2005)—is similarly lacking in democratic practice. Democratic education requires a level of participation for the Roma that is not yet realized or generally imagined. For Douglas Torgerson (2003), fuller participation in the policy-making process can lead to radical shifts in governance, from its seclusion in official and quasi-official circles to its entrance in the public domain where discourse coalitions composed of nonofficial agents of change are actually constitutive. The rationale for democratizing the policy process is threefold: the inclusion of citizens is required "to counter technocratic tendencies, either of direct expert rule or—what is usually more to the point—of experts mobilized for other oligarchic interests; . . . in the name of a communicative rationality that would counter mobilizations of bias in the policy process; [and because] . . . participation educates and empowers people as citizens" (Torgerson 2003, 124). It remains exceedingly difficult for Roma activists to access opportunities to participate and be heard in postsocialist Europe. In the Czech Republic in particular, with its small and especially disempowered, dispersed Roma population, achieving political gains has been a historical challenge (Sokolova 2008).

However, *D.H. and Others* and associated political developments have fundamentally altered the context for potential action. In many places across postsocialist Europe, individuals and local NGOs, usually with the assistance of transnational NGOs like the ERRC, have organized effectively against school segregation and/or school exclusion, providing small-scale models that can, with modification, be implemented elsewhere. It will not, we hope, take another 100 years to overcome the prejudices and the policies that have resulted in the exclusion of Roma youth from the life chances of other European citizens.

Notes

1. Student achievement in the Czech education system is generally very high, with adult literacy and high school graduation rates approaching 100 percent and student scores in math and problem solving among the highest in the world (Wößmann et al. 2007). The Czech Republic has been successful in producing highly skilled, multilingual knowledge workers, but exclusion from educational opportunity has tended to translate into poor employment prospects and low social status.

2. *D.H. and Others v. the Czech Republic*, Grand Chamber, 7325/00 (ECHR, 2007).

3. Council of the European Union, "Council Directive 2000/43/EC of 29 June 2000 Implementing the Principle of Equal Treatment between Persons Irrespective of Racial or Ethnic Origin," *Official Journal L* 180:22–26. The Czech Republic was the last nation in the EU to pass an antidiscrimination law. The law was passed following a presidential veto and under threat of action by the European Court of Justice.

4. See Wodak (1996), Chouliaraki and Fairclough (1999), Fairclough (2001), and Widdowson (2004).

5. Czech preschools serve children ages 3–6. The final year of preschool is now offered free of charge, with special preference given to students with special needs (including Roma students). Nine years of primary school (*základní školy*) attendance, which contains a presecondary component, is compulsory in the Czech Republic. Most students attend primary school for the entire period, but some begin gymnasium during the later years. Various provisions and structures exist for helping students who are not prepared for, or who do not succeed in, their studies, from providing a "preparatory" program in primary school to special education and delayed enrollment. The a priori disposition of Roma children—as a socially disadvantaged class—is under the purview of the special education division (Eurybase 2009).

6. See Guy (1977), Stewart (2001), Barány (2002), and Sokolova (2008).

7. See Wodak (1996), Bourdieu et al. (2000), Noguera (2001), and Ream and Palardy (2008).

8. See Kende (2000), Claveria and Alonso (2003), Pogány (2004), and Levinson (2007).

9. *D.H. and Others v. the Czech Republic*, Second Section, 7325/00 (ECHR, 2006); *D.H. and Others v. the Czech Republic*, Grand Chamber, 7325/00 (ECHR, 2007).

10. *D.H. and Others v. the Czech Republic*, Request for referral to Grand Chamber, 7325/00 (ECHR, 2006).

11. Ibid.

12. *D.H. and Others v. the Czech Republic*, Second Section, 7325/00 (ECHR, 2006), secs. 48, 51, 52.

13. *D.H. and Others v. the Czech Republic*, Grand Chamber, 7325/00 (ECHR, 2007), sec. 183.

14. Ibid., secs. 203, 204.

15. Ibid., sec. 207.

REFERENCES

Ahmed, Patricia, Cynthia Feliciano, and Rebecca Jean Emigh. 2007. "Internal and External Ethnic Assessments in Eastern Europe." *Social Forces* 86 (1): 231–55.

Barány, Zoltan. 2002. *The East European Gypsies: Regime Change, Marginality.* Cambridge: Cambridge University Press.

Bourdieu, Pierre. 1996. *The State Nobility: Elite Schools in the Field of Power.* Palo Alto, CA: Stanford University Press.

Bourdieu, Pierre. 2001. "The Forms of Capital." In *The Sociology of Economic Life*, ed. Mark Granovetter and Richard Swedberg. 2nd ed. Boulder, CO: Westview.

Bourdieu, Pierre, Alain Accardo, Gabrielle Balazs, Stephane Beaud, Francois Bonvin, Emmanuel Bourdieu, Philippe Bourgois, et al. 2000. *The Weight of the World: Social Suffering in Contemporary Society.* Palo Alto, CA: Stanford University Press.

Bourdieu, Pierre, and Loic Wacquant. 1992. *An Invitation to Reflexive Sociology.* Chicago: University of Chicago Press.

Chouliaraki, Lilie, and Norman Fairclough. 1999. *Discourse in Late Modernity: Rethinking Critical Discourse Analysis.* Edinburgh: Edinburgh University Press.

Claveria, Julio V., and Jesus G. Alonso. 2003. "Why Roma Do Not Like Mainstream Schools: Voices of a People without Territory." *Harvard Educational Review* 573 (4): 559–90.

Coleman, James S. 1988. "Social Capital in the Creation of Human Capital." *American Journal of Sociology* 94:S95–S120.

Council of Europe. 1950. *Convention for the Protection of Human Rights and Fundamental Freedoms.* Rome: Council of Europe.

Crowe, David M. 1996. *A History of the Gypsies of Eastern Europe and Russia.* New York: Palgrave Macmillan.

ERRC (European Roma Rights Center). 1999. *A Special Remedy.* Budapest: ERRC.

ERRC (European Roma Rights Center). 2007. *The Impact of Legislation and Policies on School Segregation on Romani Children.* Budapest: ERRC.

Eurybase. 2009. *Organisation of the Educational System in the Czech Republic.* Brussels: European Commission. http://eacea.ec.europa.eu/education/eurydice/documents/eurybase/eurybase_full_reports/CZ_EN.pdf.

Fairclough, Norman. 2001. *Analyzing Discourse: Textual Analysis for Social Research.* New York: Routledge.

Fawn, Rick. 2001. "Czech Attitudes toward the Roma: 'Expecting More of Havel's Country'?" *Europe-Asia Studies* 53 (8): 1193–219.

Fischer, Frank. 2003. *Reframing Public Policy: Discursive Politics and Deliberative Practices.* New York: Oxford University Press.

Gabal, Ivan, Karel Čada, and Jan Snopek. 2008. *Key to Bolstering Integration Policy of Municipalities: Social Exclusion of the Roma and the Czech Society.* Prague: Otevřená Společnost.

Government of the Czech Republic. 2005. *Roma Integration Policy Concept.* Prague: Government of the Czech Republic.

Guy, Will. 1977. "The Attempt of Socialist Czechoslovakia to Integrate Its Gypsy Population." PhD thesis, University of Bristol.

Hancock, Ian. 2002. *We Are the Romani People.* Hatfield: University of Hertfordshire Press.

Harvey, David. 1996. *Justice, Nature, and the Geography of Difference.* Oxford: Blackwell.

Hick, Peter, John Visser, and Natasha MacNab. 2007. "Education and Social Exclusion." In *Multidisciplinary Handbook of Social Exclusion Research*, ed. Dominic Abrams, Julie Christian, and David Gordon. New York: Wiley.

Horvat, Erin McNamara, Elliot B. Weininger, and Annette Lareau. 2003. "From Social Ties to Social Capital: Class Differences in the Relations between Schools and Parent Networks." *American Educational Research Journal* 40 (2): 319–51.

Hübschmannová, Milena. 1998. "Czech School and 'Romipen': The Core-Identities of a Rom Child." In vol. 1 of *The Roma Education Resource Book*, ed. Csaba Fényes, Christina McDonald, and Anita Mészáros. Budapest: Open Society Institute. http://www.osi.hu/esp/rei/hubschmannova_romipen.html.

Igarashi, Kazuyo. 2005. "Support Programmes for Roma Children: Do They Help Promote Exclusion?" *Intercultural Education* 16 (5): 443–52.

Johnstone, Chris. 2009. "'Stereotypes and Xenophobia Abound, Which Engenders Fear': Interview with Michael Kocáb, Czech Minister for Human Rights and Ethnic Minorities." *Europolitics*, November 9. http://www.europolitics.info/social/ stereotypes-and-xenophobia-abound-which-engenders-fear-art253550-25.html.

Kende, Ágnes. 2000. "The Hungary of Otherness: The Roma (Gypsies) of Hungary." *Journal of European Area Studies* 8 (2): 187–201.

Lacková, Ilona. 2000. *A False Dawn: My Life as a Gypsy Woman in Slovakia*. Hatfield: University of Hertfordshire Press.

Lareau, Annette. 2002. "Class, Race and Contemporary American Child-Rearing in Black Families and White Families." *American Sociological Review* 67 (5): 747–76.

Lareau, Annette. 2003. *Unequal Childhood: Class, Race, and Family Life*. Berkeley: University of California Press.

Lazarová, Daniela. 2006. "EU Says Czech Republic Discriminates against Romany Children." *Roma in the Czech Republic*, April 5. http://romove.radio.cz/en/article/20976.

Leach, Phillip. 2005. *Taking a Case to the European Court of Human Rights*. Oxford: Blackstone.

Levinson, Martin P. 2007. "Literacy in English Gypsy Communities: Cultural Capital Manifested as Negative Assets." *American Educational Research Journal* 44 (1): 5–39.

Matejů , Petr, and Michael L. Smith. 2008. "The Perceived Value of Education and Educational Aspirations in the Czech Republic: Changes in the Determination of Educational Aspirations between 1989 and 2003." *Comparative Education Review* 53 (1): 13–39.

Matejů , Petr, and Jana Strakov. 2005. "The Role of the Family and the School in the Reproduction of Educational Inequalities in the Post-Communist Czech Republic." *British Journal of Sociology of Education* 26 (1): 17–40.

MEYS (Czech Ministry of Education, Youth, and Sport). 2001. *National Programme for the Development of Education in the Czech Republic*. Prague: MEYS and Institute for Information on Education.

Noguera, Pedro A. 2001. "Transforming Urban Schools through Investments in the Social Capital of Parents." In *Social Capital and Poor Communities*, ed. Susan Saegert, J. Phillip Thompson, and Mark R. Warren. New York: Russell Sage.

Ogbu, John. 2008. *Minority Status, Oppositional Culture, and Schooling*. New York: Routledge.

Park, Hyunjoon. 2008. "The Varied Educational Effects of Parent-Child Communication: A Comparative Study of Fourteen Countries." *Comparative Education Review* 52 (2): 219–45.

Petrová, Dmitrina. 2001. "Racial Discrimination and the Rights of Minority Cultures." In *Discrimination and Human Rights: The Case of Racism*, ed. Sandra Fredman. New York: Oxford University Press.

Pogány, István. 2004. *The Roma Cafe: Human Rights and the Plight of the Romani People*. London: Pluto.

Popkewitz, Thomas. 2000. "Rethinking the Comparative Problem of Inclusion/ Exclusion." In *Historical-Comparative Perspectives: Festschrift in Honor of Andreas Kazamias*, ed. J. Boukakis. Athens: Gutenberg.

Portes, Alberto. 1998. "Social Capital: Its Origin and Applications in Modern Sociology." *Annual Review of Sociology* 24:1–24.

Ray, Douglas, and Dee H. Poonwassie. 1992. "An Assessment, Implications for Schooling and Teacher Education." *Education and Cultural Differences: New Perspectives*, ed. Douglas Ray and Dee H. Poonwassie. New York: Garland.

Ream, Robert K., and Gregory J. Palardy. 2008. "Reexamining Class Difference in the Availability and the Educational Utility of Parental Social Capital." *American Educational Research Journal* 45 (2): 238–73.

Ringold, Dena, Mitchell A. Orenstein, and Erika Wilkens. 2005. *Roma in an Expanding Europe: Breaking the Poverty Cycle.* Washington, DC: World Bank.

Sirovátka, Tomas, and Petr Mareš. 2008. "Social Exclusion and Forms of Social Capital: Czech Evidence on Mutual Links." *Czech Sociological Review* 44 (3): 531–55.

Skupnik, Jaromil. 2007. "Reflected Worlds: Marginalisation and Integration from the Perspective of the Socio-psychological Dynamics of Society." *Czech Sociological Review* 43 (1): 133–47.

Sokolova, Vera. 2008. *Cultural Politics of Ethnicity: Discourses on Roma in Communist Czechoslovakia.* Soviet and Post-Soviet Politics and Society no. 82. Stuttgart: Ibidem-Verlag.

Stewart, Michael. 2001. "Communist Roma Policy as Seen through the Hungarian Case." In *Between Past and Future: The Roma of Central and Eastern Europe,* ed. Will Guy. Hatfield: University of Hertfordshire Press.

Together to School Coalition. 2009. "2009/2010 School Year Begins, Segregation of Roma Pupils Must End." Press release, September 2. http://spolecnedoskoly .cz/wp-content/uploads/pr-together-to-school-coalition-2-september-2009.doc.

Torgerson, Douglas. 2003. "Democracy through Policy Discourse." In *Deliberative Policy Analysis: Understanding Governance in the Network Society,* ed. M. A. Hajer and H. Wagenaar. Cambridge: Cambridge University Press.

Vavrus, Francis, and Leslie Bartlett. 2006. "Comparatively Knowing: Making a Case for the Vertical Case Study." *Current Issues in Comparative Education* 8 (2): 95–103.

Večerník, Jiří. 2004. "Who Is Poor in the Czech Republic? The Changing Structure and Faces of Poverty after 1989." *Czech Sociological Review* 40 (6): 807–32.

Vaughan, David. 2004. "Ilona Ferkova—Stories That Capture Roma Life in the Czech Republic Today." *Roma in the Czech Republic,* December 12. http://romove .radio.cz/en/clanek/20268.

Vaughan, David, and Simon Evans. 2005. "We Still Breathe Their Air." *Roma in the Czech Republic,* January 22. http://romove.radio.cz/en/article/20312.

Widdowson, Henry G. 2004. *Text, Context, Pretext: Critical Issues in Discourse Analysis.* Malden, MA: Blackwell.

Wodak, Ruth. 1996. *Disorders of Discourse.* Harlow: Longman.

Wößmann, Ludger, Elke Ludemann, Gabriela Schutz, and Martin R. West. 2007. "School Accountability, Autonomy, Choice, and the Level of Student Achievement: International Evidence from PISA 2003." OECD Education Working Paper no. 13, Organization for Economic Cooperation and Development, Directorate of Education, Paris.

Yosso, Tara. 2005. "Whose Culture Has Capital? A Critical Race Theory Discussion of Community Cultural Wealth." *Race, Ethnicity and Education* 8 (1): 69–91.

*William S. New** is professor of education and youth studies at Beloit College, Wisconsin, USA.

Michael S. Merry is professor of philosophy of education at the University of Amsterdam, Netherlands.

William S. New and Michael S. Merry, "Solving the 'Gypsy Problem': *D.H. and Others v. the Czech Republic*," *Comparative Education Review* 54, no. 3 (August 2010).

Used by permission.

Chapter 7: The Scene After Battle: What Is the Victory in *D.H.* Worth and Where to Go From Here?

*by Lilla Farkas**

INTRODUCTION

Following ten years of legal battle against the misdiagnosis of 18 Romani children in the Czech town of Ostrava and their misplacement in special schools for the intellectually disabled, on 13 November 2007 the Grand Chamber of the European Court of Human Rights found that the Czech Republic had violated the right of the applicant children to education without discrimination.

As recalled in the Grand Chamber judgment in *D.H. and Others v. the Czech Republic* (judgment of 13 November 2007) (hereinafter: *D.H. II*), Roma have been a topic of discussion at the European level from the late 1960s. Over the last 15 years this discussion has been kept lively by the European Roma Rights Centre (ERRC) led NGO movement that aims at protecting the rights of Roma all over Europe. The ERRC and its allies have fought dozens of cases before European and international fora—first and foremost the European Court of Human Rights (ECtHR). None of these actions has however been as strategic, laborious and lengthy as the litigation in *D.H.* This paper examines the verdicts rendered in *D.H.* to see the journey this case has taken the ECtHR on and attempts to map out what the consequences of the final judgment may be in the European legal arena.

There will be a focus throughout this paper on the Racial Equality Directive (RED),[2] its impact on *D.H. II* and its future impact on strategic litigation against ethnic and racial discrimination in Europe. It is noteworthy in this context that although some domestic litigation—notably *actio popularis* litigation in Bulgaria and Hungary—has been made possible by the transposition of the RED, the majority of cases presently pending either predate it or fall in a sequence that pre-dates RED—eg Traveller and anti-Romani violence cases. Undoubtedly, however, a new wave of litigation is emerging and organisations engaged in such activities use the RED in their efforts. The judgment in *D.H. II* has significantly raised the profile of community law.

Over the past 13 years at the ECtHR, the bulk of anti-discrimination jurisprudence has been generated by the Open Society Institute-sponsored Roma rights movement. Other litigation, the Traveller cases, came from the UK and were limited in scope to the failure of local authorities at providing reasonable accommodation (housing but no finding of violation in relation to education), ie in essence depriving Travellers of their right to exercise their right to private and family life in full.[3] As we will see from the Court's reasoning in *D.H. II*, the Traveller accommodation cases have been instrumental in shaping the ECtHR's understanding of Roma rights.

These cases arose from (in)directly discriminatory legislation, on the basis of which Travellers had often been forced to camp illegally. On account of the 'forced illegality' prior to Connors—who had complied with the law—the ECtHR had not found violations of Article 8 of the European Convention on Human Rights (ECHR). The ECtHR had, however, been sympathetic towards Travellers and already observed in *Chapman* that "there could be said to be an emerging international consensus amongst the Contracting States of the Council of Europe recognising the special needs of minorities and an obligation to protect their security, identity and lifestyle, not only for the purpose of safeguarding the interests of the minorities themselves but to preserve a cultural diversity of value to the whole community."[4] The ECtHR also noted that "the vulnerable position of Roma/Gypsies means that special consideration should be given to their needs and their different lifestyle both in the relevant regulatory framework and in reaching decisions in particular cases."[5] The House of Lords echoed the ECtHR's concerns, when holding that the vulnerable position of Travellers as a minority group deserved more sympathetic attention and special consideration of their needs than had previously been the case in the planning and site allocation process.[6] Sadly, the practical impact of these decisions is not yet visible.

Prior to *D.H.*, however, the cases had been reactive. In the UK they reacted to individual instances of failure to accommodate Travellers, whereas in Central and Eastern Europe they reacted to violence or death inflicted on individual Romani victims by law enforcement personnel or mob violence directed against entire Romani communities. From *Assenov v. Bulgaria* (judgment of 28 October 1998) to *Stoica v. Romania* (judgment of 4 March 2008), the cases are telling of the attitudes of public officials, discriminatory administrative practice in the investigation of serious rights violations against Roma, and potential domestic judicial responses to such practices. They are also telling of the difficulties Romani victims of racial violence and discrimination may face in countries that seek to provide protection from discrimination in criminal law. Obviously, in criminal law the RED's great achievement, the reversed burden of proof, cannot be applied and it may be far more difficult to recover adequate moral damages in domestic criminal proceedings than before the ECtHR.

D. H. and Others v. the Czech Republic: THE JUDGMENTS

The ERRC hailed the judgment in *D.H. II* as bringing the ECtHR's Article 14 jurisprudence in line with principles of anti-discrimination law that prevail within the EU. Undoubtedly, since the adoption and transposition of the RED the most important and publicised legal battle relating to Roma rights covered by the RED has been fought and won in this case. And even though litigation in *D.H.* predates the RED, the length of proceedings before the ECtHR made it possible to raise arguments in this case based on the RED.

Inspired by Soviet educational dogma, in the Czech Republic, as in many other Central European countries, a system of special schools had been established during Communism and maintained for decades even after studies by social scientists, psychologists and teachers found clear patterns of system failures resulting in ethnic discrimination. In the mid-1990's the slow reconceptualisation of the issue of misdiagnosis as a legal, not only as a sociological or pedagogical problem began. The then ERRC legal director, James A. Goldston, initiated meetings with domestic stakeholders and argued that a legal challenge needed to be mounted to tackle this structural problem. In Hungary he failed to gather adequate support and it was not until 2006 that as a result of concerted efforts by Viktória Mohácsi, Member of European Parliament, and her team in this country that action for civil damages were brought on behalf of 17 misdiagnosed Romani children.

In the Czech Republic, the ERRC was successful at finding a Romani community whose members could be persuaded during months of field work to challenge their placement in special schools. However, in Ostrava, ERRC researchers did much more than identifying the victims. They systematically collected ethnic data to support the case and also to test what worth statistical data had as a piece of evidence.

The case originated with the unsuccessful filing of complaints in Czech courts in 1999 on behalf of eighteen children represented by the ERRC and local counsel. In 2000, the applicants turned to the ECtHR, alleging that their assignment to "special schools" for children with learning disabilities contravened the ECHR. According to the ERRC, "Tests used to assess the children's mental ability were culturally biased against Czech Roma, and placement procedures allowed for the influence of racial prejudice on the part of educational authorities".[7]

Statistical evidence compiled by the ERRC from Czech officials and authorities, and presented to the ECtHR demonstrated that school selection processes frequently discriminated on the basis of race; e.g. that any randomly chosen

Romani child in Ostrava was more than 27 times more likely to be placed in schools for the learning disabled than a similarly situated non-Romani child.

The case miserably failed at first instance, and that judgment (hereinafter: D.H. I)[8] did not only meddle with facts presented to the ECtHR—for instance, refusing to consider that a number of applicants had not in fact been intellectually disabled and had been placed back into normal school—but was plainly biased against Romani parents and undisciplined in its reasoning. Despite the Czech Republic's clear acknowledgement to Council of Europe monitoring bodies of structural discrimination against Romani children by way of misdiagnosis, the Chamber did not analyse the causes of such discrimination. It contented itself by finding that the legislation allowing for the maintenance of special schools was not *intentionally* discriminatory, nor could intentional discrimination be proven on the part of professionals engaged in making decisions on placement.

The Chamber judgment was nothing out of the ordinary for domestic lawyers from the CEE region, used to poorly argued cases, where legal terminology could hardly hide the prejudices of the judges themselves. They could take consolation in the fact that at least the Portuguese judge voted against the majority and argued that given the respondent State's acknowledgement of discrimination, there was no room for justification and a violation should have been found.

Similar to the Chamber judgment, in the first desegregation challenge in a Hungarian civil court—the so called *Miskolc* desegregation case—the *actio popularis* claim was dismissed at first instance[9] on the basis that the plaintiff had failed to show that the defendant local government did not only intend but directly aimed at segregating Romani children. This was, however, remedied on appeal and segregation was established as a failure to end a long-lasting spatial separation between Romani and majority children.[10] It goes without saying that intent—or in matters relating to the right to education under the ECHR— never needs to be proven to establish civil liability. However, once discriminatory intent is proven, that may be reflected in the severity of sanctions. Culpability in civil cases operates along different considerations from liability under criminal law. The Chamber ought to have noted that it was examining the liability of the Czech Republic in the field of education in a case that did not concern criminal liability at the domestic level either.

In *D.H. I*, the ECtHR Chamber was prepared to accept tacit parental consent as a potential justification for segregated education. According to the Chamber judgment, the "*needs and aptitudes* or disabilities of the children" themselves, and *parental behaviour* justified difference in treatment.[11] Regrettably, the Chamber chose not to address issues advanced by the complainants, such as the extent to which parental consent was 'informed consent', instead taking the perspective of the average majority person, who is familiar with her rights, has not experienced pressure from public authorities and has access to relevant information to make informed decisions on her own. Only from this perspective could factors such as lack of parental appeal against placement decisions be considered as evidence of genuine parental will. A similar finding in relation to parental behaviour has been made in a misdiagnosis case in Hungary as well.[12]

On appeal, the Grand Chamber, by a vote of 13 to 4, ruled that the disproportionate placement of Romani students into special schools is a form of unlawful discrimination in breach of Article 14 ECHR taken together with Article 2 of Protocol No.1. The ERRC hailed the judgment as path breaking in a number of respects, including the following:

Patterns of discrimination—For the first time, the ECtHR found a violation of Article 14 of the Convention in relation to a pattern of racial discrimination in a particular sphere of public life, in this case, public primary schools. As such, the Court underscored that the Convention addresses not only specific acts of discrimination, but also systemic practices that deny the enjoyment of rights to racial or ethnic groups.

Equal access to education for Roma is a persistent problem throughout Europe— The ECtHR went out of its way to note that the Czech Republic is not alone—discriminatory barriers to education for Romani children are present in a number of European countries.

Unified anti-discrimination principles for Europe—the ECtHR further established, clarified or re-affirmed the following principles: indirect discrimination can constitute a violation of the ECHR; in such cases, the burden of proof can shift to the respondent State; intent not required to prove violation; facially neutral law may be discriminatory in effect.

Statistics—When it comes to assessing the impact of a measure or practice on an individual or group, the use of statistics may be relevant. In particular, statistics which appear on critical examination to be reliable and significant will be sufficient to constitute prima facie evidence of indirect discrimination. The Court confirmed, however, that statistics are not a prerequisite for a finding of indirect discrimination.

No waiver of right to non-discrimination—In view of the fundamental importance of the prohibition of racial discrimination, no waiver of the right not to be subjected to racial discrimination can be accepted, as it would be counter to an important public interest.

The Special situation of Roma as an ethnic minority group—As a result of their history, Roma have become a specific type of disadvantaged and vulnerable minority who require special protection.

APPRAISAL OF *D.H. II*

It is arguable that although in *D.H. II* discrimination in the right to education has been established, there remain unresolved issues that merit further attention and action at the practical as well as theoretical levels as follows:

1. *D.H. II* could not have been won had reports from Council of Europe bodies—such as the European Commission on Racism and Intolerance and the Advisory Committee of the Framework Convention on National Minorities—not brought to light patterns of segregation and discrimination against Czech Roma in education. Given the weight afforded to these reports in the final judgment, it may be suspected that some pressure has been put on the Court to reference these reports, thus taking into due consideration the work undertaken by and according adequate acknowledgement to the respective bodies. Clearly, the referencing of political or soft law measures and reports in the final judgment is also intended to raise the profile of such endeavours.

2. Arguably, in *D.H. II* the Grand Chamber is wrong in finding indirect discrimination instead of direct discrimination, and not only because the facts do not substantiate this view. It is worthwhile recalling here that the applicants argued the case on the basis of direct as well as indirect discrimination. As is noted in the final judgment, "at the very least, there is a danger that the *tests were biased* and that the *results were not analysed in the light of the particularities and special characteristics of the Romani children* who sat them. In these circumstances, the tests in question cannot serve as justification for difference in treatment."[13] If this was the case, then obviously the tests themselves did not seem neutral, nor was the analysis of test results done in a neutral fashion—they were plainly discriminatory on the ground of ethnicity, as explained in a European Commission report.[14] Under these circumstances not only can the tests not serve as a justification, they were the primary sources of discrimination against Romani children.

   According to its jurisprudence, the Court ought to have examined whether the applicants were successful in identifying the protected ground under Article 14, less favourable treatment and a comparator group which was in an analogous situation to theirs. Once the applicants had established these elements, the Czech Republic could seek to justify its actions along the reasonable and objective justification test, or by claiming that the difference in treatment in fact arose as a result of positive action measures.[15]

Arguably, however, the Grand Chamber failed at running this test properly. The Court identified race and within that ethnic origin as a ground on which protection was due to the applicants,[16] and clearly stated that the applicants were less favourably treated because they were not tested and measured in a fashion that took their personal characteristics fully into account.[17] However, it failed at identifying properly the comparator group, that of majority Czech children whose personal characteristics were fully taken into account during testing. This failure may be the cause of controversy around the form of discrimination to be tested and justified.

In a typical case of indirect discrimination before the European Court of Justice, for instance, a difference can be discerned between groups that bear characteristics neutral to the protected ground. For instance, in *Enderby* a difference in payment was established between speech therapists and pharmacists.[18] Only at more rigorous examination could it be seen that women were grossly over represented among speech therapists, and thus indirectly discriminated by a seemingly neutral measure—the collective agreement. Differences in access to occupational pension in the *Bilka* case were revealed between full time and part time workers.[19] Again, only a closer look revealed that the vast majority of the part time workers were women as opposed to mainly male full time employees. In these cases, however, the provision or practice that resulted in indirect discrimination was indeed neutral, i.e. it was not linked to sex.

The same cannot be said in *D.H.* As the Grand Chamber noted at paragraph 201, there was a danger that the IQ tests and the professional code along which test results were analysed were not race and ethnicity neutral. Indeed, when identifying the comparator group as is suggested here, i.e., at the entry point of the testing process, the racially or ethnically loaded character of the tests and the testing process becomes apparent: The comparison is between Romani and non-Romani children, not intellectually disabled and non-disabled children. Given that there was evidence in the case as to the decade-long discriminatory impact of such testing on Czech Romani children, the Court ought to have addressed the issue of structural or systemic discrimination. Arguably, from such a system level perspective, entirely detached from the characteristics of individual Romani and non-Romani children, *D.H.* could only have been analysed as a form of direct discrimination.

3. A somewhat hidden and regrettably inconsistent argument based on eth-

nic minority rights can also be discerned in the Grand Chamber judgment. This argument flows from the ECtHR's findings in the UK Traveller cases[20] and is related to the vulnerable position of European Roma in general, and the specific ethnic minority characteristics of this ethnic group.[21] Tacitly, this argument elevates for protection Roma through their membership in a national minority group listed under Article 14 of the ECHR and specifically protected under the FCNM, and recognises a consensus, a self-imposed obligation on Member States to reasonably accommodate the said ethnic minority characteristics in relation to substantive rights protected under the ECHR.[22]

Arguably however, such a duty of reasonable accommodation is a specific, free standing form of discrimination, for which no test needs to be elaborated: It is enough to prove that the applicant is Romani, that in relation to her substantive right such a public/state duty exists and that it is not complied with. In essence the central finding of the Grand Chamber at paragraph 201 of *D.H. II* is exactly this. But why run the test for indirect discrimination then? As discussed below, the Grand Chamber went out of its way in distinguishing the reasonable accommodation duty in relation to public education from any sort of mandatory positive action measure. This distinction, however, may collapse once the ECtHR's jurisprudence evolves on this matter, and will definitely fail under the RED, which is based on a purely individualistic right to non-discrimination as opposed to a collective rights based framework of minority rights.

Certainly, this minority rights based argument shows that the Court has recognised Roma as a protected group in the area of public education, employment and the access to goods and services and indicated its willingness to strictly scrutinise measures taken against them, and its readiness to impose a duty on States to reasonably accommodate the needs and specificities of Roma in the field of education.[23]

By elevating Roma for this special protection, and grounding this protection on their status as a recognised ethnic minority, the Court at the same time limited the scope of its protection, which at the moment does not extend to other ethnic groups, or indeed racial minorities—whether or not citizens of Member States.

4. It is not yet known whether direct race or ethnicity based discrimination would be more difficult to justify under the ECHR than indirect discrimination. What is known and relevant now that the ECtHR has taken the RED into consideration in its deliberations is that under the RED indirect

discrimination can be far more easily justified than can direct discrimination. Moreover, even the test for indirect discrimination in the RED is more rigorous than that applied by the ECtHR in *D.H. II* (paras. 196–204). This said, the difference between the approaches under Community law and the ECtHR jurisprudence may not be significant, as in subsequent cases—as is already indicated in the *Sampanis and Others v Greece* judgment—the ECtHR may limit justification to that known under the RED. When assessing how progressive future case law may be, it is also important to note that the ECtHR Grand Chamber did not find it difficult to break away from the 'intent doctrine' so cheerfully applied in *D.H. I* by the Chamber.

5. The Court in *D.H. II* correctly assesses the specific situation of Romani parents vis-à-vis average non-Romani persons. Although tacitly, in mapping out this specific situation the ECtHR adopts a multifaceted view of Roma as a dual racial and ethnic minority (particularities and characteristics of Romani children, members of disadvantaged community, often poorly educated, making decisions under constraint, social and cultural differences (possibly including language), risk of isolation and ostracism in majority settings),[24] as elaborated in the *Segregation Report (chapter 2.1.)*.

In order to avoid stereotyping and generalisations, there is a need, however, to explain in full this multi-facetted nature of Romani identity—among which social deprivation is an important element, an element that internalises in the definition of Romani identity the impact of long standing, historic discrimination that some may otherwise view as a result of present indirect discrimination. The ECtHR still owes us this explanation, in fact in *D.H. II* it may itself have come a bit too close to stereotyping and generalising. Regrettably, when discussing the reasons of discriminatory application of the Czech law, the ECtHR did not maintain its definition of Romani identity as a multifaceted one.[25]

6. *D.H. II* could and ought to be argued differently in domestic courts and/or before the ECJ. First and foremost, litigators have a role in ensuring that courts have firm knowledge of discrimination against Roma in the given field. Second, they ought to advocate for principled reasoning. Third, all players should further the multifaceted definition of Roma as a dual racial and ethnic minority. Last, they need to argue for effective, proportionate and dissuasive remedies—in the form of reasonable accommodation duties or other types of mandatory positive actions if need be.

The ECtHR in the UK Traveller cases has developed a minority rights based definition recognising the special needs of Travellers, which is beneficial in that it is also able to capture Romani identity as a multifaceted one. The applicants in *D.H.* were conscious not to characterise their case as demanding positive action.[26] The ECtHR adopted this line of reasoning and ruled that positive action was not required vis-à-vis misdiagnosed Romani children, but that the respondent State was at fault when failing to take "into account these children's special needs as members of a disadvantaged class."[27]

In reality, however, these special needs cannot be taken into account by simply refraining from discrimination. In other words, unless reasonably accommodating the special needs of Roma in public education legislation, making special financial investments into developing new tests and training professionals including teachers in normal schools that formerly misdiagnosed Romani children now allegedly attend, the Czech Republic cannot facilitate the special interests of Romani children.

Under the RED, the reasonable accommodation of such special ethnic minority needs amounts to positive action, which hitherto has been rather narrowly defined in sex discrimination cases by the ECJ. It seems at the same time that on the ground of race and ethnicity, many Member States provide a broader reading to positive action.[28] Indeed, the question that needs to be resolved under the RED, i.e. mandatory positive action, is already on the table in relation to housing rights. In the UK and France, where Travellers are primarily itinerant, the key issues relate to the extent to which positive provision should be made for the special needs of Traveller families and the implementation of reasonable accommodation duties.

7. Consequently, in cases of structural discrimination, such as *D.H. II*, pursuant to Article 15 of the RED (proportionate, effective and dissuasive remedies for race and ethnic discrimination) domestic courts and/or the ECJ ought to impose positive action as the only effective, proportionate and dissuasive remedy. In failing to do so itself, the ECtHR failed to provide the applicants and tens of thousands of Romani children across Europe effective judicial protection. Just as the reversal of the burden of proof in indirect sex discrimination cases was "judge made law" introduced by the ECJ to ensure effective judicial protection, a similarly bold step needs to be advocated in relation to Roma and mandatory positive action.

8. Dissenting opinions in *D.H. II* warn us about the politics that underlie and can trump any Roma—let alone immigrant racial minorities—related litigation effort at the domestic as well as the EU level, notably in the relations of new versus old Member States. In this regard, the Czech judge Jungwiert's remarks cannot be overlooked. In his dissenting opinion (particularly in

paragraphs 6–8), Judge Jungwiert elaborated at length on how old EU Member States have been unable to resolve issues relating to the education of Travellers and suggested that they ought to then exercise more self-restraint in criticising the Czech Republic (paragraph 15).

Furthermore, the Slovenian judge Zupancic in his dissenting opinion concludes that "No amount of *politically charged* argumentation can hide the obvious fact that the Court in this case has been *brought into play for ulterior purposes* [emphasis added], which have little to do with the special education of Romani children in the Czech Republic. The future will show what specific purpose this precedent will serve." This is even more troubling, as his position is that only the Czech Republic has done something about the education of Romani children, thus it cannot be held in violation of anti-discrimination principles. The sheer level of ignorance on this topic is astonishing especially in light of the work of other Council of Europe bodies, such as the Advisory Committee of the Framework Convention on National Minorities and the European Committee on Racism and Intolerance—or indeed the Fundamental Rights Agency (formerly EUMC) at the EU level.

That out of the four dissenting judges only the Slovak judge, Sikuta, made an attempt at providing a legal, instead of a political, argument suggests structural problems at the level of the ECtHR in the selection and impartiality of judges, especially from the CEE region. One might wonder about the adequacy of domestic judgments and the attitudes of judges in the CEE region in similar cases. These are not concerns to be taken lightly as a hostile judiciary may undermine any reasonable attempt at strategic litigation for Roma and racial minority rights.

9. The ECtHR's perception of de facto discrimination resulting from (in)directly discriminatory legislation and the tacit understanding supported by relevant Council of Europe treaties and mechanisms that minority rights are collective rights virtually transformed *D.H.* from an application brought by 18 individual applicants into an *actio popularis* or collective complaint; hence the finding that there was no need to examine the applicants' individual cases. It is a shame therefore that the ECtHR did not accord a remedy suitable for structural discrimination or a collective complaint. On the other hand, the transformation of the applications into a virtual collective complaint shall definitely be advertised and followed as best practice. It ought to be borne in mind though that domestic courts may find adopting the same line of reasoning difficult in a case brought by individual applicants seeking (non) pecuniary damages on account of misdiagnoses.

There are a dozen cases initiated in 2006 in Hungary, in which individual Romani children seek compensation from Expert Committees and special schools for misdiagnoses and inadequate education. There are no final judgments yet. The first case rejected on first instance has been appealed using arguments as well as the judgment in *D.H. II*, and was sent back for retrial on account of procedural shortcomings. However, it is feared that, following *D.H. II* as an analogy, domestic courts will try these cases as indirect discrimination and thus defendants will find it easier to put forward justification defences. What is benefiting this case from *D.H. II* is that the Hungarian court, previously rejecting evidence on structural discrimination, is now ready to entertain sociological studies and data from the Ministry of Education.

In case these individual actions are rejected at the domestic level, litigators will have a difficult choice to make. They may compromise the achievements of *D.H. II* if they complain to the ECtHR seeking a finding based on direct discrimination.

CONSIDERATIONS FOR DOMESTIC ACTION FOLLOWING *D.H. II*

Given that a dozen cases similar in fact to *D.H.* are pending before Hungarian courts, and that other *actio popularis* claims relating to segregation in normal schools are being heard in Bulgarian and Hungarian courts, it is timely to analyse how they could and should be argued pursuant to the RED, and to highlight in what way the final judgment in *D.H.* may not necessarily be beneficial in these cases.

Under the RED it is arguable that the special education of intellectually sound Romani children that results from the lack of race neutral psychological testing is direct discrimination.[29] Psychological tests or any other method of pre-school screening that fail to accommodate the racial differences that arise from the social attributes of Roma (language, deprived social status and other ethnicity based special characteristics) in fact do not impose apparently neutral criteria. These tests and screening methods treat Roma less favourably than majority children on account of failing to accommodate their special minority needs and adequately measure their intellectual abilities. Thus it is direct, rather than indirect discrimination, and is not subject to a justification defence.

The fact that the bias in tests and screening methods is not expressly based on race including ethnicity, but arises on account of various essential minority characteristics, such as culture, history and social status does not mean that it is not racial or ethnic bias, since all these characteristics fall neatly under the notion of race. Clearly, a Romani child who fails a test administered in the majority language because she/he speaks her/his minority language is being treated less favourably than a majority child speaking the majority language. Again, it is preferable to conceptualise this as direct discrimination based on race, rather than indirect discrimination based on the application of an exclusionary condition, namely the majority language, which disproportionately discriminates against Roma and is unjustifiable. This is because, firstly, language is part of the definition of Roma, and therefore discrimination on grounds of their language is nothing less than discrimination on grounds of their race and ethnicity. Secondly, the justification for the majority language might appear plausible unless it is accepted that language is one of the many elements of Roma identity.

The same holds true to Romani children whose parents pursue a travelling way of life: A test or screening method which is based on local culture, local educational achievements and the assumptions of a settled way of life would amount to less favourable treatment of Romani children on account of their racial and ethnic origin. There may well be situations outside of the field of educational segregation where indirect discrimination is an appropriate tool, but it is argued here that direct discrimination is the most appropriate way of understanding school segregation.

In practice one of the most common arguments for separate (be that equal or inferior) education is not free and informed parental choice, but often tacit parental consent. However, there is a significant distinction between choice and consent, as the former denotes a free standing parental decision, whereas the latter more often than not attaches to a recommendation from teachers, psychologists etc. Parental consent cannot *generally* be construed as a legitimate justification under RED, because direct discrimination cannot be justified under RED (except potentially under the provisions for a genuine occupational qualification or positive measures). In this respect one needs to bear in mind that in *D.H. II* the ECtHR Grand Chamber found that there could be no waiver—whether or not coming from parents—from the right not to be discriminated against. Furthermore, the FCNM Advisory Committee in its thematic report on education highlighted that the issue of consent should be very carefully examined.[30]

Institutional discrimination could also be conceptualised as direct discrimination, given that it "consists of the collective failure of an organisation to provide an appropriate and professional service to people because of their colour, culture or ethnic origin. It can be seen or detected in processes, attitudes, and behaviour which amount to discrimination through unwitting prejudice, ignorance, thoughtlessness and racist stereotyping which disadvantage minority ethnic people."[31] Institutional discrimination adds up from individual acts that do in fact differentiate between Roma and non-Roma on the basis of racial stereotypes—even if such stereotyping is concealed as applying the 'majority' norm. In actions involving schools, the argument that Romani children are lazy, that they have lower expectations, that Romani girls fall pregnant at an earlier age, that Romani families are not supportive enough are commonplace. Such arguments in fact conceal teachers' and education decision-makers' attitudes that are based on racial grounds. As the UK House of Lords held in the *Prague Airport Case*,[32] acting or stereotyping on racial grounds is wrong, not only if it is untrue—otherwise it would imply that direct discrimination can be justified.

STRUCTURAL REMEDIES FOR STRUCTURAL DISCRIMINATION: THE HAJDÚHADHÁZ DESEGREGATION CASE, 2007

This Hungarian case deals with the admissibility and collection of ethnic data on Roma in the face of restrictive data protection laws. The trial court appointed a forensic education expert to collect school level data in collaboration with members of the Hajdúhadház Roma Minority Self-Government, based on membership of the local Roma minority community, perception thereof, and place of residence as proxies for the ethnic origin of Romani children.[33] The trial court found that the two schools and the local government segregated Romani children in buildings other than the main school buildings, and directly discriminated them by providing inferior physical conditions. The court ordered the local government to publish an apology through the Hungarian Press Agency, ordered the schools to end segregation by 1 September 2007, and the local government—the maintainer of the two schools—to refrain from interference with desegregation.[34]

On appeal, the Debrecen Appeals Court upheld the finding of direct discrimination and ordered an end to it, but quashed the remaining part of the first instance judgment. The case is pending judicial review before the Supreme Court which has been asked to refer the following questions to the ECJ: 1. Does spatial segregation in the instant case amount to direct discrimination contrary to Article 2.2(a) RED? 2. If the answer to question 1 is yes, can the respondents justify such direct discrimination under provisions other than Article 5 RED (positive action)? 3. If the answer to question 2 is no, then can the respondents justify their conduct on the basis of Romani ethnic minority education or small classes, or special education as provided in the respondent schools? Given that facts in the case are based on ethnic statistics compiled during litigation, it is also hoped that through guidance to domestic courts, the ECJ will facilitate the use of such statistics and flesh out the procedural framework for requiring such evidence from respondents and assessing it. The admissibility of ethnic data in *D.H. II* will support this point.

ERRC v. the Bulgarian Ministry of Education and Science, the 103rd Secondary School and Sofia Municipality, 2007

The first instance domestic court found that "In the instant case since all students of the 103rd school are of Romani origin, there exists a separation on the basis of ethnic origin.[35] It is not, however coercive in the meaning of [Article 6 Supplementary Provision of the Protection against Discrimination Act, Bulgaria]. It is so since the separation is not a consequence of circumstances beyond the will of the students, respectively—their parents or guardians and is not entirely against their will—it does not follow a normative or administrative act, containing an obligation to enrol the students of Romani origin in a specific school, therefore it does not obstruct their education in other schools." Bulgarian law prohibits racial segregation, but defines it as forced division, separation or isolation.[36]

It is unknown whether this case has been or will be referred to the ECJ, where the definition of segregation as direct discrimination could be sought in line with the ECtHR's reasoning in *D.H. II*, i.e. that there can be no waiver from the right not to be discriminated against.

Sampanis and Others v Greece[37]

The *D.H. II* judgment has already had an impact in the ECtHR's jurisprudence. In *Sampanis* the Chamber unanimously found a violation against Greece for effectively denying education to Romani children for a certain period of time and then providing primary education in segregated special classes of lower physical conditions. The Court awarded just satisfaction to each applicant in the sum of 6,000 EUR which exceeds awards made in *D.H. II*. This may be explained by the facts of the *Sampanis* case, which revealed a more active engagement of Greek authorities (Ministry of Education and the school) in discrimination which effectively denied the applicants the right to any education for a whole academic year.

The Court emphasised that not only did the applicants have a right to education but that education in primary schools is obligatory.[38] This is a significant consideration which the Court will hopefully have an opportunity to elaborate on in the future for two reasons. First, the right to education is not only unique as a substantive social right covered under the ECHR, but the right to public education is coupled with the individual's obligation to attend school and a state duty to provide schooling. In this context the duty to reasonably accommodate specific Romani needs in public education is all the more apparent.

In *Sampanis* the Court indeed called for such reasonable accommodation in providing access to Romani children to Greek schools, and noted that such measures—including initial enrolment in lieu of a birth certificate—were in effect in the respondent State but not availed of in the instant case.[39]

The protest of non-Romani parents against the inclusion of Romani children and the blockading of the local school was particularly noted by the Court, that clearly spelt out how integration in schools is a necessary element of integration into local society as a whole.

The *Sampanis* judgment reproduced the *D.H. II* line of reasoning in relation to soft law measures at the Council of Europe level, as well as the legal argument and the test for discrimination and its justification.

Even though the Court found that the placement of the applicants in special classes amounted to segregation in the given case, and that de facto segregation in other schools was tolerated by the authorities,[40] it failed to distinguish this form of discrimination as the most severe, gravest form which clearly allows for an extremely restricted justification defence on the part of the respondent State. It is noteworthy that the Court's analysis of the placement in special classes indicates that such measures would only be admissible if there were clear and non-discriminatory criteria for placement, regular assessment tests to monitor development and that such placement could only be provisional as a reasonable objective to enable children to enter ordinary classes in due course.[41]

The judgment is also promising, because alongside the Greek judge the Cypriot and the Croatian judges also voted against Greece. Judge Vajic has done so while certainly being aware of a similar case pending before the Court against Croatia.[42]

ACTIO POPULARIS, COLLECTIVE COMPLAINTS AND COLLECTIVE MINORITY RIGHTS

As was argued above, the ECtHR in *D.H. II* in effect transformed the case of 18 individual applicants into a collective complaint based on minority rights and by leaving the examination of each individual applicant's case aside, focussed on structural, systemic problems. By doing so, it followed a procedure similar to the European Committee on Social Rights, which has rendered decisions in various Roma rights cases revealing structural discrimination. But whereas the ECSR is dependent on the Committee of Ministers for sanctions, the ECtHR is free to impose sanctions that may go beyond the payment of individual compensation. It is to be seen whether a succession of cases similar to *D.H.* can persuade the Court to adjust the remedies it renders to the form of discrimination it finds.

When transposing the RED, Romania, Bulgaria and Hungary have introduced a procedural invention that is open to NGOs, i.e., the right to bring *actio popularis* claims. Similar standing is given in many Member States on the ground of disability, or in the field of consumer protection and environmental rights. As could be seen in the first instance judgment brought in the *Hajdúhadház* desegregation case, domestic courts have the power to impose sanctions that are adequate to address structural problems. Whether case law at the domestic level as well as before the ECJ will evolve in this direction remains to be seen.

The following characteristics make *actio popularis* a unique and most attractive tool: there is no need for an individual victim as the case is brought by NGOs demonstrating an interest in rights protection and instead of injustices suffered by individual victims it focuses on patterns, trends and scenarios of discrimination. Thus, *actio popularis* is ideal in tackling institutional, structural, or *de facto* discrimination. In lieu of an individual client, there is a minimal risk of victimisation—in fact no client needs to be identified for the case. Perennial costs, such as maintaining contact with the client or indeed maintaining a client service for case selection can be saved. And as counsels for the applicants explained to the ECtHR in *D.H. II*, if a case is not about the violation of the rights of an individual victim, then remedies ought also to be tailored accordingly, i.e. they have to tackle 'system failures'.

Ostrava represents the ERRC's greatest strategic litigation action. It cost approximately 150,000 EUR and lasted for ten years (1998–2007). Primary research in the case was carried out by 12 people—staff members and local community and NGO activists—and lasted for eight months. Drafting the answer to the Government's first observations on first instance engaged six staff members for two weeks. In 2006, following the admissibility decision, six researchers spent another one month in Ostrava, doing additional research. Excluding the core legal team (Lord Lester, David Strupek and James A. Goldston), ERRC staff spent about 1,000 hours with case work after filing the application with the ECtHR.[43] They recovered 10,000 EUR in costs.

Disregarding the operational costs of the litigating NGO, the contrast between actual and recoverable legal costs is enormous. It may in part explain why many domestic NGOs do not even consider litigation as an option. In any case, when Open Society Institute-funded litigation projects present their results at different European fora the most frequently asked question—regardless of the protected ground—is this: Where did you get the funding? If stakeholders at the European level wish to see Romani cases in domestic courts, the ECtHR and the ECJ, they ought to bear these considerations in mind and do their best to facilitate necessary domestic and regional litigation.

Roma Rights Litigation After *D.H. II*

The Grand Chamber judgment in *D.H. II.* and the transposition of the RED has fundamentally changed the European legal landscape and Roma rights defenders should explore it, travelling as far as possible. An in-depth study of how litigation strategies may change is beyond the scope of this article, so let me just flag a number of obvious points here.

I. The Scope of Litigation

It is submitted here that following the ECtHR judgment in *Stoica v Romania*, where violations of both substantive and procedural branches were found, there is not much left for Roma rights defenders in improving jurisprudence under Article 3 of the ECHR.[44] Regrettably, horrendous cases of racially motivated deaths or ill treatment may surface any time, but as it has clarified legal arguments in this regard, it may not any longer be the ERRC's call to engage in these cases. Also, in *Stoica* the ECtHR has made it abundantly clear that it will not tolerate racially motivated violence against Roma.

It is submitted that the transposition of the RED and *D.H. II* have created a momentum for breaking away from retroactive, individual complaint based legal defence work. There are ample opportunities to initiate collective actions, no matter whether civil or political or economic and social rights are at stake. Indeed, if racial violence within certain police forces is deeply embedded, if it is supported by local high ranking officials—such as the local mayor in *Stoica*— and if public prosecution continues to turn a blind eye on these practices, then the payment of compensation to an individual Roma victim may not be the remedy the Roma rights movement wishes to seek.

Anti-Romani hate speech and the threat or actual physical and verbal violence has been on the rise within the EU. Although freedom of expression is not covered by the RED, it is precisely this instrument whose implementation has created a greater potential in fighting racially motivated verbal or physical violence. For instance, in Romania, the National Council for Combating Discrimination proceeded against President Basescu on account of his anti-Romani speech under domestic law transposing the RED.[45] In Hungary, it is arguable that *actio popularis* action could be taken against members of the extreme right Hungarian Guards and ECHO TV, a private TV channel supporting extremist behaviour. Last, questions decided on preliminary referral by the ECJ in relation to the RED may also have an impact in litigation against anti-Romani hate speech—see in this regard the issue raised in the *Feryn* case of whether or not a 'speech act', i.e. a statement by an employer to the effect that he will not employ workers from a certain racial background is potential or actual discrimination and as thus prohibited under the RED and actionable under transposing national legislation by an equality body.[46]

II. Actio Popularis and Collective Action

Actio popularis action in the fields covered by the RED (employment broadly meant including equal pay, education, social security including social protection and health care, social advantages, and access to and supply of goods and services including housing) can be brought in Bulgaria, Romania, Hungary and possibly in other EU Member States. To map the scope of collective action across Europe, procedural and charity laws should be closely studied.

Given that domestic legislation transposing the RED may not limit collective action rights to the fields covered by the RED, there is room to litigate in the field of civil and political rights, and social rights whose coverage is not straightforward under community law. In some fields, the ERRC itself has published studies detailing system level failures and putting forward proposals for structural changes—most lately for instance in relation to child protection.[47] In other fields, such as in the field of ethnic profiling by the police, domestic or regional NGOs or academic institutions have produced reliable data. Similar to domestic *actio popularis* litigation, these data can substantiate a legal action, and proposals can be transformed into remedies sought before domestic courts.

Moreover, there are a much greater number of EU and Council of Europe Member States that allow collective actions under the Revised European Social Charter (ESC)—e.g. France, Greece, Finland, Sweden, Belgium, Ireland, Italy, the Netherlands and Portugal. Similar to *D.H.*, arguments based on the RED

can be raised in proceedings under the ESC as well, and structural remedies going further than a mere adoption of government programmes for Roma can be
sought. Information and lobbying from other Council of Europe bodies—such
as ECRI and the FCNM Advisory Committee—should be relied on and generated here as well. It is arguable that given the hard law obligations flowing
from the RED in the field of social rights, the reference to the RED could raise
the profile of social rights litigation and change the way stakeholders view the
justiciability of such rights.

The great thing about collective action is that in case of a failure on the
part of governments to provide the remedies ordered, such an action can be
repeated. This has in fact been done with regard to the housing rights of Roma
in Greece: In 2003 the ERRC brought and won a collective complaint,[48] which
in 2008 was followed by another complaint by Interights, claiming that the government continues to forcibly evict Roma without providing suitable alternative accommodation and that Roma in Greece continue to suffer discrimination in access to housing.[49] It remains to be seen whether or not the Committee of
Ministers will go further in 'remedying' the situation as it had in 2005 when it
resolved the issue as follows:

• Having regard to the information communicated by the delegation of
Greece during the 924th meeting (20 April 2005) of the Ministers' Deputies,
• Takes note that the implementation of the Integrated Action Plan (IAP)
for the Social Integration of Greek Roma is still in progress, that evaluation
and reform of the IAP is currently ongoing in order to ensure more effective
coordination of the IAP between all partners involved (including the local
authorities),
• Takes note of the extension and revision of the housing loans programme
for Greek Roma,
• Takes note that a Commission for the social integration of Greek Roma
has been established,
• Decides not to accede to the request for the reimbursement of costs
transmitted by the European Committee of Social Rights.[50]

III. Reasonable Accommodation and Ethnic Minority Rights

With respect to the duty to provide reasonable accommodation to Roma in
public education and their right of housing falling under Article 8 of the ECHR,
the ECtHR has been remarkably progressive. There is further room for manoeu-
vre in this regard. Litigation should go deeper and wider: 1. It should focus on
seeking judgments rendering detailed and effective injunctions ensuring reason-

able accommodation; and 2. It should litigate in all fields that are covered by the ECHR—e.g. child protection under Article 8 and further cases in the field of education under Article 2 of Protocol No. 1—and the RED.

Structural problems arising in the field of child protection may flow from, for example, structural concerns in the field of housing. It has been reported by the ERRC that in Hungary for instance the lack of adequate housing, eviction, or inadequate financial resources may result in taking Romani children into state care—which is in violation of Article 8 of the ECHR.[51] Clearly, such a situation cannot be remedied by simply refraining from taking children into state care but by providing some sort of housing. Possibly, this issue can be argued on the basis of a reasonable accommodation duty under Article 8 of the ECHR. Even though the ECHR does not cover the right to housing *per se*, given the inter-linkages between the fields in which discrimination against Roma occurs, litigation before the ECtHR may still in effect make it actionable.

NOTES

...

2. *Council Directive 2000/43/EC implementing the principle of equal treatment irrespective of racial or ethnic origin.*

3. *Beard v. the United Kingdom, Application No. 24882/94; Buckley v. the United Kingdom, judgment of 25 September 1996; Chapman v. the United Kingdom, judgment of 18 January 2001; Connors v. the United Kingdom, judgment of 27 May 2004.*

4. *Paras. 93–94.*

5. *Para. 96.*

6. *In the cases of South Buckhamshire v Porter, Wrexham CBC v Berry and Chichester DC v Keet and Searle.*

7. *See: http://www.errc.org/cikk.php?cikk=2945.*

8. *Chamber judgment of 7 February 2006.*

9. *See trial records in case No. BAZ Megyei Bíróság, 13.P.21.660/2005.*

10. *Judgment of 9 June 2006, Debreceni Ítélotábla (Debrecen Appeals Court) No. Pf.I.20.683/2005.*

11. *Para. 49 and paras. 10–11 and 49–51, respectively.*

12. *Bács-Kiskun Megyei Bíróság, 2.P.21.843/2006, on file with the author.*

13. *Para. 201, D.H. II [emphasis added].*

14. *European Commission. July 2007. Segregation of Romani Children in Education: Addressing structural discrimination through the Race Equality Directive. Chapter 2.3. Available online at: http://ec.europa.eu/employment_social/fundamental_rights/policy/aneval/legnet_en.htm. (hereinafter: "Segregation Report").*

15. Harris, D.J., O'Boyle and Warbrick. 1995. Law of the European Convention on Human Rights. Butterworths, pp. 462–488.

16. Para. 176, D.H. II.

17. Para. 201, D.H. II.

18. Enderby v Frenchay Health Authority, C-127/92 ECJ.

19. Bilka-Kaufhaus GmbH v. Karin Weber von Hartz, case 170/84 ECJ.

20. Beard v. the United Kingdom, Application No. 24882/94; Buckley v. the United Kingdom, judgment of 25 September 1996; Chapman v the United Kingdom, judgment of 18 January 2001; Connors v the United Kingdom, judgment of 27 May 2004.

21. See at para. 181, D.H. II, a recapitulation of the finding that Roma are a vulnerable group whose situation and different lifestyle merit special consideration.

22. Paras. 31 and 182, D.H. II.

23. Para. 194, D.H. II.

24. Paras. 201–203, D.H. II.

25. See conclusions in paras. 205–210, D.H. II.

26. Para. 183, D.H. II.

27. Para. 207, D.H. II.

28. See, for example, positive action measures listed in Chapter 5 of the Segregation Report.

29. For this and other arguments under the RED relating to the segregation of Romani children in public education see the Segregation Report.

30. Advisory Committee on the Framework Convention for the Protection of National Minorities. Commentary on Education under the Framework Convention for the Protection of National Minorities. ACFC/25DOC(2006)002, p. 11.

31. The Stephen Lawrence Inquiry. Report of an inquiry by Sir William Macpherson of Cluny. CM4262-I, para. 6.34. The report concluded an investigation into police practices in the UK following a racist murder of a black teenager.

32. R. v. Immigration Officer at Prague Airport and Anor ex parte ERRC and others, [2004]UKHL 55.

33. See trial records in case No. Hajdú-Bihar Megyei Bíróság, 6.P.20.341/2006.

34. Hajdú-Bihar Megyei Bíróság, judgment No. 6.P.20.341/2006/50.

35. Judgment of February 2007 by the Sofia District Court, Civil College, IV B Division.

36. PADA Additional Provisions para. 1.5: "Racial segregation" shall mean the issuing of an act, the commission of an action, or an omission leading to forced division, separation, or isolation of persons on grounds of their race, ethnicity or skin colour.

37. ECtHR judgment of 5 June 2008 (hereinafter: "Sampanis").

38. Para. 66, Sampanis.

39. Paras. 86–87, Sampanis.

40. Para. 81, Sampanis.

41. Paras. 88–91, Sampanis.

42. For details on the so-called Croatian school case, see: www.errc.org.

43. *Information provided by Andi Dobrushi, ERRC legal officer in charge of the Czech Republic.*

44. *Stoica v. Romania, judgment of 4 March 2008, ECtHR.*

45. *Decision 92 of the National Council on Combating Discrimination, 23 May 2007. On 19 May 2007, the President of Romania was recorded during a discussion with his wife in his car, calling a journalist who allegedly harassed him "filthy Gypsy," after publicly calling her "birdie" (păsărică), a pejorative with demeaning and sexual connotations. The NGO Romani CRISS filed a complaint with the National Council for Combating Discrimination for the racist remarks of the President. (The video recording and the press articles are available at http://www.antena3.ro/Basescu-despre-o-jurnalista-tiganca-imputita_act_ 32833_ext.html, accessed on 21 May 2007.) The NCCD decided that the expression "filthy Gypsy," is "discrimination according to Art.2.1 and 4 of the GO 137 from 2000 . . . and that the use of this expression damaged the dignity of persons belonging to Roma community." Mr Băsescu subsequently contested the decision before the courts of law arguing that the decision was illegal. The NCCD found that a) the act reported by the plaintiff in terms of discrimination on grounds of gender does not fall under administrative liability; b) the act reported by the plaintiff in terms of discrimination on grounds of ethnicity amounts to discrimination as per Article 2 (1 and 4) of the Governmental Ordinance 137/2000, republished and decided that Mr Traian Basescu will be sanctioned with an administrative warning. The Court of Appeal upheld the NCCD decision in Dosar Nr. 4510/2/2007, Curtea de Apel Bucuresti, sentinta civila nr.2799, 8 November 2007. The decision of the Court of Appeal was quashed by the High Court of Justice and Cassation. At the time of writing this article the decision has not published yet. The President won by demonstrating the privacy of the speech and the lack of intention to discriminate.*

46. *Opinion of Advocate General Poiares Maduro delivered on 12 March 2008 (1), Case C-54/07, Centrum voor Gelijkheid van Kansen en voor Racismebestrijding v Firma Feryn NV (Reference for a preliminary ruling from the Arbeidshof te Brussel (Belgium)), para 16.*

47. *European Roma Rights Centre. December 2007. Dis-Interest of the Child: Romani Children in the Hungarian Child Protection System. Available at: http://www.errc.org/cikk.php?cikk=2930.*

48. *ESC, collective complaint No. 15/2003*

49. *ESC, collective complaint No. 49/2008.*

50. *Resolution ResChS(2005)11, Collective complaint No. 15/2003 by the European Roma Rights Centre (ERRC) against Greece.*

51. *Op. cit, p. 42.*

***Lilla Farkas** is a practicing attorney mainly involved with OSI-sponsored *actio popularis* litigation against segregation in public education at the Budapest-based Chance for Children Foundation.

Originally published in European Roma Rights Centre, *Roma Rights* 1, 2008, Roma Education: The Promise of D.H., available at: www.errc.org. Reprinted with permission by the European Roma Rights Centre.

Section III:
Roma Representation: The
Question(ing) of Roma Identity

Roma identity has been increasingly politicized through the emergence of: Roma political parties and interest groups, Roma activists and Roma elites; legislation, policies, and welfare strategies addressing specific Roma needs across Europe, and increased media visibility—particularly surrounding controversial relocations, expulsions, and crimes. The clear negative image of much of the Roma populations across Europe has been explained, on the one hand, in terms of the increased negative stereotyping of these communities by the media and, on the other, in terms of a deep-seated resistance to the Romani lifestyle and culture, which is often perceived as unassimilable.

The articles in this section address both the causes of these increasingly negative stereotypes as well as the issue of whether a diminishing of such stereotypes would necessarily lead to an increased acceptance of what is perceived to be Romani culture and lifestyle. Thus, the authors debate whether current perceptions of Romani culture and lifestyle as dangerous and inassimilable are a direct result of these negative stereotypes or whether they are the result of a more fundamental rejection of close-knit, internally oriented traditional communities that see themselves as separate from wider communities.

Chapter 8: Talking About Gypsies: The Notion of Discourse as Control

by Joanna Richardson*

Gypsies and Travellers are increasingly part of a debate by politicians and the media in the UK. This discourse is not a benign reflection of events; instead it is part of a complex mechanism of control. There is a difficult relationship between the settled and travelling communities which inhibits political discussion of a strategy for site provision. In this context, the paper examines the links between discourse and control, by paying attention to Foucauldian notions of the 'gaze', amongst other explanations. Drawing on findings from analysis of the media, focus groups with Travellers and a case study in one local authority planning consultation exercise, the paper proposes a theoretical explanation for the link between the discourse used around Gypsies and Travellers and the control that is exercised over them, particularly in inhibiting their right to a travelling lifestyle.

INTRODUCTION

Gypsies and Travellers have been used by politicians, such as Michael Howard in his 2005 election campaign, as a way of highlighting groups in society that need controlling. It is seen as a vote-winner to crackdown on these and other 'folk-devils' (Cohen, 1980) such as asylum seekers and young, single mothers. Local authorities are under pressure to ensure that the needs of Gypsies and Travellers are analysed (for example, the duty to assess accommodation needs under Section 225 of the Housing Act 2004), yet there is no legislative duty to build new sites (this was removed by the Criminal Justice and Public Order Act 1994). Research for the Office of the Deputy Prime Minister (Niner, 2003) has highlighted a shortage of suitable local authority sites, yet Gypsies and Travellers are not given planning permission to build their own. Recently, there seems to be an increasing debate around unauthorised development, where Gypsies and Travellers are building sites without permission, and submitting retrospective applications. The government has responded to this with Circular 02/2005 on Temporary Stop Notices. The social housing sector faces a difficult time in balancing the needs of settled and travelling communities to promote cohesion; the discourse used by politicians and the media highlights the tension between the two. It is a problematic base from which to devise a forward strategy for accommodation provision and, as such, there is a need to understand how discourse is used as a tool to control.

The discourse around Gypsies and Travellers is part of a wider, ambiguous, discussion on equality and diversity in current policy and practice. The government is keen to promote concepts of citizenship and community within a 'British' identity, and it 'cracks down' on those seen to be anti-social. However, a parallel discourse includes diversity of culture and the need to address institutional racism in public institutions.

The debate surrounding Gypsies and Travellers is current in Whitehall, town halls and in the media. It is also discussed increasingly in the housing press (Gardiner, 2004; Snow, 2004) and issues of site provision and discrimination are examined in papers such as *The Guardian* (Barkham, 2004; Bowers & Benjamin, 2004). These examples of coverage of the issues are largely positive, as is the news (Beunderman, 2004) that the first Roma MEP was elected to the European parliament. Despite positive moves to debate the issues, there is also an increase in negative discursive debate (Greenhill, 2004; Kelly, 2004; Levy, 2004, *Lincolnshire Free Press*, 2004; Long, 2004; *The Sun*, 2005). To a large extent, this negative coverage is centred upon the issue of the cost of dealing with Gypsies and Travellers, a theme that is central to this paper. There is also recognition that Gypsies and Travellers are subject to negative, discriminatory discourse that would not be acceptable against other black and minority ethnic communities (Asthana, 2004).

The current discursive debate is not just limited to the press, but is manifested in recent legislation such as the Anti-Social Behaviour Act 2003. There is also the Planning and Compulsory Purchase Act 2004, and Circular 02/2005 was published in March 2005 which gave guidance on Temporary Stop Notices, allowed for in Part four of the Act, on unauthorised developments. Political and legislative debate continues around the Criminal Justice and Public Order Act 1994, which took away the duty from local authorities to provide sites. The Office of the Deputy Prime Minister (ODPM) Planning, Local Government and the Regions Select Committee published their report in November 2004, calling for a duty to be reinstated. The response in early 2005 was that the government did not feel that a duty was needed. This official response was prompted in a statement given at the end of 2004:

> A duty to provide sites is not necessarily an appropriate solution. A duty has been tried before and often did not produce sufficient or appropriate provision. (Johnston, 2004, p. 4)

However, ODPM have still asked councils to provide extra sites, in their good practice guide *Diversity in Equality and Planning* (March 2005). Commentators suggest this will not be possible without enforcing a duty (Hilditich, 2005). Additionally, local authorities should also adhere to the Homelessness Act 2002 which requires them to carry out homelessness reviews and to formulate and publish strategies; plus the Housing Act 2004 includes Section 225 which places a specific duty on local authorities to assess the accommodation needs of Gypsies and Travellers. The ODPM has already reprimanded one council in Brentwood (Inside Housing, 2005), for not including the needs of this group in their local development plans.

Housing providers need to make sense of their duties under a mixed raft of legislation. This is not easy within the current discourse, which is positive in some areas of the press (particularly the housing press) but extremely negative in the more popular press (see *The Sun* campaign in March, 2005). This discourse affects strategies for providing accommodation for Gypsies and Travellers. Therefore, there is a need to understand the discourse surrounding the group and to see how it can be controlling. To do this, a theoretical approach is examined next, and this is followed with analysis of primary research undertaken within the framework.

THEORETICAL FRAMEWORK

There is an existing body of work that examines frameworks of control or discursive frameworks; for instance Akerstrom Anderson (2003) and Clegg (1989). The framework detailed in this paper focuses on Foucault's theory of gaze and links this with explanations of discourse. A further component of the framework is an analysis of society, norms and folk devils. This is in an attempt to explain why control of Gypsies and Travellers, through discourse, is seen as necessary in society. Neither Akerstrom Anderson (2003) nor Clegg (1989) tackle this issue; they concentrate on the how, rather than the why. Clegg states as much in his work:

> The circuit of power framework enables us to analyse how this is so. Why it should be so is another question, suited to more polemical occasions than this text allows. (Clegg, 1989, p. 272)

The framework has three main areas: first, power and control (Foucault's gaze, 1969), second, theories of discourse (and the links between theories on discourse and control, Foucault, 1976) and, thirdly, theories on society, norms and folk devils (Bauman, 1989; Cohen, 1980).

Power and Control

For the purposes of this paper, the examination of theories on control and power focuses on Foucault. In particular, his work on the gaze is important. It might best be described as the eye of power and control. Foucault describes gaze, thus:

> . . . the gaze is not faithful to truth, nor subject to it, without asserting, at the same time, a supreme mastery: the gaze that sees is a gaze that dominates. (Foucault, 1969, p. 39)

The crucial element in the gaze is the interpretive element. Foucault (1969) was discussing it in relation to doctors looking at illnesses in their patients. He explained that doctors no longer passively viewed symptoms, but instead started to actively interpret them. This is important because this research attempts to link theories of the gaze with those of discourse and it raises the notion of discourse as control. The gaze is not passive surveillance, but involves active interpretation and domination. Words and terms used in the discourse around Gypsies and Travellers are not passively describing a situation but instead they are interpreting them. The interpretation involved in discourse is based on a variety of variables including the ontology of the speaker and their social norms and characteristics.

There are a number of examples of explicit surveillant gaze over Gypsies and Travellers. For instance, during a project to assess Supporting People needs in the South West of England, a Gypsy/Traveller Liaison Officer showed the researcher where a closed circuit television camera had been hidden on a neighbouring property to the site, to record images for the police.

Foucault's (1969) research on surveillance was inspired by Bentham's Panopticon principle in his 18th century prison designs. Cohen (1985) explains panopticism:

> Surveillance and not just punishment became the object of the exercise. The all seeing world of Bentham's panopticon is the architectural vision of the new knowledge/power spiral: the inmate caught in a power which is visible (you can always see the observation tower) but unverifiable (you must never know when you are being looked upon at any one moment). The prison is the purest form of the panopticon principle and the only concrete way to realize it. (Cohen, 1985, p. 26)

But there are other ways of realising it. Partly, this is through society's gaze, which is dominating through active interpretation rather than passively watching. Additionally, there may be other concrete ways of realising it; such as the architecture of the built environment (Dovey, 1999).

To help understand how the 'gaze' dominates the individual, Nikolas Rose (1999) examines the connections between individuals and 'society', through his concept of 'grammars of living':

Individuals are now to be linked into a society through acts of socially sanctioned consumption and responsible choice, through the shaping of a lifestyle according to grammars of living that are widely disseminated, yet do not depend upon political calculations and strategies for their rationales or their techniques. (Rose, 1999, p. 166)

Rose (1999) is also useful in clarifying that the 'gaze' is not exercised by one particular person or organisation. He appears to support Foucault's (1980) notion of networks of control and power and he states that there are multiple actors involved. Rose (1999) uses an example of 'government of madness' (p. 278) and says that the controlling authorities are 'diverse and disputatious'.

A multitude of other groupings and collectivities have also had their say in the government of madness—press campaigns, pressure groups, groups established by individuals whose family members have been damaged psychiatric patients or damaged by psychiatric patients [sic], local residents protesting ...(Rose, 1999, p. 278)

This multitude of other groupings could also be applied to the governance of Gypsies and Travellers. It is important to include Rose here to remind us that there is no singular application of a steadfast discourse. Instead, there are multiple actors involved in a circularity of power and control.

Foucault (1969) did not just believe in the manifestation of the gaze in physical things, such as Bentham's panopticon, or a modern day example, surveillance cameras; he believed that the gaze was internalised. This internalisation would normally manifest in a person inculcating a social norm, to the extent that they did not know that it wasn't their own original thought or idea. The problem of understanding why the gaze is internalised by some people and not others comes back to the issue of different group and individual norms: why do some individuals believe in different norms to the rest of a group, or to other individuals? If internalisation of the gaze, as a tool of power, is dependent on everyone internalising the same values then there will never be internalisation wholesale of one value of society, because of different individual and group norms. Gypsies and Travellers could be viewed as eschewing the norm of living a settled life in a house. However, this meta-norm of society, of house dwelling, docs not accord with the long history of the norm of nomadism of the Gypsies and Travellers. In some current examples Gypsies are forced to accept the settled norm because there is no alternative accommodation provision, but others refuse to do this and will not give up their norm of nomadism. Cowan & Lomax (2003) highlight this pressure to conform:

> We argue that both policing and welfare require and reinforce conformity to particular norms as preconditions to legal entitlements, and socially exclude those who fail to conform. (Cowan & Lomax, 2003, p. 284)

They further discuss this implicit surveillance and the pressure to internalise the gaze:

> Equally important, however, is the dispersal of policing processes and practices into the enquiries and assessments made by welfare professionals ... Submission to assessments by health, housing and social services implies a submission to their own individual surveillance and policing techniques. (Cowan & Lomax, 2003, p. 306)

McNay (1994) reinforces the view that control is exercised indirectly through normalisation techniques:

> Control in modern societies is achieved, therefore, not through direct repression but through more invisible strategies of normalization. Individuals regulate themselves through a constant introspective search for their hidden 'truth', held to lie in their innermost identity. (McNay, 1994, p. 97)

Discourse

In housing research, discourse tends to be discussed in two ways, as a theoretical subject (Clapham, 2002) and as a method of analysis (this occurs across a number of social science fields, including housing studies). In this paper, the link is made between discourse and control at a theoretical level, but critical analysis methods, such as through the use of NVIVO help to examine themes in the media and in public debate. Discourse analysis is increasingly being used in housing, and also specifically in the field of Gypsies and Travellers. Of particular importance in this area are: Erjavec (2001); Holloway (2003); Leudar & Nekvapil (2000); Shuinear (1997); Turner (2000, 2002). Turner's work in particular is discussed further on in the paper, as certain themes have resonance with this research. In addition, Shuinear (1997) helps to understand the Gypsy as folk devil.

The main premise of Foucault's work on discourse and language is that it is not reactive. Discourse does not just describe an action or thought. Indeed, for Foucault, discourse is productive. By talking, or writing, about a particular entity it is possible to recreate it.

Clapham (2002) helps to understand the importance of discourse:

> In this way language and knowledge are not copies of reality, but constitute reality, each language constructing specific aspects of reality, on interpretation and negotiation of the meaning of the lived world. (Clapham, 2002, p. 61)

However, it is the link between discourse and control that is the focus of this paper. Foucault specifically links discourse and surveillance:

> The examination that places individuals in a field of surveillance also situates them in a network of writing; it engages them in a whole mass of documents that capture and fix them. The procedures of examination were accompanied at the same time by a system of intense registration and of documentary accumulation. A 'power of writing' was constituted as an essential part in the mechanisms of discipline. (Foucault, 1977, p. 189)

Although a theoretical link can be made between discourse and control, this paper will later analyse research that sought to test whether this theoretical relationship applied to Gypsies and Travellers. First, however, it is necessary to discuss further the issue of social norms, and those seen to live outside them.

Society, Norms and Folk Devils

> Objective reality can readily be 'translated' into subjective reality, and vice versa. Language, of course, is the principal vehicle of this ongoing translating process in both directions. (Berger & Luckmann, 1966: 153)

Berger & Luckmann define society as subjective reality which, through language, links in with 'objective' reality, each defining the other. Not only is this useful in thinking about what society means, but it shows the links between society, the gaze and discourse. It helps to explain how the objective 'reality' of Gypsies and Travellers is internalised into subjective reality, but then enters a dialectical process with objective reality again; a cycle of definition and social construction of reality continues.

The circular route that Berger & Luckmann discuss is key to the theoretical framework in this paper. In addition, there is an emphasis on the importance of society, what it means and what is seen to be real in society. A useful debate is that of social 'norms', this is necessary in order to understand that there are people who are seen to exist outside of the norm. Elster (1989) provides an appropriate base. He states that a norm is social because it is shared with other people, but also enforced by other people (p. 99). Living in a permanent dwelling may be seen as a social norm, and as such Gypsies and Travellers, and home-less people, fall outside of this; these 'outsiders' can be described as 'folk-devils' (Cohen, 1980). Bauman (1989) examines the importance of 'proximity' in the context of 'othering'. He explains that 'othering' and the notion of proxim-ity leads people to accept adverse treatment of 'others'. In Bauman's study he looked at the treatment of Jews in Germany during the Second World War, as an example.

> Being inextricably tied to human proximity, morality seems to conform
> to the law of optical perspective. It looms large and thick close to the
> eye. With the growth of distance, responsibility for the other shrivels,
> moral dimensions of the object blur, till both reach the vanishing point
> and disappear from view. (Bauman, 1989, p. 192)

Cohen (1980) and Bauman (1989) have discussed the notion that folk devils serve a purpose by being different. Shuinear (1997) also supports this function-alist explanation for distancing Gypsies and Travellers as folk devils (it should be noted that Gaujo is the name that Gypsies and Travellers give to members of the 'settled' community):

> This need is so overpowering that time after time, in place after place,
> Gaujos create situations forcing Gypsies to fill this role.

> It is important to remember that what we're talking about here are not
> 'alien' faults and problems but Gaujo's own; therefore, the people onto
> whom these are projected must be clearly distinct from the Gaujo main-
> stream, but not utterly foreign to it: just as in cinema, the screen must
> be neither too close nor too distant if the image projected onto it is to
> remain sharply focused. (Shuinear, 1997, p. 27)

This begins to provide a reason for the control of the group, through discourse, and begins to answer the question of why there is a perceived need for the con-trol of Gypsies and Travellers.

The framework brings together the above three key areas (see Figure 1). The diagram shows three stages of a circular route of power and control: what, how and why. It is circular, rather than linear, because there is no set start and end point. Additionally, there are no arrows to denote direction of the route, as it is multi-directional and can flow in any direction.

The question of 'who' is controlling and being controlled is different, accord-ing to which marginalised group the framework is being applied to. It is possible to apply the main theoretical model to any marginalised group, for instance, asy-lum seekers. In applying the framework to the empirical material in this paper, the 'who' particularly sees the government and the media as controllers. Gypsies and Travellers are seen as mostly subject to control. It is important to remember from explanations of resistance by Clegg (1989) and research in housing policy by Marston (2004), and also Foucault's description of power (1980), that a 'target' of power can also apply power. Rose (1999) also explained that there is no singular person or organisation doing the controlling: "Programmes and technologies of government, then, are assemblages which may have a rationality, but this is not one of a coherence of origin or singular essence" (p. 276).

Power is relational. A contextual example of this relational, changing power is the Gypsy Traveller Media Advisory Group (GTMAG). This group monitors media representations of Gypsies and Travellers in an attempt to see a more positive portrayal. The act of those under media surveillance, forming a group to monitor the media, demonstrates a resistance to the flow of power and exemplifies the circular route discussed by Foucault (1969, 1980).

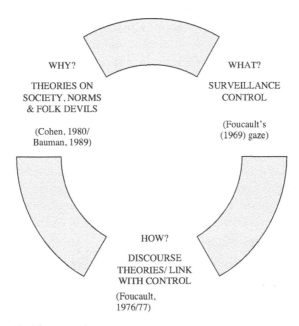

WHY?
THEORIES ON
SOCIETY, NORMS
& FOLK DEVILS

(Cohen, 1980/
Bauman, 1989)

WHAT?
SURVEILLANCE
CONTROL

(Foucault's
(1969) gaze)

HOW?
DISCOURSE
THEORIES/ LINK
WITH CONTROL
(Foucault,
1976/77)

Figure 1: Theoretical framework

There are also links with the definition and redefinition of groups through discourse. For example, Berger & Luckmann (1966) discuss the social construction of reality as broken into subjective and objective reality. This is especially true when one looks at the question of who is being controlled. Gypsies and Travellers are defined according to societal norms and then kept under surveillance through societal discourse which controls and redefines the group according to new subjective realities. This subjective reality is then taken as a new objective reality and so the definition and redefinition, through discourse, continues.

The motivation of government and the media to define and redefine 'other' groups is not explicit, however, a number of researchers moot different ideas. For instance, Cohen (1980) analyses the need for government to move a general fear into something more tangible, in order to allow for political shifts. It is possible to see examples of this in national security issues, post 9/11. The fear of terrorist attack is heightened by government rhetoric in order that policy and legislative shifts can be made under the guise of protecting the population. A similar explanation can be found for the government in their discourse around Gypsies and Travellers. By 'othering' them, particularly on the issue of cost, the theory of proximity (Bauman, 1989) means the general population is less concerned with adverse treatment of them. It should be noted that there is a differentiation between government 'actors'. In this paper, 'government' largely refers to central political government, which is concerned with retaining party political control. However, local officers, and indeed quasi-governmental officers will have different motives for their discourse around, and treatment of, Gypsies and Travellers. The local gate-keeping role (Lipsky, 1980) would be an interesting area for future research in Gypsy/Traveller discourse.

The reason for the media 'othering' Gypsies and Travellers is perhaps not as clear as that of government. However, one suggestion is that by perpetuating the stereotype of Gypsies and Travellers as 'folk-devil' it enables more newspapers to be sold (and thus the link with cost as motive is further enforced). The 'othering' discourse surrounding Gypsies and Travellers serves to heighten their presence in society, which makes it easier to monitor them. This discourse redefines Gypsies and Travellers further, as folk devils, and refuels the motive to 'other' them, and so the cycle continues.

The theoretical framework enables some of the concepts such as power, control, gaze and discourse to be operationalised in the analysis of the empirical material. It outlines what type of power and control is being used (surveillance/gaze), how it is being used (through discourse) and why it is being used (to 'other' those that don't conform to societal norms).

Talking About Gypsies

To begin, a literature review was undertaken; this examined key texts. The primary research focused on the way that people talk about Gypsies and Travellers, and how this forms part of a controlling discourse. Three elements were involved in the primary research strategy: media analysis, public consultation in Colchester, and focus groups with Gypsies and Travellers (see Table 1).

Table 1. Summary of methodological approach

Approach	Methodology
Media analysis	Search of English and Welsh national and local newspapers for the month of October 2003, using Lexis Nexis database. 54 articles were found, eight were discounted (e.g. they referred to a football team called the Gypsies), 13 articles were viewed as being largely positive, with the remaining 33 articles having a negative focus. Coding and analysis of the articles was conducted using NVIVO software.
Planning consultation in Colchester	Effectively this part of the research analysed 100% of the sample frame as Colchester was the only local authority debating new site provision at the time (December 2003). The meeting allowed for the researcher to be observer, without any direct involvement in the discussion. Ongoing communication with the Planning Officer also facilitated access to previous consultation information where 598 responses from the public had been received by the council.
Gypsy/Traveller focus groups	A series of four focus groups was held, with a mixture of Romany Gypsies and Irish Travellers, from November to early December 2003. Meetings were held at a Community College, in the East Midlands.

This approach aimed to triangulate the methodology to enable the talk about Gypsies and Travellers to be analysed from a number of angles. A number of themes emerged from the literature review, and these were used as key words in the analysis and explanation of the discourse:

- Mess and cost.
- Site provision, including size and location of sites.
- Labelling—Gypsies or Travellers?
- Folk Devils.
- Who is talking about Gypsies and Travellers? (This final theme was analytical, rather than discursive.)

It is important to remember that these themes are not merely describing the views of the media, the public and Gypsies and Travellers. Instead, they construct new social 'truths' about them (see Clapham, 2002). The use of language seems to precipitate further action. It is not the saying of the words that is the ultimate control, but instead is where it may lead to extra vigorous policing, or renewed focus on trespass legislation or planning legislation. Examples of this can be physical action (Lodge, 2004), implementation of legislation (Morris, 1998), or increased visibility and surveillance that dominates the travelling community.

Having included a brief summary of the research methodology, the paper now gives an analysis of the findings, on a thematic basis.

THEMES OF DISCOURSE AND CONTROL

Throughout the primary research, a number of themes were identified. Each of these themes is discussed, below.

Mess and Cost

One of the most significant themes to come out in the findings of the media coding and analysis was that of mess and cost. In the findings from the media analysis, there were a number of 'negative' articles that discussed mess. This is a common theme across all three elements of the primary research. The public consultation linked mess and cost with Gypsies and Travellers. During the focus groups with Gypsies and Travellers, they too knew that they were linked with mess but they felt unable to defend themselves and change this perception.

The theme of mess was linked closely with cost. The issue of cost and mess was couched in a way to tell the reader 'you are paying for all this through your council tax'. Examples of this include: "Mess left by travellers over the last two years has cost Redditch taxpayers £50 000 to clean up" (*This is Worcestershire*, 2003, p. 9). "Birmingham taxpayers have forked out tens of thousands of pounds to evict [Travellers] and clear up their mess and litter" (*Birmingham Evening Mail*, 2003, p. 5). A headline in one local newspaper said "£60 000 to keep them out" and it went on to describe the years of work and the amount of money spent in clearing a greenfield site, and then making it 'traveller-proof' for the future (*This is Wiltshire*, 2003, p. 1). Another newspaper carried a similar article in which it stated that "On Wednesday Camarthenshire County Council completed a two-day clean-up of the site, removing rubbish—including nappies and tyres—in an operation reputedly costing more than £6000" (*South Wales Evening Post*, 2003, p. 2).

The discourse of the cost of Gypsies and Travellers is powerful. It quantifies the expense of 'otherness' in a way that could make the settled community feel the travelling lifestyle is too expensive to society. The particular examples from newspapers, discussed above, make the cost of Travellers personal to the reader. This 'costing' of the lives of Gypsies and Travellers was examined by Morris & Clements (2002). They looked at the cost of not providing sites, rather than focusing on the cost of provision. They also made the point that a lifestyle could not really have a numerical value placed upon it and indeed, by trying to cost a lifestyle, this heightened the 'otherness' (costliness) of that lifestyle.

Cost was a key theme in public speech at the planning meeting, and information from a prior consultation exercise (which saw 598 responses received by the council) also reflected the importance placed on cost and mess. Although, in Colchester, the issue of cost did not just relate to the cost of clearing up mess; it also seemed to relate to the perceived cost of reduced value in property prices. Examples of some of the quotes from previous written objections, provided by the Planning Officer, included:

- "What would you think if you bought a £150K house from Barratts to find your neighbours were Gypsies?"
- "The value of my property which I work hard to pay for would drop in value overnight. Perhaps the Council would be prepared to compensate people living close to this site".
- ". . . put them back in Haven Road with a site warden to keep them and the site clean and hygienically tidy".
- "These Travellers contribute nothing, only filth".
- "MESS, *THIEVING* AND POLLUTION".
- "The Police admit they have no control as to when or where they turn up, or any control of Travellers what-so-ever".
- "Surely cost should be one of the most important factors? After all, it's someone else's money you are spending".
- "Looking at the last location near the Hythe river, the mess they left, the horses wandering around and the general squalor of the site appals me and we DO NOT want it here".
- "I have first hand experience of Travellers and the carnage they leave behind". (Colchester Borough Council, Relocation of Gypsy/Travellers Site Report to Council, 30 September 2002, Appendix One)

Negative speech was the dominant discourse around cost, however, there was a resistant discourse (Clegg, 1989; Marston, 2004) from Gypsies and Travellers. There is an assumption that Travellers settle on green fields and then leave a mess. It is further suggested that any rubbish left on a Travellers' site was left there by Travellers; however, this is not always the case, as was highlighted by a Traveller in his letter to *The Cornishman* newspaper:

1. We did not force any padlock or gate to enter the site; we merely lifted off the chain and opened the gate which is left unlocked . . .
2. We do not drive untaxed vehicles.
3. We have not caused any damage to the land (or gate) and intend only to enhance the site.

This is not rural pastureland but a 'brownfield site'—and a highways dump and local fly-tipping spot which has been cleaned up, cared for and enhanced by a community of people who have appreciated living here and becoming part of the community and have felt, on the whole, very welcome. (*The Cornishman*, 2003b, p. 35)

Cost and mess is the most important theme to come out of this research, it links with findings from other empirical research (Morris & Clements, 2002) and it is also explained by two stages of the theoretical framework (see Figure 1). 'Cost' is a unique theme in that it can be placed in the 'how' or 'why' section of the framework. It is possible that reduction of cost is a motive for the government to 'other' the Gypsy/Traveller lifestyle in its rhetoric. However, the language of 'cost' is also the method of achieving a 'folk-devil' status for the travelling community amongst the public and in the media.

Site Provision and Facilities

Gypsies and Travellers wanted to talk about the benefit of new site provision, a theme not found in the media analysis or public consultation. The current lack of site provision (Crawley, 2004; Niner, 2003) is a further manifestation of public discourse. Gypsies and Travellers are seen as vote-losers by politicians, and the government of the day does not want to be seen to pay 'taxpayers' money' to an unpopular cause (Michael Howard, in his 2005 election campaign, attempted to make political capital out of 'othering' Gypsies and Travellers and distancing them from any expenditure plans the Conservatives may have had). The issue of new site provision is a double-edged sword. If enough sites were provided it would reduce unpopular, unauthorised encampments. This is not to suggest that new site provision would provide a Utopian ideal where there would be no more divisions between the travelling and settled communities. It would, nevertheless, reduce illegal development and unauthorised encampments that do give rise to friction. However, to provide more sites the government would have to spend money on a group that is unpopular in public discourse and is seen as 'costly' to society.

The Travellers in the focus groups felt they were being controlled by lack of site provision and lack of services. Some of the women in one of the groups said that their privately run site, owned by Travellers, did not have washing facilities and that the nearest public shower facility was eight miles away. One of the women said that each of her four children was charged £2 every time they had a shower and she was charged a little bit more. She felt cheated by the cost of the shower but said she was a clean person and was aware of the public perception of Gypsies and Travellers as dirty and messy. By charging so much, the owner of the facility was almost challenging this woman's family not to wash every day, as was the site owner who did not provide arrangements for washing. They felt that what was needed was more council site provision with toilet and washing facilities. All of the Travellers in the focus group agreed that increased site provision would reduce unauthorised encampments and would perhaps reduce the tensions between the settled and travelling communities.

The theme of site provision also extends to the location and size of existing and proposed sites. During the Colchester consultation, the framework examining potential sites used a points system. Proximity to residential and commercial sites carried negative points in the consultation process. Additionally, the public were clear that they wanted the number of pitches on the new site to be limited; the preference for smaller sites is echoed by Gypsies and Travellers.

Bauman's theory of proximity (1989) is important in explaining the concern over the location and size of Travellers' sites. Sites need to be physically distant from the settled population; this allows Gypsies and Travellers to be seen as 'other' and prevents them from being known as 'real'. This means the 'truth' about them can be socially constructed and reinterpreted through discourse. The issue of distancing and the theory of proximity is an important component in explaining how discursive control is exercised, according to the theoretical framework.

Labelling: Gypsies or Travellers?

The desire to classify, characterise and label satisfies a fundamental human need ... The processes of defining, labelling and representing Gypsies are much the same as those involving any group, especially minority groups. The stereotypical descriptions adopt and adapt the language and concepts of any given period, and so reveal the nature and distribution of power in society...(Mayall, 2004, p. 276)

A theme which runs through the media, public and Gypsy/Traveller discourse is labelling. This is an issue that applies not just to Gypsies and Travellers but particularly also the debate on asylum seekers where the term 'bogus' has been common currency in previous political debate.

Two newspaper articles, in the media analysis, focused on the distinction between Gypsies and Travellers. Both of these were in fact letters from local people in the settled community and they were negative in their portrayal:

> . . . Some of these people are threatening in their behaviour, aggressive. There may be the odd family group who are genuine but in my experience they don't often 'park up' with larger groups.

> Penwith please be realistic, stop calling this group 'travellers'—they're hardly of the Benedict Allen variety of 'Romany Ryes'—gypsies never camp with 'travellers'. Save Penwith from becoming an easy place to doss. (*The Cornishman*, 2003a, p. 35)

As well as marking out a distinction between Travellers and Gypsies, fake and genuine, the author of the article also heightens the Travelling community as 'other'. Terms such as 'these people' followed with negative associated characteristics, again serve to heighten the presence of the Gypsy or Traveller in the local population and to mark them out for surveillance and control. Terms like 'these people' also link in with the theory of proximity (Bauman, 1989) which discusses the 'othering' of people who are perceived to be different, in order to make it easier to treat them badly. 'These people', Gypsies and Travellers, are not like 'us' and therefore do not need to be treated with the respect that 'ordinary people' would expect.

The second letter is also negative, but specifically against Travellers as opposed to 'real' Gypsies.

> . . . Gypsies are members of the Romany tribe. They are extremely honest, hard- working and clean. Unlike gypsies, travellers are thieves, liars, lazy and dirty—as we have learned to our cost here in Eldene. (*Western Daily Press*, 2003b, p. 12)

It is virtually impossible to imagine a published piece of writing about any other ethnic group, describing them as 'thieves, liars, lazy and dirty', being allowed past the editorial control of the newspaper. Why then, does it seem to be acceptable to talk about Gypsies and Travellers in this way? The writer of the letter also assumes to be blessed with the knowledge that allows them to distinguish between 'real' and 'fake' Gypsies, just by looking at them (Acton, 1994). In providing a distinction, the writer of the letter is making the job of the surveillant society even easier. 'Do not worry about the good traditional Gypsies: concentrate on the dirty, thieving Travellers—they are the ones who need controlling', is what this distinction is saying. Mayall (2004) discusses the issue of labelling and Gypsies and Travellers. One of the problems he identifies is the dual definition of Gypsies and Travellers, on the one hand, according to race, and on the other, to nomadism. This confusion in political and legal terminology exacerbates the problem of labelling in other areas of discourse, such as media debate.

One letter, published in the local press, gave a Gypsy/Traveller view of the labelling issue:

> There is still an enormous amount of prejudice. In fact, we are treated like the Red Indians of America. People want us to keep to reservations. There has always been an inbred fear of the Romany. If Romanies move into a village and people find out, many will start saying that the gypsies will be stealing diesel and so on. When I put in for planning permission in the same village where my parents had lived for 30 years, I faced a huge amount of prejudice and people collected money to try to buy me out. (*Western Daily Press*, 2003a, p. 6)

The focus groups with Gypsies and Travellers echoed the problem with labelling. Romany Gypsies and Irish Travellers mainly wanted to be known as Gypsies and Travellers, respectively. However, some Romany Gypsies felt that the word 'Gypsy' had been tarnished with negative connotation, and preferred the more generic term of 'Traveller'. This is different to the perception of the letter writer from Eldene, above, who has a very clear idea that Gypsies are acceptable and Travellers are not. The word 'Gypsy' has been shortened, in some colloquial language, to 'Gypo'. This is a derogatory term and it could be this that has tarnished the word Gypsy.

The lack of objection to discriminatory language and labelling in news reports and public speech, demonstrates public acquiescence (Zelizer, 1993). Negative labelling of Gypsies and Travellers does not meet resistance from readers or listeners because they are agreeing to the social construction of the 'truth' about Gypsies and Travellers through the discriminatory discourse.

Folk Devils

This theme follows on from the issue of labelling and it, again, links with Cohen (1980) and Bauman (1989). In a discussion with the Planning Officer at Colchester Borough Council, the image of Gypsies and Travellers as 'other', as folk devils, was examined. From historical information on site provision, it became apparent that there had been an issue with one particular site, which since closed. Originally this was populated and managed by Romany Gypsies, but the Gypsy manager then left and Irish Travellers started to move in. The Romanies and Irish were not at ease with each other and the Romany Gypsies left. At the same time, the previously unpopulated surrounding area started to build up both commercially and residentially:

> As a result the two communities [settled and travelling] were thrown together. Interestingly, if you talk to people today there are a lot of urban myths of how bad the Travellers were, from murders to eating people's pets. At the time however, very few complaints were raised. Without a doubt the criticism of Travellers has grown over the intervening years.

> Local populations have difficulty in distinguishing between unauthorised camping and staying on an authorised site. They assume that Travellers are all dirty and trouble. Quite clearly the majority of residents have a prejudice related to Travellers which is now being fuelled by stories that have either no evidence or no way of determining who could have been responsible. (Planning Officer, Colchester Borough Council, 2004)

The history of people's views of Travellers in Colchester helped to contextualise the objections raised by the public in the consultation exercise; and the views of local people seemed to categorise Gypsies and Travellers as folk devils. It is interesting to see that the views have become more extreme in the years since the site was closed. This echoes Bauman's theory of proximity (1989) in that it seems the longer the period of time from the site being inhabited, the more 'other' the Gypsies and Travellers were. There are also links with Morris' research (2000, 2002). It seems that the more extreme the characteristic— murdering, eating pets—the less like 'normal' settled members of the community Gypsies and Travellers are. This makes it easier for the settled community to deny them decent homes, access to schools or welcoming neighbours. The myth of local discourse, as with the socially constructed 'truth' of the media, is so strong that they cannot remember the reality.

There has been some research conducted in Scotland which looks at views of Travellers' sites, which may back up this theory of proximity. Duncan (1996) examined neighbours' views of three proposed sites for Travellers. He examined public opposition to the planning permission, and then revisited some of the complainants to ask their views after the site had been up and running for a while:

> We have to conclude that the three sites which were the subject of this study have had far less impact on their 'neighbours' than these people anticipated before the sites were set up. The picture we obtained is that

the sites have generally fitted into their chosen surroundings better than people living in the neighbourhood anticipated. . . .

It would be fair to say that our study backs up the view that official sites do settle down to a large extent after they are developed. In none of the sites examined were the number and intensity of objections an appropriate response in retrospect. (Duncan, 1996, p. 14)

The Gypsies and Travellers that the Scottish neighbours were objecting to were the mythical messy, costly, troublesome Travellers that are the subject of local discourse and media social construction. However, the Gypsies and Travellers who actually populated the three sites were not like the people the neighbours had been imagining. The 'otherness' of the Gypsies and Travellers seemed to be less marked. There is some merit in replicating Duncan's (1996) methodology in Colchester. It would be interesting to find out the views of the neighbours to any new sites, once approved and developed; they may show similarities to the Scottish example.

The stereotyping of Gypsies and Travellers as folk devils was discussed, in the theoretical framework, as part of the motive behind the media's negative discourse. Erjavec (2001) also found this in her empirical work, of their representation in the Slovenian media. She found that unless they were stereotyped, they were not newsworthy. The Gypsy, as costly and messy, sells more newspapers than the Gypsy who is represented as 'normal'.

Who Is Talking About Gypsies and Travellers?

As part of the coding of the newspaper reports on Gypsies and Travellers, the origins of direct quotes were examined. Speech was put into 'ownership' nodes, for example: Travellers, local people, and politicians (councillors and Members of Parliament). The 'negative' comments in the articles were then analysed according to who had said them. In 14 instances it was a local person quoted with a negative comment, but in nine instances it was a local councillor or MP. Of the negative comments 26 per cent were from political representatives of local constituencies, people who had been voted in by local members of the public to best represent their needs. Therefore, they could be seen to be speaking on behalf of local constituents.

It seems that the very people who should carefully consider what they say are the ones expounding negative images about Gypsies and Travellers. One such comment, from a Swindon Councillor, said: "Hopefully, after all these years, we'll finally see an end to the illegal invasions which have caused so much misery and anger in this area" (*Western Daily Press*, 2003a, p. 25). A Councillor, in Grimsby, talked about the costs associated with Travellers, and said: ". . . increased costs of educating extra children and the potential tension caused by possibly hundreds of travellers moving into the area" (Turner, 2003, p. 10). The Chair of Stowe Town Council talked about abusive Gypsy youths and how female shopkeepers had to be protected from their intimidation during the Stowe fair (*Gloucestershire Echo*, 2003, p. 5). Two Birmingham Councillors showed their impatience in an article about moving Travellers on. They suggested that evictions were delayed because Traveller women claimed they were pregnant and one of the Councillors referred to an example where a Traveller family was not moved on because one of their children was in hospital (Bell, 2003, p. 5).

Because of their status in the local community, what local Councillors and MPs say bears significance on the public discourse on Gypsies and Travellers. When elected officials use discriminatory language about Gypsies and Travellers it has the appearance of sanctioning the discriminatory discourse. This may be partly due to the fact that, as a group, Gypsies and Travellers can lose votes and as such politicians are not interested to support them. Crawley suggests as much: "What was lacking was the political will to ensure that the accommodation needs of Travellers and Gypsies were addressed" (Crawley, 2004, p. 19). Indeed, the Conservative 2005 election campaign relied partly on a tough approach to Gypsies and Travellers, for example, by suggesting that European Human Rights legislation should not be adhered to in the case of Gypsies and Travellers (Article 8 of the Human Rights Act 1988 is one of the main defences used in Traveller cases).

In some instances senior politicians have been as acquiescent as the public in allowing discriminatory discourse to unfairly label Gypsies and Travellers and mark them out for surveillance by society. In one extreme example of discriminatory discourse used in the House of Commons in 2002, the Conservative MP for Bracknell, Mr Andrew MacKay said:

> The cost to council tax payers, where there are natural budgetary
> restraints, is great. Ordinary, innocent people—hard-working, normal,
> straightforward people who live around Bracknell—want to get on with
> their lives in peace, but they want protection under the law *when they
> are invaded by this scum. They are scum*, and I use the word advisedly.
> People who do what these people have done do not deserve the same
> human rights as my decent constituents going about their everyday lives.
> (MacKay, 2002) (Emphasis added)

MacKay's use of inflammatory and discriminatory language was not picked up by other Members of Parliament. Indeed, Angela Eagle (Under-secretary of State for the Home Office at the time) spoke of her gratitude to the Right Honourable Member for raising this. Eagle did state that Travellers should be seen as part of society, but she did not comment on the use of language by MacKay (Eagle, 2002).

Therefore, it should not be surprising that the language of local politicians and officials, as exemplified in the October 2003 news reports, discriminates against Gypsies and Travellers. The example from the House of Commons is that it is acceptable to talk about Gypsies and Travellers in discriminatory language. This public discourse about Gypsies and Travellers contains so many socially constructed 'truths' that it does not seem to be noticed or commented upon.

Therefore, whilst at first the fact that 26 per cent of the negative comments quoted in the October 2003 press were from local councillors and MPs may seem high, an examination of national political and public discourse goes some way to explaining it. This finding is supported by research undertaken by Turner (2002) who found parliamentary language to be overwhelmingly negative. He analysed a number of speeches, including one made by Anne Widdecombe:

> Miss Widdecombe was very explicit about the need for 'control'. It was mentioned by her several times. Indeed, the British way of life itself was threatened. She closed her speech by arguing that there was a need to find a means of 'controlling the menace before it becomes a greater one, when it will no longer be so easy to bring it within the laws that apply to the rest of civilised Britain'. (Turner, 2002, pp. 7–8)

CONCLUSION

One of the strongest themes to come out of the research was the association of 'mess' and 'cost' with Gypsies and Travellers. This was not evidenced by those who spoke of mess in the media or the public meeting, in any systematic way (although a cost was attributed to mess), but instead it demonstrated a socially constructed 'truth' both in the media and the local population in Colchester.

It was discussed, earlier, how 'mess' and 'cost' seemed to be emotive language that made the settled community more prejudiced over the travelling community. The media makes the links between 'mess' and 'cost' and Gypsies and Travellers, as does the settled community; this was exemplified in the Colchester debate. The former did so because of proprietorial pressure to use emotive headlines to sell newspapers (Kundnani, 2004). The latter seemed to do it in order to win their objections against neighbouring planning proposals for Travellers' sites. Although 'mess' and 'cost' was the strongest theme in research for this paper, the newspaper and current political debate seems to have moved on, since 2003, to a current discourse of 'unfairness'. This is particularly centred upon unauthorised development of new private sites. This may be linked to a perception of an increase in more Travellers building sites on their own land and breaching planning legislation (following which ODPM issued Circular 02/2005), rather than a previous concern of 'unauthorised camping' on road-sides and common ground.

Whatever the individual motive of the speaker of the negative terms and phrases, there seems to be an overall desire to mark the Gypsy or Traveller out as 'other'; as different to the people in the settled community. Whether they are creators of mess and rubbish (media analysis), eating people's pets (Colchester folk devils), or whether they are 'getting away' with breaching planning control (current debate in national and local press) the aim of the discourse is to high-light their 'otherness' and to increase their visibility in society.

The theoretical framework is a useful aid to interpret the empirical data. It explains the circuitous route of discourse as control and it serves as an example of how the motive to 'other' reinforces the stereotype and that this reinforced image causes a moral panic and a need for further surveillance. This then pro-duces more discriminatory discourse that reinterprets the Gypsy/Traveller ste-reotype; and on it goes.

REFERENCES

Acton, T. (1994) Modernisation, moral panics and the Gypsies, *Sociology Review*, 4, September, pp. 24–28.

Akerstrom Anderson, N. (2003) *Discursive Analytical Strategies, Understanding Foucault, Koselleck, Lacalau and Luhmann* (Bristol: The Policy Press).

Anti-Social Behaviour Act (2003) (London: HMSO). Available at www.hmso.gov.uk/acts/acts2003/30038- h.htm (accessed 24 April 2004).

Asthana, A. (2004) Gypsies are new race hate target, *The Observer*, 15 November, p. 5.

Barkham, P. (2004) Gypsies worker, 80, to return MBE in anger at policy, *The Guardian*, 10 August, p. 5.

Bauman, Z. (1989) *Modernity and the Holocaust* (Oxford: Polity Press).

Bell, D. (2003) Gypsy curse, *Birmingham Evening Mail*, Midland Independent Newspapers plc, 24 October, p. 5.

Berger, P. & Luckmann, T. (1966) *The Social Construction of Reality, A Treatise in the Sociology of Knowledge* (Harmondsworth: Penguin Books Ltd).

Beunderman, M. (2004) *Roma MEP urges Commission to act for her people*. Available at www.romea.cz/ english/index.php (accessed 11 August 2004).

Birmingham Evening Mail (2003) Brum is Gypsy capital, Midland Independent Newspapers plc, 24 October, p. 5.

Bowers, J. & Benjamin, A. (2004) Pitch battles, *The Guardian Society*, 28 July, pp. 2–3.

Clapham, D. (2002) Housing pathways: a post modern analytical framework, *Housing Theory and Society*, 19, pp. 57–68.

Clegg, S. (1989) *Frameworks of Power* (London: Sage).

Cohen, S. (1980) *Folk Devils and Moral Panics, The Creation of the Mods and Rockers* (Oxford: Martin Robertson).

Cohen, S. (1985) *Visions of Social Control* (Oxford: Polity Press).

Colchester Borough Council, Relocation of Gypsy/Travellers Site Report to Council, 30 September 2002, Appendix One.

Cowan, D. & Lomax, D. (2003) Policing unauthorised camping, *Journal of Law and Society*, 30, pp. 283–308.

Crawley, H. (2004) *Moving Forward, The Provision of Accommodation for Travellers and Gypsies* (London: Institute of Public Policy Research).

Criminal Justice and Public Order Act (1994) (London: HMSO).

Dovey, K. (1999) *Framing Place, Mediating Power in Built Form* (London: Routledge).

Duncan, T. (1996) *Neighbours' Views of Official Sites for Travelling People* (Glasgow: The Planning Exchange).

Eagle, A. (2002) *House of Commons Hansard Debates*, Part 5, 15 January. Available at http://www.publications. parliament.uk/cgi-bin/ukparl_hl (accessed 16 June 2003).

Elster, J. (1989) *The Cement of Society, A Study of Social Order* (New York: University of Cambridge).

Erjavec, K. (2001) Media representation of the discrimination against the Roma in Eastern Europe: the case of Slovenia, *Discourse and Society*, 12, pp. 699–727.

Foucault, M. (1969) *The Birth of the Clinic: An Archaeology of Medical Perception*, translated by A. M. Sheridan (London: Tavistock Publications).

Foucault, M. (1976) *The History of Sexuality: 1 The Will to Knowledge* (London: Penguin Books Ltd).

Foucault, M. (1977) *Discipline and Punish, The Birth of the Prison* (London: Penguin Books Ltd).

Foucault, M. (1980), in: C. Gordon (Ed.) *Power/Knowledge* (Harlow: Pearson Education Ltd).

Gardiner, J. (2004) Corporation will pay RSLs to build and manage Gypsy sites, *Housing Today*, 30 July, p. 9.

Gloucestershire Echo (2003) Hotline will curb Fair problems, 18 October, p. 5.

Greenhill, S. (2004) March of the Gipsy camps, *Daily Mail*, 15 November, p. 1.

Hilditch, M. (2005) ODPM takes Gypsies and Travellers' side in sites row, *Housing Today*, 11 March, p. 9.

Holloway, S. (2003) Outsiders in rural society? Constructions of rurality and nature-social relations in the racialisation of English Gypsy-Travellers, 1869–1934, *Environment and Planning D: Society and Space*, 21, pp. 695–715.

Homelessness Act (2002) (London: The Stationery Office).

Inside Housing (2005) Government set to use new gypsy land powers, *Inside Housing*, 11 March, p. 6.

Johnston, P. (2004) MPs in call for more official gipsy camps, *The Daily Telegraph*, 8 November, p. 4.

Kelly, T. (2004) £350,000 That's the bill (so far) to evict 450 travellers from their illegal camp, *Daily Mail*, 1 November, p. 31.

Kundnani, A. (2004) Express newspaper faces criticism from its own journalists for anti-Roma stance, Independent race and refugee news network, 4 February. Available at http://www.irr.org.uk/2004/february/ak000006.html (accessed 6 February 2004).

Leudar, I. & Nekvapil, J. (2000) Presentations of Romanies in the Czech media: on category work in television debates, *Discourse and Society*, 11, pp. 487–513.

Levy, A. (2004) Village in dread of travellers who sent the builders in first, *Daily Mail*, p. 27.

Lincolnshire Free Press (2004) Travellers' site ruling 'invitation to anarchy', 5 October, p. 3.

Lipsky, M. (1980) *Street-Level Bureaucracy, Dilemmas of the Individual in Public Services* (New York: Russell Sage Foundation).

Lodge, A. (2004) What happened next?, *Observer Magazine*, 28 March, p. 65.

Long, R. (2004) Travellers vow to fight to stay at site, *Lincolnshire Free Press*, 14 September, p. 5.

MacKay, A. (2002) *House of Commons Hansard Debates*, Part 5, 15 January. Available at http://www.publications.parliament.uk/cgi-bin/ukparl_hl (accessed 16 June 2003).

Marston, G. (2004) Managerialism and public housing reform, *Housing Studies*, 19, pp. 5–20.

Mayall, D. (2004) *Gypsy Identities 1500–2000, From Egipcyans and Moon-Men to the Ethnic Romany* (London: Routledge).

McNay, L. (1994) *Foucault, a Critical Introduction* (Cambridge: Polity Press).

Morris, R. (1998) Gypsies and the planning system, *Journal of Planning and Environmental Law*, July, pp. 635–643.

Morris, R. (2000) Gypsies, Travellers and the media: press regulation and racism in the UK, *Communications Law*, 5, pp. 213–219.

Morris, R. & Clements, L. (2002) *At What Cost? The Economics of Gypsy and Traveller Encampments* (Bristol: Policy Press).

Niner, P. (2003) *Local Authority Gypsy/Traveller Sites in England* (London: ODPM).

ODPM (2004) *Select Committee Report: Gypsy/Traveller Sites* (London: The Stationery Office).

ODPM (2005) Circular02/2005(London: ODPM).

ODPM (2005) *Diversity in Equality and Planning* (London: ODPM).

Planning and Compulsory Purchase Act (2004) (London: The Stationery Office).

Planning Officer (2004) Colchester Borough Council, interview by telephone, 10 February.

Rose, N. (1999) *Powers of Freedom, Reframing Political Thought* (Cambridge: Cambridge University Press).

Shuinear, S. (1997) Why do Gaujos hate Gypsies so much, anyway?, in: T. Acton (Ed.) *Gypsy Politics and Traveller Identity* (Hertfordshire: University of Hertfordshire Press).

Snow, E. (2004) Nomad's land, *Housing Today*, 3 September, pp. 21–24.

South Wales Evening Post (2003) Stones moved as Travellers arrive, 3 October, p. 2.

The Cornishman (2003a) I don't think so, 23 October, p. 35.

The Cornishman (2003b) Come and meet your nomadic neighbours, 23 October, p. 35.

The Sun (2005) Stamp on the camps, 9 March, p. 1.

This is Wiltshire (2003) £60,000 to keep them out, 6 October, p. 1.

This is Worcestershire (2003) £50,000 mess bill, 27 October, p. 9.

Turner, L. (2003) Benefit reforms to present problems, *Grimsby Evening Telegraph*, 11 October, p. 10.

Turner, R. (2000) Gypsies and politics in Britain, *The Political Quarterly*, 71, pp. 68–77.

Turner, R. (2002) Gypsies and British parliamentary language: an analysis, *Romani Studies*, 5(12), pp. 1–34.

Western Daily Press (2003a) The end of the road for Travellers in town, 10 October, p. 25.

Western Daily Press (2003b) Travellers are not Gypsies, 15 October, p. 12.

Zelizer, B. (1993) Narratives of self-legitimation, in: D. Mumby (Ed.) *Narrative and Social Control: Critical Perspectives* (London: Sage).

*Joanna Richardson is principal lecturer at the Centre for Comparative Housing Research, De Montfort University, Leicester, United Kingdom.

Joanna Richardson, "Talking About Gypsies: The Notion of Discourse as Control," *Housing Studies* 21, no. 1 (January 2006).

Chapter 9: Ethnic Minority Identity and Movement Politics: The Case of the Roma in the Czech Republic and Slovakia

by Peter Vermeersch*

The level of political mobilization among ethnic minorities in Central and Eastern Europe has often been regarded as directly dependent on the strong or weak ethnic identity of the groups involved. Less attention has gone to the role of ethnic leaders in creating ethnic group identities for political purposes. This article explores the influence of political mobilization on ethnic group formation in the case of the Roma (Gypsies) in the contemporary Czech and Slovak Republics. It examines the various ways in which Romani activists in these two countries have "framed" Romani identity. The article suggests that activists' conceptions of Romani identity are closely tied to their political strategies. At the same time, Romani activists have not been able to gain complete control over the production of Romani identity. They have had to deal with powerful schemes of ethnic categorization promulgated by the media, public officials and policy documents.

Throughout the last decade, political scientists and popular commentators have increasingly recognized ethnicity as an important element of politics in Central and Eastern Europe. This has produced a large body of literature debating the ethnic interests of political parties, leaders and activists in the region. At the same time, however, relatively few empirical studies have examined how politicians and activists in Central and Eastern Europe have influenced ethnic boundaries. In fact, not many observers of the region have regarded ethnic politics as a factor that contributes to the *production* of ethnic minority groups.

It is the aim of this article to examine precisely this factor in the case of the Roma (Gypsies). The Roma are popularly viewed as one of the most immutable and traditional ethnic groups in Central and Eastern Europe; they seem 'unconstructed' and unaffected by the larger political environment. This article challenges this depiction and aims to show that the institutional and discursive dimensions of politics do have a strong impact on the process of Romani identity formation. To study this process I rely on insights from social movement literature. Social movement scholars have emphasized the utility of analysing group identity as the product of 'group-making projects' (Brubaker 2002, p. 12). Group identities, they have argued, are produced and continuously re-defined by the process of collective action (della Porta and Diani 1999, p. 87). Translated to the area of ethnicity research, this means one should concentrate not on 'ethnic groups' as supposedly 'substantial entities to which interests and agency can be attributed' (Brubaker 2002, p. 2), but on the role of activists, organizations, political institutions and political discourses in bringing about ethnic groups.

A number of reasons underpin the choice to focus on the Roma in the Czech Republic and Slovakia. First, while in recent years the Roma in these two countries received an unprecedented amount of attention, the descriptions in the media and in international studies have mostly been one-sided. Much attention has gone to the Roma as victims of human rights breaches and economic deterioration, but there has been little reflection on the link between collective action and Romani identity. Yet it seems not unreasonable to assume that activists have played a role in producing public conceptions of Romani identity. Since 1989 the number of ethnically-based interest organizations in the Czech Republic and Slovakia that have engaged in Romani political mobilization has increased dramatically (see e.g. Barany 1998). Moreover, a number of Romani activists have managed to voice their concerns in the international media and have found a positive response from a number of domestic and international politicians.

Secondly, the case of the Romani movement in the Czech and Slovak Republics is interesting because it is characterized by what seems to be a contradiction. On the one hand, activists have been successful in getting the term 'Roma' adopted in mainstream politics. Moreover, they have been able to find access to the domestic policy-making process. On the other hand, however, the Romani movement has manifestly failed to attract large constituencies. Some observers have argued that this shortcoming is related to the exceptional nature of the Roma as an extremely heterogeneous conglomerate of ethnic sub-groups. As one journalist argued: 'They belong to many different, and often antagonistic, clans and tribes, with no common language or religion' (*The Economist* 2000, p. 62). According to Barany (2002, p. 203), 'the absence of a strong ethnic identity has been one of the key reasons for the deficiencies of Romani mobilization'. The evidence in this article suggests, however, that the ethnic heterogeneity can be understood, not as a cause of failing ethnic mobilization, but as a *consequence* of it. The process of Romani mobilization itself has given rise to competing understandings of Romani identity. Thus, it is my contention that Romani mobilization has been hindered, not by the alleged universally low levels of Romani ethnic awareness, but by crucial factors of political organization such as strategic disputes between movement elites about how to conceptualize Romani identity, how to promote their conceptualizations, and how to organize around them.

The article consists of four parts. The first part briefly describes the historical background of the emergence of Romani political activism in the 1990s in the Czech and Slovak Republics. The second part introduces the concept of 'framing', which in social movement literature refers to the attempts of movement organizers to define and promote a particular understanding of reality (a 'frame') as a basis for collective action. In the third part, the concept of 'framing' is employed to explore Romani activists' descriptions of collective identity. The empirical basis of this part consists of interviews with Czech and Slovak Romani activists about their movement activities, conducted during field research in 2000 and 2001.[1] The fourth part examines the way Romani identity has been framed in recent government reports.

THE ROMANI MOVEMENT IN THE CZECH LANDS AND SLOVAKIA

Historical Background

Although Romani activism in the Czech and Slovak Republics has largely been a post-1989 phenomenon, some of its roots date back to the communist period. In 1969 the Czechoslovakian authorities temporarily abandoned the policy of cultural assimilation and allowed the establishment of a Romani organization, the Association for Roma-Gypsies (*Svaz Cikánů-Romů*/*Sväz Cigánov-Rómov*) (Guy 2001, p. 291). This organization was tasked to promote Romani folklore, music and literature, and to bolster the Roma's participation in the mainstream economy. Although the organization fell under the control of the communists, it should not be discounted as meaningless. For the Romani activists involved it represented one of the first institutional channels through which nationality status could be demanded (although the communist authorities would never comply with this demand). Moreover, it enabled the participation of an official Romani delegation from Czechoslovakia to the first World Romani Congress [WRC], held in London in 1971. This congress was a historical meeting of Romani activists from various European countries and represented one of the first well-documented attempts at organizing an international Romani movement. After the sudden abolition of both the Slovak and Czech branches of the Association in 1973, the communist authorities in Czechoslovakia did not again allow experimenting with ethnically-based institutions. Nevertheless, the Association had set the aims for future mobilization.

One of the aims had been the distribution of a new name. The term 'Roma' (meaning 'man' or 'husband' in the Romani language) was put forward to encompass a variety of communal-based identities across different countries—such as Servika, Romungro, Vlach, Sinti and so forth—which had in common that they all were subject to external categorization under the exonym 'Gypsies' (Gheorghe 1991). The dissemination of the 'new' ethnic label and the eradication of the 'old' designation was considered especially necessary with regard to the words for 'Gypsy' in the Slavic languages (e.g. 'cikán' in Czech, 'cigán' in Slovak), which are almost invariably used in a derogatory way.[2]

After the changes of 1989, individual Romani activists and emerging Romani political elites across several Central European countries resumed the promotion of a common Romani ethnicity. Puxon (2000, p. 94) has argued that with the end of communism the 'shocking increase in anti-Gypsy violence and racial intolerance, evident throughout Europe, has begun to politicise and unite a new generation to a degree not seen before'. It is no doubt true that deteriorating economic conditions and the increase of anti-Romani behaviour in the Czech and Slovak Republics have stimulated the increase of Romani movement activities. However, important additional elements of the explanation are to be found in the institutional and political circumstances of the post-1989 period, which offered Romani individuals unprecedented opportunities to organize around ethnic claims. First, since they were able to build alliances with former dissident organizations, the Roma gained support from the new political elite. In 1990 a number of Romani activists in Czechoslovakia publicly identified themselves as a separate group of participants to the anti-communist movement, and joined the coalition parties that won the first democratic elections (Civic Forum and Public against Violence). Secondly, the new political environment functioned as a breeding ground for ethnopolitical mobilization in general, and thus not surprisingly also for Romani mobilization. As Wolchik (1995, p. 240) has argued, political leaders in Czechoslovakia were able to channel the dissatisfaction and uncertainty that accompany large-scale economic and political changes into support for ethnic claims.

This was still the case after the break-up of Czechoslovakia. In Slovakia, the issue of the rights of the ethnic Hungarian minority began to dominate party competition (Evans and Whitefield 1998). Throughout the 1990s, the popular party Movement for a Democratic Slovakia [HZDS] of the former premier, Vladimír Mečiar, mobilized around the issue of Slovak national identity in opposition to Hungarian identity. Although the language of the HZDS was not as harsh as the xenophobic rhetoric of the far-right Slovak National Party [SNS], which was twice a coalition partner in a government led by the HZDS, the party was certainly not averse to tapping into anti-Hungarian sentiments (Haughton 2001, p. 752). The nationalist discourse and Mečiar's authoritarian style of government between 1994 and 1998 aroused fierce criticism from human rights organizations at home and abroad.

In the Czech Republic, the ethnic dimension to domestic political competition was less prominent. After the break-up the country was more than ever perceived as ethnically homogeneous. However, ethnic mobilization surfaced also there both in the margins and at the centre of domestic politics. The electoral results of the radical-right Republican Party [SPR-RSC] were poor throughout the 1990s, but this did not prevent mainstream politicians parties from playing out hostile sentiments towards the Roma from time to time. Precarious statements were made by members of the Civic Democratic Party [ODS] of the former prime minister, Václav Klaus. For example, some decried the choice of an increasing number of Roma to seek asylum in other countries; others denounced the international indignation about the situation in Ústi nad Labem, where the local government in 1999 attempted to fence off a block of flats inhabited mostly by Romani families (Fawn 2001, p. 1203). In both countries ethnic Romani claims received support from international and domestic advocacy organizations. Moreover, political concern for the countries' international reputation in recent years frequently moved the Romani issue to the centre of the political debate. As European Union candidate countries the Czech Republic and Slovakia tried to enhance their international standing by emphasizing that they attached particular importance to the principles of minority rights protection.

Failing Mass Mobilization

Despite the organizational growth and the increase of international attention, the Czech and Slovak Romani movements continued to struggle with obstacles hindering mass mobilization. This was most obvious in electoral politics. The only Romani party that ever ran on its own in Czech nationwide elections was the Romani Civic Initiative [ROI] in the elections for the 1992 Federal Assembly and Czech National Council, in the 1996 Senate elections, and in the 2002 elections for the Chamber of deputies; in all cases it attained results far below 0.1 per cent. During the 1990 elections a coalition of the Democratic Union of Roma and the Party for the Integration of Roma in Slovakia [DÚRS] filed candidates for the Federal Assembly and the Slovak National Council, but its electoral support reached no more than 0.73 per cent. The Romani parties ROI-SR and the Party for Labour and Security [SPI] stood separately in the 1992 Slovak elections, but reached no more than 0.6 per cent and 0.97 per cent of the vote—far below the 5 per cent threshold. In the 1994 elections, ROI-SR enjoyed support from one of Slovakia's most popular parties, the HZDS, but again it attracted a low number of voters (0.67 per cent) (for election results see Popescu and Hannavy 2002). Various Romani activists also tried to achieve political representation through their involvement in mainstream political parties; but these activists, too, failed to persuade voters. After the elections of 1992, when the anti-communist alliance had splintered, Romani political representation on national level almost disappeared. Romani elites received more attention from the mainstream media with the passage of time, but the gap between them and their constituencies in many cases proved to be unbridgeable.

Furthermore, the Czech and Slovak Romani elites grappled with the reluctance of their target audiences to identify themselves as Roma in official registrations. The official 1991 census figure for the Romani population was 80,627 (1.5 per cent) in Slovakia and 32,903 (0.3 per cent) in the Czech part of the country—this being the result of the first census in which the Roma obtained the right to proclaim themselves as a distinct national minority (Cesky statistický úřad 2002; Štatistický úrad Slovenskej republiky 2002). However, both the Czech and Slovak government have admitted that the actual rate of people who identify themselves as Roma in daily life must be substantially higher (Vláda České republiky 1999a; Slovak Government 1999). Independent researchers and Romani organizations have claimed that the Roma constitute around 7 to 8 per cent (up to 500,000) of the Slovak citizens and around 3 per cent (up to 250,000) of the Czech citizens (Druker 1997, pp. 22–23). These authors have not made clear how their estimations were carried out, but their numbers are often cited, have been accepted by the international community, and therefore have gained the status of the 'truth'. The results of the 2001 censuses, however, were again far below the estimated figures. In the Czech Republic the number decreased to 11,716 (barely 0.1 per cent of the total population), while in Slovakia there was only a slight growth to 89,920 (1.7 per cent of the population). These figures came as a disappointment to many Romani activists, who had promoted Romani identification and had even demanded the government to make census forms available in the Romani language.

Low official rates of Romani identification do not necessarily indicate, as some authors have suggested, a 'low level of ethnic awareness' among Roma (Plichtová 1993, p. 17). Other authors, for example, have explained the matter by referring to bureaucratic irregularities during the official registration (Druker 1998) or by referring to people who identify themselves as Roma in daily life, but refuse to do so in an official form for fear of some kind of reprisal (Clark 1998). Although it is difficult to establish the definitive influence of such factors, the discussion at least points to a potential problem surrounding the perception of the public 'image' of Romani identity.

In what follows I will consider the responses of Romani activists. I will discuss (a) their attempts at formulating convincing conceptions ('frames') of Romani identity, and (b) the difficulties that they have encountered when attempting to promote particular identity frames. A comparison of the two countries, then, will allow one to explore factors of the political context that influenced identity disputes within the Czech and Slovak Romani movement.

FRAMING ETHNIC GROUP IDENTITY

Before embarking upon all of this, however, a few words of explanation may be in order with regard to the concept of 'framing'. In various types of research the term 'frame' has been used to denote, in its most general sense, a schema of interpretation. 'Framing', then, refers to the activity of reproducing meaning. Most studies in social science that use the concept of framing offer a definition derived from the writings of Erving Goffman, in particular his book *Frame Analysis* (Goffman 1975). Goffman used the designation 'primary framework' to refer to what he called a 'conceptual structure' that organizes interpretation, or a 'mental set' through which people understand and construct social events. Goffman's concept provided an important source of inspiration for scholars who studied social movements (McAdam, McCarthy and Zald 1996). These scholars shifted the focus away from frames as pure cognition and concentrated on the power of deliberate framing by activists. According to these authors, frames do not only perform an interpretative function, as suggested by Goffman. Certain patterns of interpretation are promoted with a specific intention 'to mobilize potential adherents and constituents, to garner bystander support, and to demobilize antagonists' (Benford and Snow 2000, p. 612).

Social movement scholars have been interested in framing when understood as the way in which movement actors disseminate their understanding of social reality in order to appeal to a constituency. Different authors have often highlighted different aspects of the framing process. Some authors have centred attention on the individual control over framing processes. In their view, research has to focus on the ability of activists to assign meaning to social reality, promote a certain understanding of reality and intentionally choose a frame for mobilization. McAdam, McCarthy and Zald (1996, p. 6) define framing as 'the conscious strategic efforts by groups of people to fashion a shared understanding of the world and of themselves that legitimate and motivate collective action'. Others have emphasized that the process of framing is not taking place in a vacuum (Benford and Snow 2000, p. 628). For them, research should not discard the fact that framing is always negotiated and to a certain degree shaped by the complex, multi-organizational, multi-institutional arenas in which it takes place. These authors have emphasized that frame diffusion (how do frames spread?) and frame resonance (how do frames become effective?) is affected by the cultural and political environment.

The concept of framing provides a useful contribution to the study of ethnic minority mobilization since it directs attention to cognition and persuasion. According to the framing approach, the boundaries of ethnic minority identity are continuously reconstituted in the light of the present circumstances, even in cases where there are seemingly 'objective' historical and cultural foundations of this identity. Thus, an ethnic minority is not simply a group of people that differs from the rest of society in terms of language, tradition and so forth, but rather the result of a process in which such differences are deemed socially and politically meaningful and are acted upon. By employing Benford and Snow's concept of framing to the subject area of ethnic mobilization, an opportunity is created to examine the element of choice in the construction of ethnic identity (the use of intentional frames) as well as the element of designation (the presence of countermobilizing frames or the (in)ability of a particular frame to resonate in a given context).

ROMANI IDENTITY AND FRAME ALIGNMENT IN ROMANI ACTIVIST DISCOURSE

Since 1989 a growing body of descriptions of the way in which the Roma are treated in the new democracies of Central Europe have become available to the regional specialist. These descriptions contain various assumptions about what constitutes Romani identity. Often the Roma in Central Europe have been conceptualized as a mixture between an 'immigrant minority' and a 'national minority', but neither of the two types exactly, because it was observed that only a limited number of them had migrated in recent times and that they did not have a connection to an external homeland (Kymlicka 2000, p. 204). Others have pointed to certain customs and traditions that—even if they are not observed—constitute in their view the basis of 'orthodox' Romani identity (Barany 2002, p. 13). In the majority of the descriptions the alleged Indian origin has served as a main source for identifying them.

Exploration of the interviews and texts produced by Romani activists in the Czech Republic and Slovakia led to the observation that in both countries mainly three types of Romani identity frames have been used to describe and promote Romani collective action.

A Non-Territorial Nation

The first frame defines the Roma as a 'non-territorial nation'. The Romani activists who subscribed to this perspective in order to talk about their collective identity emphasized the view that all Roma in Europe possess a common history and, especially, a common origin. The apparent fragmentation has in their view been caused by time periods of aggressive assimilation and repressive policies implemented by non-Romani authorities. They argued that all Romani communities are deeply connected, not through territory, but through blood ties, common history, and culture; and that therefore they should be granted a special legal position in Europe—although they usually had only vague ideas about what kind of legal protection this special status would need. To some extent this frame reflects the experience of what Soysal (1996) has called 'postnational citizenship', a practice of citizenship that is increasingly defined according to entitlements emerging from the transnational discourse and the practice of international human rights protection. Arguably, the growing attention of human rights organizations to the position of the Roma in both countries stimulated the popularity of this perspective.

The frame has been vigorously promoted by organizations that claim to represent a cross-border Romani constituency, such as the German-based Roma National Congress. Since its foundation in 1977 it has also been the perspective promoted by the International Romani Union [IRU], a non-governmental organization that has attempted to become the predominant forum for international Romani activism. Until recently, the attempts of the IRU to gain a dominant position in the Romani movement and attract a larger constituency were rather unsuccessful. Moreover, in the 1990s the organization was plagued by internal dissidence and leadership struggles (Acton and Klímová 2001, p. 162). In 2000, however, activists were able to revive the IRU through a new World Romani Congress [WRC] held in Prague. The initiative had been encouraged by calls from international organizations (in particular, the Council of Europe and the Organization for Security and Cooperation in Europe [OSCE]) for a unified international Romani actor as negotiating partner. There had also been a need for a legitimate international Romani agency to put forward a restitution claim for pre-war financial deposits of Roma that were made available by Swiss banks.

Clearly, the election of the former leader of the Czech part of the Romani political party ROI, Slovak-born Emil Ščuka, to the presidency of the IRU at the fifth WRC in Prague, played a significant role in the promotion of this frame in both the Czech and Slovak Republics. During the latest WRC a declaration was adopted that conceptualized the Roma as a 'nation' on the basis of their common culture, language and origin. The IRU claimed not to be just an international Romani organization, but *the* representative organization for 'all the Roma in the world' (article 1 of the IRU Charter; Acton and Klimová 2001, p. 201). The language of the latest WCR was clearly that of 'national liberation', although dissimilar to many other national liberation movements since it explicitly excluded *territorial* liberation as a goal. Defining the Roma as a non-territorial and 'transnational' ethnic group has clearly been an effective strategy. In the latter half of the 1990s the OSCE and the Council of Europe established special institutions to raise the level of awareness concerning the problems facing the Roma within the respective member states (respectively, the Contact Point for Roma and Sinti Issues and the Specialist Group on Roma/ Gypsies). Thanks to good contacts of the IRU's Commissar for Foreign Policy (Paolo Pietrosanti) with the Transnational Radical Party and the Lista Emma Bonino in the European Parliament, the IRU was able to establish an office at the European Parliament buildings in Brussels.

Ščuka's ideas have been widely distributed among Czech and Slovak Romani activists; all activists surveyed were aware of the existence of the IRU. Especially activists who had been present at the fifth WRC—such as, for example, Ivan Veselý and Gejza Adam—recognized the symbolic importance of representing the Roma in a Europe-wide forum. Other Romani activists who advocated this frame usually maintained connections with the IRU or the Roma National Congress, although their connection and knowledge of the organizational development of Romani activism in countries outside the Czech and Slovak Republics was usually quite limited. For all these activists the 'nation' frame represented a useful tool for activism towards international organizations. Indirectly this strategy contributed to higher levels of external pressure and scrutiny on both the Czech Republic and Slovakia.

However effective the idea of the Roma as a non-territorial nation has been on the international level, it has had limited concrete implications for domestic Romani mobilization in the Czech Republic and Slovakia. Some concrete influence of the fifth WRC could be detected in Slovakia during attempts of Romani political parties in October 2000 to unite in an electoral platform. Emil Ščuka, as the IRU president, was present at the meeting in Košice where thirteen Romani political parties and twenty-five non-political Romani organizations decided to join together in a unified Romani electoral platform for the parliamentary elections of 2002. However, the role of the IRU in this case should not be overestimated; the plan had been initiated by ROI, a Romani political party with no international goals, and was unambiguously formulated as an attempt to stimulate Romani political mobilization, not on the European level, but in the Slovak political arena.

Many local activists in both the Slovak and Czech Republic questioned the connection between the international level and the local needs of Romani communities. According to one Slovak activist,

> There is a growing division between the needs of the Romani population and the activism of the Roma. Today, it is even more difficult than in the past to attract Romani voters. The main reasons are poverty and the fact that people are disillusioned by politics. They don't regard activists as their representatives. When I go to Eastern Slovakia, the Romani people there don't see me as their representative, but as an important person from Bratislava (Personal interview).

The 'non-territorial nation' frame was criticized for other reasons as well. One criticism was that 'Indian origin' and 'transborder cooperation' are very academic notions, and thus poor tools for bolstering domestic mobilization. As one Czech Romani activist stated,

> We are a national minority (…). The fact that the Roma are a worldwide and a European nation is only important to stress towards other countries where the Roma are not yet acknowledged as a national minority (Personal interview).

Another contention relates to the symbolic consequences of considering the Roma a separate nation. Some have wondered what it would mean to be treated as a nation *within* another nation. As one activist asked, 'Would this mean that, in the Czech Republic, for example, the Roma are no longer Czechs?' (PER 2001, p. 37). One Czech respondent even claimed that 'ordinary' Roma are not interested in being regarded as a nation: they do not want Romani schools, they want to be regarded as Czechs with Havel as *their* President, too (Personal interview).

Several Romani activists were also suspicious of the Slovak and Czech governments' strong verbal support for the WRC and the IRU Charter, even though the IRU actively sought the support of those governments. Many agreed with the opinion that the whole process of promoting the Roma as a nation was primarily in the interest of individual states, since it shifted the focus of attention away from the responsibility of domestic governments. Thus a number of Czech and Slovak Romani activists perceived the strategy of the IRU as potentially undermining the position of the Roma as a national minority in the domestic context.

The Discourse of National Minority Rights

The second way in which Romani identity was presented by activists was through a 'national minority' frame. Although as in the previous frame activists centred attention on the difference between the Roma and the ethnic majority, they did not demand a special 'European' status for the Roma. They maintained that the Czech and Slovak Republics were to be regarded as the 'homelands' of the Czech and Slovak Roma. They also believed that when the Roma would be conceptualized as a national minority, they would more easily find support from other national minorities and non-Romani supporters of minority rights. This was an important element especially for the Roma in Slovakia. More than once the political success of the Hungarian minority was referred to as an example.[3] The frame was also reflected in attempts by Slovak Romani activists to form ethnically-based political parties. As mentioned, the attempts of ROI in October 2000 to unite Slovak Romani political parties in an electoral platform can clearly be read as an effort to strengthen the position of the Roma as a national minority and bring it to the level of that of the Hungarian minority.

Other Slovak Romani activists found this frame of Romani identity problematic, and this for a number of reasons. First, the experience of the Roma has often been very different from that of other national minorities. For example, the Roma have never voiced demands for political autonomy or territorial self-determination. Secondly, parties and interest groups from other national minorities have often distanced themselves from the Romani perspective. Slovak Romani activists have estimated that just a small portion of the Hungarians in Slovakia identifies itself with the plight of the Romani minority. In the Czech Republic there has even been less opportunity to ally with other national minorities. The Roma have not felt any affiliation with the demands for self-government rights sometimes voiced by Moravian and Silesian civic organizations and political parties.

There is also a third reason. Some Romani activists have been hesitant about bringing Roma under the discourse of national minority rights, because they fear that national minority rights do not primarily reflect Romani interests, but rather the interests of the authorities. According to their argument the issue of national minority rights plays a fundamental role in the negotiation of the relationship between the European Union states and the candidate countries, and is therefore not driven by a real concern for the position of the Roma. Although this criticism was only implicitly present in the accounts of some of the Romani activists interviewed, it is one that has been most clearly expressed in the international Romani movement. In 1997 Nicolae Gheorghe, a Romanian Romani activist and currently the head of the Contact Point for Roma and Sinti Issues of the OSCE's Office for Democratic Institutions and Human Rights [ODIHR], formulated the matter as follows:

> I personally am critical towards this trend in the Romani movement which seeks to fashion Romanies as a national minority because I consider that in reality, the true concept of national minority is only a byproduct of nation-state building (…). Ethnic minority policies are exhibited as if in a display cabinet, like a showcase in international politics to make sure that the Council of Europe and the Western democracies think that things are good in eastern Europe. (Gheorghe 1997, p. 160)

The Roma as an Ethnoclass

The third frame conceptualizes the Roma as what could be called an 'ethnoclass'. Gurr and Harff (1994, p. 23) have defined an ethnoclass as an ethnic group which resembles a class. According to Gurr and Harff members of ethnoclasses are disproportionately concentrated in occupations at or near the bottom of the economic and social hierarchy. Romani identity in this frame is characterized by a low social position. Romani activists who use this frame emphasized the detrimental social circumstances of Romani life: the need for education, better housing and employment. The protection of cultural aspects of Romani identity was seen as less important; these matters were mostly regarded as strictly private. In general, activists advocated a certain degree of ethnic anonymity. The view has been expressed quite clearly by a Slovak Romani activist who in the beginning of the 1990s was involved in the establishment of a Romani party called Party for Labour and Security [SPI].

> We disagreed with ROI because we saw that they didn't make any progress in integrating the Roma. (…) We wanted a party which would not represent only the Roma living in the East of the country [where the main support for ROI is located]. We wanted to focus on social issues in general, and most importantly, on unemployment (Personal interview).

Another Romani activist has formulated a similar perspective as follows:

> For at least two decades now, the IRU agenda has been packed with such ideas as developing a 'Roma codex', codifying the language, and 'renewing' old traditions and values—ideas the Romani masses really didn't

care all that much about. The Romani leadership bears a responsibility to address the central problem of providing Roma with security. How the Roma will live their lives is a secondary concern. This is a matter of individual choice. (PER 2001, p. 38)

This frame has had a certain appeal to people who experienced that receiving attention as a national minority does not necessarily diminish popular stereotypes. Romani activists who emphasized ethnoclass identity sought to avoid presenting themselves as too closely associated with Romani identity. They considered it not beneficial to stress a form of identity that is generally perceived as pathological. Instead, they tried to mobilize on the basis of their social situation as poor or disadvantaged citizens. Many Roma who advocated this frame had positive memories about the communist period. For them post-communism has only meant a substantive decline in living standards and exclusion from economic opportunity.

The problem, however, is that this framing has not visibly created links of solidarity between Roma and the poor non-Romani population. Those Roma who favoured diminishing the importance attached to ethnic differences, and chose instead to demand economic support for poor communities in general, hoped to find more successful lobby groups outside the Romani movement. Moreover, none of the attempts by Romani activists to capitalize upon feelings of nostalgia for the communist period have proved successful. Some Romani activists were reminded of the less attractive sides of the communist approach. They referred to the fact that overall approach of the communist authorities in Czechoslovakia had been ambiguous on the status of 'Gypsy' identity. For example, the designation 'Gypsy' was officially approached as a social group identification, a remnant of a previous social order, and was simply meant to disappear by a transformation of the social and economic status of the group. This inspired a harsh assimilation campaign at the end of the 1950s and a targeted 'dispersal and transfer' scheme from 1965 to 1968 (Guy 2001, p. 291).

ROMANI IDENTITY AND POLICY FORMULATIONS

Frames of Romani identity are shaped not only by the internal circumstances of the Romani community or by strategic considerations, but also by external circumstances such as institutional context and cultural meanings and, most importantly, by formulations of public policy. In order to gain insight into the latter aspect, I will now briefly consider the conceptions of Romani identity that can be discerned in recent Czech and Slovak government reports and resolutions.

Czech Republic

Two elements of Romani identity framing in Czech government reports and in the more general Czech political discourse have attracted attention. The first element concerns the allusions made to objectionable identity characteristics; the second relates to the increasing tendency of Czech governmental actors to support the idea of the Roma as a European nation. The sources that I refer to here are in the first place documents that have been produced with the participation of the Interdepartmental Commission for Romani Community Affairs (later, the Government Council for Romani Community Affairs) under the government led by Miloš Zeman. In 1999 the Interdepartmental Commission finished a document presenting the policy concept of 'Romani integration'. In April 2000 this concept was adopted by the government as the principal component of a new strategic 'Romani policy' (Resolutions 279/1999 and 599/2000).

The first point to be noted is that the resolutions shaped by the Interdepartmental Commission do not contain any explicit definitions of Romani identity. These texts depart from the assumption that Roma should be regarded as a national minority. This assumption, then, is regarded as a sufficient motivation to devote attention to the group. However, the texts make clear that there are some crucial differences between the Roma and other national minorities. These differences are presented as motivations for the construction of a *special* policy for this group. In essence, then, the differences described express an implicit top-down conception of Romani identity. The resolutions 279/1999 and 599/2000, together with their explanatory reports, contain indications of a conception that links Romani identity with condemnable social behaviour. This does not necessarily mean that Czech policy-makers have deliberately wanted to stimulate negative views on Romani identity. What it does show, however, is that negative aspects of Romani identity (as implicitly defined in the resolutions) are seen as a core element of the policy problem that these resolutions want to address. This implicit connection is visible, for example, in the passages that describe the need for better motivations to work and the active prevention of illegal behaviour. For instance, the Czech authorities have defined Romani integration in the following way:

> Integration, then, is understood to mean the Romani community's full-scale incorporation into society while preserving most of the cultural specificities and different features which characterize this community and which it wishes to adhere to *so long as these distinctive features are not at variance with the laws of the Czech Republic.* (Vláda České republiky 1999b, emphasis added)

By referring to illegal behaviour as a distinctive feature, this definition suggests that some features of Roma identity *are* indeed at variance with the laws of the Czech Republic. With the exception of some brief considerations on Romani language, the documents do not provide any further descriptions of Romani traditions or 'cultural specificities'.

The problematic character of certain alleged traits of Romani identity are also suggested by the dubious position in the texts on whether the development of Romani culture is a desirable strategy. The government document on Romani policy, on the one hand, states that the emancipation of Romani identity is the ultimate goal. In a translation of the draft resolution distributed by the Czech government it is stated that 'the more Romas [sic] will feel being Roma, the more emancipated and responsible citizens they will be' (Vláda České republiky 1999b). But at the same time, the first three pages of that same draft already contain four statements to qualify this. These statements indicate that assimilation (quite the opposite of what is proposed in the above quote) is not necessarily a bad strategy either, at least for individuals. The resolution further argues that assimilation is generally what 'the majority of the Czech citizens' expect of the Roma, and that the government should certainly not discourage the phenomenon.

> [The government] is aware that the majority of the Czech citizens is able and willing to accept Romanies only when they adapt to the majority and assimilate into it.
>
> (...)
>
> The government will not refuse support to those Romanies who voluntarily wish to assimilate. (Vláda České republiky 1999b)

In one of the drafts the statement that emancipation is a prerequisite for integration is preceded by a qualification arguing that 'it cannot be denied that assimilation can also lead to meaningful citizenship'.

With regard to the 'Europeanization' of Romani identity, one can refer to the Czech Ministry of Foreign Affairs' activities and statements that have been related to the Roma. In December 1998 the Ministry of Foreign Affairs supported a conference organized by the Czech Institute for International Relations under the title, 'The Roma community and multi-ethnicity in the countries of Central Europe—A European problem?' The contribution of the then Czech deputy minister of foreign affairs, Martin Palouš, indicated clearly that the purpose of the conference was to place the Czech 'Romani problem' in a European context.

> As the title of the conference reveals, it is an all-European problem (...)

We must always bear in mind that the successful solution of our domestic difficulties as regards the integration of the Romany ethnic group will to a large extent be inseparable from these broader links. (Palouš 1998a, pp. 11–12)

Palouš also mentioned the reason why he believes we should examine the 'Romani problem' in a European context: the European character of Romani *identity*. Because of their European identity, the Roma should, according to Palouš, expect more help from Europe than other European nations, which have their own state. In the following passage a boundary is constructed between 'the Czechs' as a 'European nation with a state of their own' and 'the Roma' as 'the most European nation' *without* a state and for whom the transnational level (European institutions) should bear more responsibility than the Czech Republic.

If the Roma are the most European nation, then the reason could well be that they hold up a kind of specific mirror to Europe in which Europe can see itself, and where they can expect from European institutions a little bit more than other European nations which have their own European states and enter the process of European integration precisely in the light of their experience. (Palouš 1998b, p. 16)

The ministry has supported the Europeanization of Romani identity in more than words alone. Symbolic and financial support was offered by the Ministry of Foreign Affairs to the fifth World Romani Congress, and a 'Memorandum of Understanding and Co-operation' was signed by both the Ministry and the IRU. Furthermore, in 2000, the Ministry of Foreign Affairs prepared a document entitled 'the Ministry of Foreign Affairs' conception of the Roma issue', meant inter alia to clarify the official Czech response to international criticism about the situation of the Roma. In this document the 'Europeanization' of the Romani problem was literally referred to as the preferential way of framing the issue. Point 65 of the document defined a number of goals towards which Czech foreign policy should be oriented. The first goal was:

Promotion of the concept of the Europeanization of the Romani problematic on all levels of Czech foreign policy. We understand Europeanization here, as to grasp the Romani issue as an affair which concerns every European state where a Romani minority lives today. From this follows also the will to seek a solution for the Romani issue at the international/European level, and this includes a financial safeguard for such a solution. (A copy of a part of this document is published in Sobotka 2001, p. 68).

Furthermore, the document suggested that the Czech Republic needs to reject more consistently the criticism from abroad that anti-Romani racism in the Czech Republic is a ubiquitous phenomenon.

Slovak Republic

In 1996, before the refugee crisis of 1997 and 1998, the Slovak coalition government under Vladimír Meciar adopted a resolution pertaining to the situation of the Roma. Slovakia introduced new policy initiatives on this subject before the Czech Republic did, plausibly as a result of the attitude of Meciar's right-wing populist party HZDS (Movement for a Democratic Slovakia) towards the Roma. Unlike in the Czech Republic the Roma in Slovakia form a substantial part of the electorate. By emphasizing preference for a strong social policy the HZDS has more than once tried to attract Romani voters. Not surprisingly, the 1996 resolution on Roma entitled 'Activities and Measures in Order to Solve the Problems of Citizens in Need of Special Care' (Vláda Slovenskej republiky 1996) was very much in keeping with a 'socio-economic view' on Roma: it treated the name 'Roma' and the phrase 'citizens in need of special care' as synonymous concepts.

The responses to this government resolution were varied. On the one hand, it was welcomed by a part of the Romani activists since it made funds available for initiatives in the fields of education, employment, housing and health. At the same time, much to the frustration of Romani activists it did not refer to discrimination as one of the problems to be addressed. On the contrary, it explicitly linked Romani ethnic or cultural identity and social inferiority by attributing the roots of the 'Romani problem' to their 'socially retarding environments' (paragraph E) or their 'negative social behaviour' (paragraph F). Romani activists also perceived the whole government's approach as paternalistic, because it did not acknowledge the responsibility of the majority and neither did it plan to address the under-representation of the Roma in the policymaking process. For these reasons it was also heavily criticized by international human rights organizations.

The government of Mikuláš Dzurinda, which came to power in 1998, prioritized the 'Romani issue'. The newly appointed deputy prime minister for human rights, minorities and regional development, the Hungarian Pál Csáky, established the position of Government Commissioner for the Solution of the Problems of the Romani Minority, a position filled first by Vincent Danihel and later by Klara Orgovánová, both Romani activists. The government commissioner's office, responsible for bringing Romani concerns to the governmental level, completed a policy paper in June 1999 entitled 'Strategy of the Government for the Solution of the Problems of the Roma', which was later adopted by the government (Vláda Slovenskej republiky 1999).

The view on Romani identity produced by the 1999 resolution is ambiguous. On the one hand, the accompanying explanatory report is careful not to generalize, and consistently qualifies the 'Romani problem' as the problem of *a part* of the Romani population. Nevertheless, the document vaguely suggests that Romani culture and lifestyle are indeed problematic by stating that, 'Some aspects of life of a certain part of this minority *cause* social distance in the majority society' or that problems are '*caused* by the specific way of life of a part of the Romani national minority' (Vláda Slovenskej republiky 1999, emphasis added).

The suggestion of a natural overlap between 'Romani identity' and the 'Romani problem' has also been reflected in the political debate surrounding the new government resolutions. Especially when one considers statements made by politicians in power, one sees that the dominant political discourse still suggests that 'Romani identity' and 'Romani culture' are deemed an integral part of the 'Romani problem'. Consider, for example, Csáky's description of the reason why the government has not yet been able to tackle the problematic situation of the Roma:

> The Roma problem arises from the absence of a model for mutual coexistence between completely different cultures. If you had an unimaginable amount of money, could you change India into a modern European country in four years? No. Roma mentality, culture, thinking, reactions do not stem from the classic Slovak culture. We have to look for mutual coexistence, and we need time to make Roma in the Czech Republic & Slovakia 897 changes inside ourselves—both Roma and non-Roma citizens. (Reynolds and Habšudová 2001)

Another characteristic of the resolutions and the surrounding political discourse is that the 'Romani problem' is considered to be a 'European problem'. One easily sees the strategic interest that the authorities have in describing the 'Romani problem' as a problem that exists, not only in Slovakia, but also in other countries where Roma live. In this way Slovakia attempts to get rid of its anti-Romani image. The Europeanization of the Romani problem is a strategy that is readily usable, since it implicitly relies on the argument promoted by some Romani activists themselves that the Roma are a European nation. Consider again the 1999 resolution.

> [T]he Roma are considered a pan-European specific non-territorial ethnic minority whose different way of life traditionally (historically)

wakes intolerance among [the] majority population. (Vláda Slovenskej republiky 1999)

As a whole the document presents itself not as a document addressing the difficulties of disadvantaged groups in society in general, or as a document about the protection of ethnic minorities in general; it is a document that *specifically* targets the Roma, conceptualizing them as a European ethnic group *and* as a socially problematic layer of society.

Top-Down Formulations of Romani Identity: Implications

The above descriptions are not a full-scale investigation of governmental discourse on Romani identity. Nevertheless, they indicate two basic trends: (a) There is a tendency in both countries to recognize the Roma as a European minority, (b) the meaning of Romani ethnic identity in policy reports carries the strong suggestion that problematic social behaviour and deplorable material circumstances are crucial defining elements of that identity. The implication of this top-down construction of Romani identity for the Romani movement is that it creates a *double bind* situation for activists desiring to engage in ethnic mobilization.

On the one hand, the tendency of both governments to recognize the specific character of the problems that face the Roma represents a positive response to the demands of the Romani movement. In both the Czech and Slovak case the recent resolutions have been drafted through a process that involved the consultation of selected Romani 'representatives'. Arguably, with the assistance of external pressure Romani activists have been able to gain some control over the production of documents on Romani policy. As a result, the conception of the Roma as 'one ethnic group' has been supported by the state. To give just one example, all Romani policy documents apply to both Vlach and Romungro communities (both groups have become subject to one Romani policy). Although government reports have mentioned that ethnic divisions among the Roma exist, policy-makers have not based differentiated policies on these divisions.

On the other hand, the top-down conception of Romani identity is to a large extent based on observations of social behaviour. This has confronted Romani activists with new difficulties. The identification between social behaviour and ethnic identity can easily be maximized in public discourse and can lead to support a 'discourse of otherness'. For example, when speaking about Romani policy, certain politicians in power have attributed problems of social disadvantage to a reified notion of the 'Romani way of life'.

Unsurprisingly, it has become difficult for Romani activists to promote alternative understandings of themselves and to capture their predicament in an alternative way. The Czech and Slovak governments' ways of framing Romani culture as 'substantially different' neatly fits images of them in mass media and public opinion. Thus, when Roma want to mobilize protest 'in the name of their ethnicity', they are confronted with narratives that question a positive framing of this very same ethnicity. The more they emphasize their ethnic identity, the more they appear to be held responsible for what is typically called the 'Romani problem'. The double bind that Roma are confronted with may have strong implications for the resonance of new frames of Romani identity proffered by the Romani elite. Because of highly salient counterframes, some Roma have already become ambivalent towards the postulated 'Romani identities'. People who express a Romani ethnic identity in the private sphere, may be reluctant to emphasize that ethnicity in public, because they fear that precisely this identification will allow others to discredit them even more. Dominant rhetoric associating Romani identity with social marginality can lead them to reject Romani political mobilization altogether.

Conclusion

I have argued that political mobilization is a crucial aspect of the ethnicity of a minority group since it deeply affects the public self-definition of such a group. In this view it is likely that ethnic identity will be the result of the institutional environment shaping mobilization and the internal strategic choices of aspiring minority leaders which underpin this mobilization.

This is the case for the construction of Romani ethnic identity in the Czech Republic and Slovakia. There are three ways in which activists have framed Romani identity. These frames vary according to the degree in which they emphasize ethnic differentiation or assimilation, and they represent competing strategic positions. Furthermore, they are to some extent dependent on the dominant ways in which Romani identity has been understood in society at large and the ways in which the 'Romani problem' has been constructed in political discourse.

Comparison between the Slovak and the Czech Republic indicates that contextual aspects of Romani identity play an important role in the creation of Romani mobilization. Even when, as is the case in both countries, international attention has stimulated a process of ethnic mobilization, there is no guarantee that a unified movement will gain ground domestically. In a similar vein, even when, as in the case of Slovakia, ethnic claims are an important element in mainstream political competition and when activists believe they have a large potential constituency, it may still not be easy to mobilize a group around an ethnic minority identity. The complex discursive struggles surrounding the 'Romani problem' seem mostly to have rendered a powerful negative valuation of the concept of Romani identity. Policy documents that were meant as responses to the demands of Romani activists have offered a further basis for such negative understandings. As a result, many Romani activists are today confronted with a crucial question: How to build a movement on what is regarded by many as a 'stigmatized' identity? By paying attention to this double bind situation, this article shows that the difficulties of Romani mobilization should not necessarily be regarded as problems that are related to the nature of the Roma as a heterogeneous collection of immutable ethnic sub-groups. Rather they have to do with the obstacles that activists encounter when they attempt to turn Romani identity, with all its stigmas, into a mobilizing identity.

Acknowledgements

Research for this article has been funded by the National Fund for Scientific Research [FWO], Flanders (Belgium). I thank Colin Clark, Will Guy, Fried Swenden, Ilona Klímová, Bart Maddens and Jan Beyers for their useful comments on earlier drafts.

NOTES

1. Representatives of the following organizations were interviewed about their movement activities (in alphabetical order): Athinganoi; The Civic Organisation for the Emancipation and Integration of the Roma; The Democratic Movement of Roma in Slovakia (DHR); Dženo; Inforoma; The International Romani Union; The Party for the Protection of Roma in Slovakia (SOPR); The Party of Romani Democrats in the Slovak Republic (SRD); The Romani Civic Initiative Czech Republic (ROI); The Romani Civic Initiative Slovakia (ROI-SR); The Romani Intelligentsia for Co-existence (RISZ); The Romani Parliament for Human Rights and Romani migration; The Slovak Romani Initiative (RIS); The Society of Roma in Moravia.

2. Czech and Slovak nouns that refer to ethnic and national groups are normally capitalized; nevertheless, there is a tendency not to do this with the words 'cigán'/'cikán'. This reflects the popular usage of the word as an insult or a term with negative connotations.

3. One Slovak Romani activists mentioned claims for cultural rights similar to those of the Hungarian minority: 'Not far from Dunajská Streda there is a kindergarten only for Romani children. Some Romani parents there were angry about this, because according to them putting the Roma in separate education is a form of discrimination. They are ashamed of being Roma. I say: the Hungarian minority has its own schools where they teach their children Hungarian, so why should we be ashamed of creating a Romani school?' (Personal interview). Such statements have not been consonant with the concerns of other activists

and international NGOs, which have strongly advocated the integration of Romani pupils in mainstream education.

REFERENCES

ACTON, THOMAS and KLÍMOVÁ, ILONA 2001 'The International Romani Union: an East European answer to West European questions?', in Will Guy (ed.), *Between Past and Future. The Roma of Central and Eastern Europe*, Hertfordshire: University of Hertfordshire Press

BARANY, ZOLTAN 1998 'Ethnic mobilization and the state: the Roma in Eastern Europe', *Ethnic and Racial Studies*, vol. 21, no. 2, pp. 308–27

—— 2002 *The East European Gypsies. Regime Change, Marginality and Ethnopolitics*, Cambridge: Cambridge University Press

BENFORD, ROBERT D. and SNOW, DAVID A. 2000 'Framing processes and social movements: an overview and assessment', *Annual Review of Sociology*, vol. 26, pp. 611–39

BRUBAKER, ROGERS 2002 'Ethnicity without groups', <http://www.sscnet.ucla.edu/soc/faculty/brubaker/index.htm> [March 2002]

CLARK, COLIN 1998 'Counting backwards: the Roma "numbers game" in Central and Eastern Europe', *Radical Statistics*, vol. 69, pp. 35–46

CESKÝ STATISTICKÝ ÚŘAD, *Sčítání lidu, dom a byt* , <http://www.czso.cz> [March 2002]

DELLA PORTA, DONATELLA and DIANI, MARIO 1999 *Social Movements: An Introduction*, Oxford: Blackwell Publishers

DRUKER, JEREMY 1997 'Present but unaccounted for', *Transitions*, vol. 4, no. 4, pp. 22–23

EVANS, GEOFFREY and WHITEFIELD, STEPHEN 1998 'The structuring of political cleavages in post-communist societies: the case of the Czech Republic and Slovakia', *Political Studies*, vol. 46, no. 1, pp. 115–39

FAWN, RICK 2001 'Czech attitudes towards the Roma: "expecting more of Havel's country"?', *Europe-Asia Studies*, vol. 53, no. 8, pp. 1193–1219

GHEORGHE, NICOLAE 1991 'Roma-Gypsy ethnicity in Eastern Europe', *Social Research*, vol. 58, no. 4, pp. 829–35

—— 1997 'The social construction of Romani identity', in Thomas Acton (ed.), *Gypsy Politics and Traveller Identity*, Hertfordshire: University of Hertfordshire Press, pp. 153–63

GOFFMAN, ERVING 1975 *Frame Analysis: An Essay on the Organization of Experience*, Harmondsworth: Penguin books

GURR, TED ROBERT and HARFF, BARBARA 1994 *Ethnic Conflict in World Politics*, Boulder, San Francisco, Oxford: Westview Press

GUY, WILL 2001 'The Czech lands and Slovakia: another false dawn.?', in Will Guy (ed.), *Between Past and Future. The Roma of Central and Eastern Europe*, Hertfordshire: University of Hertfordshire Press, pp. 285–323

HAUGHTON, TIM 2001 'HZDS: The ideology, organisation and support base of Slovakia's most successful party' *Europe-Asia Studies*, vol. 53, no. 5, pp. 745–69

KYMLICKA, WILL 2000 'Nation-building and minority rights: comparing West and East' *Journal of Ethnic and Migration Studies*, vol. 26, no. 2, 183–212

MCADAM, DOUG, MCCARTHY, JOHN D. and ZALD, MAYER N. (eds) 1996 *Comparative Perspectives on Social Movements. Political Opportunities, Mobilizing Structures and Cultural Framings*, Cambridge: Cambridge University Press

PALOUŠ, MARTIN 1998a 'Forward', in Mesfin Gedlu (ed.), *The Roma and Europe. Romové a Evropa*, Štiřín Castle: Institute of International Relations, pp. 11–12

—— 1998b 'Opening remarks', in Mesfin Gedlu (ed.), *The Roma and Europe. Romové a Evropa*, Štiřín Castle: Institute of International Relations, pp. 15–19

PER (Project on Ethnic Relations) 2001 *Leadership, Representation and the Status of the Roma*, Princeton: Project on Ethnic Relations

PLICHTOVÁ, JANA 1993 'Czechoslovakia as a multi-cultural state in the context of the region', in Minority Rights Group (ed.), *Minorities in Central and Eastern Europe*, London, pp. 11–18

POPESCU, MARINA and HANNAVY, MARTIN 2002 *Project on Political Transformation and the Electoral Process in Post-Communist Europe*, <http://www.essex.ac.uk/ elections> [March 2002]

PUXON, GRATTAN 2000 'The Romani movement: rebirth and the first World Romani Congress in retrospect', in Thomas Acton (ed.), *Scholarship and the Gypsy Struggle. Commitment in Romani Studies*, Hertfordshire: University of Hertfordshire Press, pp. 94–113

REYNOLDS, MATTHEW and HABŠUDOVÁ, ZUZANA 2001 'Pál Csáky: SMK not "byzantine swindlers" (interview)', *The Slovak Spectator*, vol. 7, no. 4

SLOVAK GOVERNMENT 1999 'Report submitted by the Slovak Republic pursuant to article 25, paragraph 1 of the Framework Convention for the Protection of National Minorities', Bratislava: Office of the Government

SOBOTKA, EVA 2001 'Crusts from the table: policy formation towards Roma in the Czech Republic and Slovakia', *Roma Rights*, no. 2–3, pp. 66–70

SOYSAL, YASEMIN N. 1996 'Changing citizenship in Europe', in David Cesarani and Mary Fulbrook (eds), *Citizenship, Nationality and Migration in Europe*, London, New York: Routledge, pp. 17–29

ŠTATISTICKÝ ÚRAD SLOVENSKEJ REPUBLIKY 2002, *Sčitanie obyvateľov, domov a bytov*, <http://www.statistics.sk> [March 2002]

THE ECONOMIST 2000 'Are they a nation?', *The Economist*, vol. 357, no. 8198, pp. 61–62

VLÁDA ČESKÉ REPUBLIKY 1999a 'Report submitted by the Czech Republic pursuant to article 25, paragraph 1 of the Framework Convention for the Protection of National Minorities', Praha: Uřad Vlády České republiky

——— 1999b 'Conception of the government policy towards members of the Roma community to facilitate their social integration, 279/1999', Praha: Uřad Vlády České Republiky

VLÁDA SLOVENSKEJ REPUBLIKY 1996 'Resolution to the proposal of the activities and measures in order to solve the problems of the citizens in need of special care, 310/ 1996', Bratislava: Úrad Vlády Slovenskej republiky

——— 1999 'Resolution on the strategy of the government of the Slovak Republic for the solution of the problems of the Roma national minority and the set of measures for its implementation, first stage, 821/1999', Bratislava: Úrad Vlády Slovenskej republiky

WOLCHIK, SHARON 1995 'The politics of transition and the break-up of Czechoslovakia', Jiří Musil (ed.) *The End of Czechoslovakia*, Budapest, London, New York: Central European University Press, pp. 225–44

***Peter Vermeersch** is postdoctoral research fellow in political science and East European politics, University of Leuven.

Peter Vermeersch, "Ethnic Minority Identity and Movement Politics: The Case of the Roma in the Czech Republic and Slovakia," *Ethnic and Racial Studies* 26, no. 5 (September 2003).

Reprinted by permission of Taylor & Francis Ltd., http://www.tandfonline.com.

Chapter 10: Chimeras of Terror: Disciplining Roma Identity in Lithuania

*by Jurate Kavaliauskaite**

The article explores the proliferation of discourses on (anti)terror and the production of discursive "peripheries" that provide a rationale for social exclusion, ethnic intolerance, and governmental disciplining after 9/11. Preconditions and functionality of the vocabulary of terror in the construction of the identity of the Roma ethnic minority in Lithuania are presented in the case study. The case study focuses on the conflict in late 2004 between state authorities and the Roma community settled in the Kirtimai district of the capital city.

One might argue that mythical notions can contribute to adequate redescriptions of the political condition after 9/11. Today the figure of the Chimera, referring to the bodily disparity of an imagined ancient creature, can be turned into a viable political metaphor to define incoherent but legitimate rationalities of present social and governmental practices. An expansion, multiplication, and omnipresence of global and local discourses on terror and antiterror structure public and scholarly debates, realities of international relations, and national security policies; antiterrorism becomes an imperative of institutional order: "The danger is still out there."[1]

However, the discourse on terror seems to have a centrifugal force as it is detected in various and, sometimes, unusual realms of social relations and communal interactions. It is salient to identify and explain the production, establishment, and functionality of such "peripheries" of the discourse on terror to detect cases when this political imperative tends to mutate into a rationale of social exclusion, ethnic intolerance, and structural violence.[2]

This article presents a case study of terror as a technique of social and governmental discipline; namely, an instrument to structure relations with the ethnic Roma minority in Lithuania. The article aims to untangle a complex nexus between local discourse on terror and the social construction of Roma identity to answer the following question: How could the local Roma be overtly labeled "terrorists" by state authorities without major and effective public dissent in autumn 2004?

THE ROMA—A PRESCRIBED TERRORIST IDENTITY?

The analyzed case of discursive control of minority identity is relatively unconventional in international settings, and in Lithuania it is exceptional. The further analyzed public discourse does not concern migrants, newly established ethnic minorities, Islamic communities, or any external (foreign) threats. Rather, the Roma belong to one of the oldest ethnic groups in the country, having exercised an official right "to roam Lithuanian lands" since 1501.[3] The Roma community of fewer than three thousand people makes up less than 1 percent of Lithuania's total population. Roma are among the least numerous of ethnic minorities, along with the Latvian, German, Tatar, and Armenian communities.[4] Some 25 percent of the Roma community is located in the Kirtimai suburb on the outskirts of Vilnius, the capital city of Lithuania. Today the Roma community of Lithuania is not homogenous, although divisions and relationships inside the community are hardly known about by nonmembers, except for a language variation.[5]

In spite of a durable and relatively nonviolent historic interethnic cohabitation, the vocabulary of terror was evoked in a conflict with the Roma in autumn 2004. It represented the peak of tensions after unsuccessful attempts of the Vilnius municipality and police department to intensify a surveillance system in the Kirtimai settlement in Vilnius on the grounds of crime reduction and prevention of drug trafficking.

First, the Roma representatives expressed overt discontent with the installation of video surveillance cameras in their living area. Second, on October 6, 2004, a police station, newly established at the entrance to this Roma settlement, was burned down. The very next day, without an arsonist having been found, the police proclaimed the arson "an act of terror," a failed attempt to intimidate police officers and society.[6] A process under the respective article on terrorist activities of the criminal code of the Republic of Lithuania has been launched with a promise to "withstand the challenge of criminals" and "reinforce the control of the Roma settlement[7] with heavier police forces."[8] Arturas Zuokas, a former mayor of Vilnius city, declared: "The reaction to municipal attempts to curtail drug trafficking showed the criminal structures have been hit, reassurance of security in Kirtimai settlement means an impediment of the 'death trade.'"[9] Although the "criminals" were discursively differentiated from the Roma community, in December 2004, several shelters in Kirtimai were put under demolition on the order of the Vilnius municipality, on the grounds that these constructions were illegal.

One may argue that the official "hard" definition of arson was to increase the seriousness of a breach—to downplay the voice of Roma advocacy and to legitimate state efforts to regain control of the opaque and ungovernable city space. Moreover, the negligence of official charges received a queer consent of other actors in the public sphere. Lithuanian mass media, the civic "watchdog," also confined itself to official interpretations of events; even the major daily news outlets took the Roma as the main target for incrimination. The breaking news came under titles such as "Revenge of Gypsies to the Police,"[10] "Gipsies Tolerated the Police Station for One Day,"[11] "Gipsy Terrorists Attacked the Police of the Capital,"[12] "Gipsies Rebuffed with Lightning Speed,"[13] "Inhabitants of Shantytown Are Inflamed with Anger Toward Order-makers,"[14] "A Fire Revenge of Gypsies Do Not Stop the Police."[15] In such a media-saturated environment the countervoice of the Human Rights Monitoring Institute (Lithuania) has been relatively weak in undermining the hegemonic accusatory discourse.

How could the notion of "terrorist" be evoked and discursively inscribed into the identity of the Roma minority? Before proceeding with the analysis, a couple of points are to be stressed. Firstly, the legal case on the arson was closed in summer 2006 after an arsonist was found and sentenced to twenty months in jail (both for the arson and another crime, a protection racket).[16] However, the news did not indicate the arson was an act of terror. Secondly, the media noted that the guilty person was not of Roma origin at all, but the scarcity of subsequent internet commentaries showed a lack of public attention and relative disinterest in a "true story" about the crime that contravened established popular narratives about the local Roma people.

Further discussion demonstrates that the combination and synergetic sociopolitical effects of at least three factors empowered peculiar governmental strategies of conflict management in Kirtimai settlement in late 2004. The lack of a domestication of discourse on (anti)terror in Lithuania, dominant and persistent negative popular attitudes toward the Roma minority, as well as ineffective state policies of social cohesion and minority integration, enabled an arbitrary grotesque extension of the notion of terror.

TERRORISM AS A PHANTOM OF THE PUBLIC SPHERE

Jacques Derrida suggested being attentive to the phenomenon of language (naming, labeling, dating), arguing that, after the catastrophe in New York in 2001, 9/11 started to circulate as a bare index that represented more than a date: It revealed the absence of an adequate concept to identify and describe what happened. It unfolded the impotence of our language to overwhelm the density of meanings attached to the event.[17] Since then, *terror* and *terrorism* as semantic signs have been denied singularity of meaning and transparency. The notions are repeated, replicated, multiplied, and redefined in different ways and various contexts. We encountered a dissemination of meaning, in the words of Jean Baudrillard. *Terrorism* as a sign became fractal, operating by "contiguity, fascination, and panic . . . a chain reaction by contagion."[18] However, the United States made great efforts to repress the multitude of interpretations of 9/11. The symbolic order of "antiterrorism" has been established on the international arena, backed by the establishment of the Coalition of the Willing and military campaigns. Antiterrorism became an imperative of security policies of states under a US-led NATO umbrella, and the domestication of (anti)terror discourse became a priority task for security and the makers of foreign policy in Lithuania, too.

I would argue that the domestication process of discourses on (anti)terror has not been completed in Lithuania because of its poor association with a manifest existential threat perceived by the society. The issue of terrorism and antiterrorism was promoted into the national political agenda by external political pressures; it was not securitized in the broader national public setting. Popular attitudes on the status of alleged terrorists and the means to fight this threat represent the ambivalence of discourse. Results of a global survey, "Voice of the People, 2004," showed that a larger share of the Lithuanian population was keen on rendering terrorists the same rights as exercised by indictable offenders and downplayed the efficiency of military action against terrorism if compared to the global moods or attitudes in neighboring Baltic states.[19]

The discourse on terror gained significance several times in the political life of Lithuania in the 1990s. Two streams of discourse can be identified during the period. The first trend concerns the discourse of building state sovereignty and symbolic delimitation from the former occupant. It refers to sabotage actions against the state allegedly backed by Russia. The second stream was mostly related to blackmailing and scuffling cases of local criminal forces in the early 1990s. At that time, the press noted that nobody knew where the line separating a terrorist act, criminal act, and hooliganism was drawn.[20] Besides, Lithuania endorsed the European Convention on the Suppression of Terrorism (1977) in 1997, and in 1998 introduced an article on terrorism into the country's criminal code. But until 9/11, the discourse on terrorism loomed only in relatively closed administrative routines and was not effective in the wider social arena. In summer 2001, a deliberate act of damaging railing on Lithuania's national day has been officially put under the criminal code title "Other National Crimes," and no reference to terrorism were made.[21]

The events of 9/11 presented a challenge to redefine the phenomenon of terrorism in legal, administrative, and state-security mechanisms. The ratification of a number of United Nations antiterrorist conventions, participation of Lithuanian military forces in the US-led antiterrorist campaigns in Afghanistan and Iraq, and curtailment of illegal financing of terrorist organizations (money laundering) constituted an official discourse of antiterrorism. Curiously enough, political authorities both downgraded and gave prominence to the issue, but they did not publicly present the legal definition of terrorism and the scope of potential antiterrorist activities. On the one hand, terrorism was considered an exogenous threat because the domestic situation and historical experience of the country was not conducive to the formation of local terrorist structures. On the other hand, the long-term National Program Against Terrorism[22] remained inaccessible to ordinary citizens, therefore an explicit and nationally enforced notion of terrorist activities was restricted to the limited "security community." Moreover, experts note that the definition of terrorism is rather incoherent in Lithuania's criminal code.[23] The combination of the dominant perception of terror as an exogenous, distant threat, the closure of official discourse, and its irrelevance to ongoing Lithuanian domestic political and social life allow the consideration of terrorism as a communication phenomenon—a product of the public sphere.

The public sphere implies social networking wherein the engagement in debates over the general rules governing political community takes place.[24] The social notions and meanings are negotiated, contested, and formed in the complex polyphony of the public dialogue, at interchanges of opinions and a saturation of rumors. If we consider communication to be a symbolic process whereby reality is produced, maintained, repaired, and transformed,[25] this interaction shapes meanings of terror and images of actors facing and debating political realities. In the absence of direct encounters with debated phenomena, the social centrality of "the window to the outer world"—mass media—is vitally important. "The myth of mediated centre"[26] functions as a means of symbolic production, a channel to witnessing manifestations of distant violence and imagining oneself safely entering the world of terror.

In the case of Lithuania, an absence of direct and severe violence (similar to attacks in New York, Madrid, or London) on the national territory allows definition of terrorism as an intersubjective communication phenomenon, mostly enforced by practices of mass mediation. The dynamics and variation of discursive notions of terror in the Lithuanian media-saturated public sphere is a complex issue; however, it is to be noted that even after 9/11, media practices hardly established rules of when and how the peculiar vocabulary of terrorism was to be evoked. The permanent references to the faraway lands of outlaw, violence, and death (Afghanistan, Iraq, Russia, the Caucasus) and strikes in the vicinity (Spain, the United Kingdom) construct terrorism as a heavily value-laden notion with poor attachment to the local existential space. Violence as an attention-pulling phenomenon prone to what is considered to be newsworthiness becomes an outcome of habitual process and functions as a peculiar technical routine of public mediators.[27] The negativity combined with repetitiveness, and irrelevance for the daily life of citizens, characterize the mainstream public communication on terror in Lithuanian upmarket mass media, and in the national tabloids human-interest stories can be terror-related.[28]

The lack of effective domestication of the discourse on (anti)terror resulted in the absence of rigid principles and rules of "Who, when, and how" can use discourses on terror in the national public sphere. In a nutshell, the control mechanisms of the discourse were relatively weak. Under these circumstances, the state authorities could take advantage of the fluidity of such a discursive formation in the conflict with the Roma community. On the one hand, in late 2004 the police were relatively unrestricted in setting up the content of terrorism and temporally fixing it to include meaning a deliberate malign arson and infringement of legitimate policing of public order. The surplus of meaning of the term *terrorism* was reduced, anchoring it to a "malicious attempt by criminals to intimidate law-enforcement structures and society,"[29] even if the validity of this anchoring was not apparent. On the other hand, the vocabulary was deliberately chosen to exploit the normative aspects of the discourse: The naming of the arson as a terrorist act intended to give the event an utmost salience and importance, to stress the extremity of the malignancy so as to make it worthy of the strictest punishment.

However, only Lewis Carroll's Humpty Dumpty could freely choose and play with meanings of words.[30] The indeterminacy of the discourse on terror does not mean the total arbitrariness of its exercise, because the power to redescribe depends on the resistance potential of the entity under redescription as well as upon the legitimacy of this attempt in the wider political and cultural arena.

POPULAR IMAGE OF THE ROMA: INEVITABLE INSIDE OUTSIDERS

Burdens of Interethnic Cohabitation

During the 2007 European Year of Equal Opportunities for All, the Roma remained the least wanted members of the community in Lithuania. Tolerance toward representatives of this ethnic minority remained extremely poor.

Human rights experts note that attitudes of Lithuanians toward the Roma people are explicitly negative.[31] They remain the least wanted neighbors, encountering stronger social rejection than minorities based on sex orientation, the Chechen minority, refugees, and Muslims.[32] Nearly 80 percent of respondents asked about the subject do not wish Roma people in their neighborhood, and the numbers grew from 59 percent in 1990 to 77 percent in 2005. Nearly 70 percent of respondents indicated their opinion about the Roma had become worse or definitely worse over the past fifteen years. Moreover, the recent surveys show the majority of the population thinks that the present situation of the Roma is not worse at the moment if compared to earlier periods, that international organizations overstate factual problems of this minority, and that the Roma themselves are to be blamed for their problems and poverty.[33]

Surprisingly enough, the level of intolerance clashes with the popular perception of ethnic discrimination in the country. A 2006 Eurobarometer survey on discrimination across the European Union shows that the Lithuanian population does not perceive discrimination of minorities in the country: first, the perception of ethnic discrimination is lower if compared to the EU average; second, a substantially smaller number of respondents consider that belonging to a different ethnic origin is a disadvantage (27%, compared with the EU average of 62%); third, a smaller percentage thinks that being Roma is a disadvantage (67%, compared with the EU average of 77%).[34] The parliament, mass media, and the government are considered the most important institutions to combat discrimination, though in the EU generally it is civic society—schools and universities, families, and the media—that is given the most important role.

This tendency implies that a substantial share of the Lithuanian population does not recognize discrimination on ethnic origin, and individuals in the same group do not themselves feel responsible for eliminating social risks, vulnerabilities, and hostilities. However, sociologists note that true tolerance cannot be limited to patience and bearing: It must extend to the recognition of the other, respect, and the abandonment of violence.[35]

Reproduction of Popular Imaginary Through the Media Lens

No society is totally immune to ethnic intolerance; however, the devaluation of the problem is prominent in post-Soviet communities.[36] Empirical research proves that channelled media representations mirror as well as mold and frame ethnic relations in everyday interactions.[37] Scholars and human rights activists stress a negative bias in the selection and framing of issues related to the local

Roma community—"Their collective identity is permanently moulded by scandals, police reports and repeating stereotypes."[38]

The mass-mediated publicity enforces crude stereotyping in terms of criminalization, drug trafficking, violence, poverty, and attribution of asocial behavior. Roma are the most heavily criminalized ethnic group in Lithuanian mass media, and the Roma people are subject to the worst representations as the least socially integrated, exotic but also deviant, socially insecure, inscrutable, and manipulative group.[39] News reports on Roma are often negative, and a habit of indicating the ethnic origin of an individual in criminal news has been established. Moreover, besides reporting being reactive rather than proactive, there is a lack of debate focused specifically on the social problems of this ethnic minority—unemployment, housing, education, and discrimination. Thus Roma are not seen as genuine members, "insiders" of the social and cultural life of the country. They are visible in the public sphere, but their publicity is framed and controlled by dominating negative discourses, hardly influenced by communicative initiatives of the Roma themselves.

As comparative empirical studies show, once fixed, negative discourse on immigrant or ethnic identities is prone to domination and self-reproduction by repetition.[40] Inner conflicts in the community, relatively weak public activism, normalization of social isolation of the Roma as well as unfavorable public feelings would generate a vacuum of pressure on national policymakers if not on the activities of the nongovernmental sector.

Monologue of the Public Sphere: Images of the Roma in Internet News Commentaries

The mass-media discourse in Lithuania is seen as rather modest in terms of intolerance levels if compared to internet commentaries, which range from temperate to the strongest forms of verbal discrimination.[41] Although legal norms are relatively efficient in precluding overt discrimination in mass-media content, intolerance looms in anonymous discourses in virtual space.[42] Therefore, internet commentaries containing opinions, attitudes, and values regarding the Roma in Lithuania are the main area of interest in the research for this article. A focus on public responses to journalistic messages, not solely the content of these messages, allows a broader view on social and political conditions that allow formation of the particular images of the Roma community. In comparison with press, television, or radio, the internet offers a higher degree of interactivity and nonprescribed, relatively free commenting by publics that otherwise remain rather invisible.

The internet, specifically the website delfi.lt, the most popular news portal in Lithuanian, was chosen for the analysis of the construction of the Roma identity in the national public sphere. That website was chosen for at least two reasons: first, delfi.lt is the most popular and strongest national internet news portal. Launched at the beginning of 2000, it has a current average of 0.3 million readers per day.[43] Portals of the Delfi group in the three Baltic states attract more than 0.7 million readers per day and take 45 to 48 percent of the internet market in the region.[44] Managers of delfi.lt claim that "60 percent of delfi.lt readers are over twenty-four years old, educated individuals, receiving average or higher income."[45] Second, delfi.lt news is the most heavily commented on online by its readers, and no other national news portal enjoys such activism of its users. Therefore, public commentaries on news about the Roma in Kirtimai district, published on delfi.lt during the period from September 2004 to June 2006, are selected to reveal popular moods at the moment of the appearance of terror vocabulary in the rhetoric of state authorities regarding relationship with the Roma. Sixteen news reports have been selected on the basis of their relevance to the conflict under investigation and the amplitude of readers' comments on them. The selected reports generated more than 2,616 short commentaries from delfi.lt readers. News reports were chosen to see how images of Roma are constructed in the news and if representations of Roma in the media correlate with attitudes toward the minority, expressed in the commentaries on news reports.

Three groups of agenda-setters in media messages can be distinguished: news reports dominated by state authorities; reports questioning the position and policies of state authorities; and reports defending Roma by human rights institutions.[46] The reactions of delfi.lt readers to state actions, views on media coverage of the conflict and the Roma's advocacies, as well as strategies and types of social "labelling" of Roma, embedded in internet commentaries, are the main objects of qualitative content analysis in the following paragraphs.

One should note that an explication of the Roma identity and the construction of social exclusion in internet commentaries was a reaction to the following sequence of news: First came rumors about the authorities' intentions to relocate the Roma settlement; then came news of increased policing and installation of the video surveillance cameras at the Kirtimai site, followed by reports of the arson of the new, permanent, police station there and the official discourse on terror. Next came the anti–drug trafficking raids and the destruction of shelters at the site by order of city authorities, the Roma's claims for damage to their property, and advocacy by human rights bodies. Finally, the arson conviction was reported.

The idea to resettle Roma and to eliminate the Kirtimai site was met with great approval of delfi.lt readers, though it went together with some expressed doubts on the possibility of avoiding coexistence with this ethnic group. There were voices suggesting moving the Vilnius Roma to a poor corner of the country (Didžiasalis) or an area dominated by other ethnic minorities (Visaginas) or simply to expel all Roma from the country (to Romania or Russia). Nevertheless, it was admitted that the Roma were going to return to rich Vilnius, where making a living was easier.

The need for coexistence raised an issue of cordoning threats and risks emanating from the Kirtimai settlement. Commentators denigrated protests from Roma leaders against intensified surveillance of the site and unanimously supported arguments of the city authorities and police that increased control was legitimate: it had to help to reduce drug-trafficking "business" flourishing in the city area. The Roma's resentment was seen as a manipulative attempt to cover and sustain illegal activities. A letter to the European Court of Human Rights was parodied: "Lithuanian policemen put video surveillance cameras by our slums and we cannot sell drugs easily. Help! Stop the discrimination!"[47] An expression of regret for the damage to the young lives of non-Roma drug addicts dominated the comments. Drug dealers, specifically the Roma, were seen as guilty, but not the addicts.

The peak of tension and public resentment on October 6 and 7, 2004, in the aftermath of the arson, brought several hundred comments.[48] The event was interpreted as the launching of "war" between the town community (represented by the police and the former city mayor Arturas Zuokas) and the aggressive, threatening criminal minority. The arson was presented as a natural, expected incident, a challenge to righteous town dwellers and the state that protected their interests. Therefore, stricter means of policing, control, curfew, the introduction of military forces, and ghettoizing were welcomed. The discourse fully reinforced the position of the authorities. It was also strengthened by popular agreement that Roma were unwilling to take on any decent, legal activities: "To make a Romani work is a 'Sisyphian task,'[49] and the trait was said to be "genetically coded" in the nature of the Roma ethnic minority. Hence, any attempts to "civilize" them by creating and offering work places and introducing any other positive strategies were thought to be pointless.

The peak of conflict, in autumn 2004, coincided with general parliamentary elections that year, and Zuokas, the former mayor, led a Liberal and Central Union in the election campaign. Analysis of the controversies regarding the personality of Zuokas as a political figure is beyond the scope of this article;

however, it is to be noted that the enforcement of policing at the Kirtimai site was soon interpreted (by delfi.lt commentators) as a PR campaign in the mass media, a political spectacle to attract votes in national elections but not an attempt to solve the drug-trafficking problem in the town.[50] Nevertheless, the recognition of potential manipulation of the Roma issue by the city authorities did not alter a negative stance toward the Roma community. On the contrary, their imagined identity was "enriched" by the suspicion that Roma deceived the whole city community by secret collaboration with Zuokas—informal backing of their illegal business by political power. Other voices welcomed any attempts to "establish order" at the Kirtimai site, disregarding the political rationalities of such activities.

On December 2 and 3, the Vilnius municipality demolished six shelters in the Kirtimai settlement, arguing that dwellings in the neighborhood of the shelters were at risk of fire and that further expansion of the settlement (where drug trafficking was allegedly increasingly widespread) was to be stopped. The parliamentary ombudsman held that the demolition of these dwellings violated the legal rights and interests of their residents.[51] However, the initiative to raise the question of the Roma's rights, advocacy initiated by human rights bodies, and attempts by such bodies to revise the legality of the demolition of housing in December 2004 were downplayed in delfi.lt news commentaries.

Commentators dismissed arguments about minority discrimination and that there had been violation of human rights by using a peculiar conception of fairness. It was stressed that, while the same constitution, legal norms, and rules applied to all and that there was no citizenship guaranteeing rights but not requiring duties, the Kirtimai Roma demanded only rights; the Roma claimed benefits that other groups of society could not claim; an ordinary Lithuanian citizen was conceptualized as an autonomous subject, sustained by personal effort and endeavor, making no pretensions for state support.

In this argument, the responsibility for the poor social status and conditions of Roma was attributed to the minority themselves. The idea of positive discrimination of the Roma ethnic minority by the state was seen as an unfair act,[52] discriminatory to the rest of the population, while Vilnius citizens were perceived as victims of illegal activities by the Roma: "Isn't the poisoning of the nation important?"[53] The principle of the uniform application of the same rules and laws justified the demolition of "illegal" housing on state-owned land. A formal rule, applying to all, was to be the main criterion for evaluating Roma actions. The public and legal advocacy of the Roma was treated as a careless ignorance of a looming threat, an outcome of a gap between political elite and ordinary citizens in perceptions of crucial social problems, or even a conspiracy between the advocates and the criminals. The harm done by the destruction of several shelter houses was considered insignificant in comparison with the moral and social harm done by drug dealers. Therefore, claims for compensation were interpreted as an aggressive illegitimate impudence.

During the period under review, the essence of the disciplined identity was expressed by a strong refusal to use the word *Roma* instead of the traditional and vernacular *Gypsies* in internet commentaries (contemporary scholarly and legal documents use the words interchangeably). The word *Roma* is rejected as an artificial element of the discourse, a euphemism that is installed by authorities and human rights bodies to grant this ethnic minority a higher, but undeserved, social status—an attempt to mask the negative connotations of the established notion of Gypsy.[54] Overall, minor countervoices and neutral imagery of the Roma had only a very weak presence in the online commentaries, and they were met by overt hostility and seen as misunderstandings. There were attempts to equate representatives of the Roma minority with the rest of the population, to ground their behavior, to look for the roots of their present situation, or to shame radical commentators, but they were mostly ineffective in that they met with strong counteraction in the discourse.

One might argue—to use terms from the anthropological notions of Douglas[55] —that the discourse of symbolic pollution and impurity pervades the realm of the internet public sphere over the analyzed period. The concept of symbolic pollution allows conceptualization of the production and meaning of social exclusions; it explains how communities differentiate themselves from one another and meet a need to preserve social boundaries. Symbolic pollution occurs when there is a settled order, a customary arrangement of relations, and there is then a breach of that order. Public discourse then functions as a mechanism of purification, a normative cleansing of community. Delfi.lt commentaries encourage a complement to Douglas's ideas because the impurity of the Roma is constructed as a permanent, inevitable, fixed element that can hardly be changed.

Cultural geographers observe that the idea of symbolic pollution refers not only to human bodies and relationships but also to distinct sites or social spaces. The function and meaning of the space require adherence to particular modes of behavior; improper conduct may be deviant because the place determines the evaluation of an act—its appropriateness.[56] Impropriety is of a normative nature here, and the behavior that does not correspond to the symbolic requirements of a particular space (church, shop, market) is considered to be abnormal, deviant, dangerous, and polluting, thereby asking for intervention to restore and sustain the order of things. Any transgression has political implications, too: Violators may be isolated and estranged from the fabric of community by the determination of other community members to "cleanse" the space. In the case of the Roma conflict, the Kirtimai settlement—*taboras*—circles the peculiar space differentiated from the rest of the cityscape. Poverty, disorder, deviance, illegal activities, drug addicts, death are integrated into the description of taboras and naturalized. The overall symbolic order and balance between taboras space and city space is sustained until the disorder is contained within the space of Roma community. The containment is guaranteed only by the permanent control of the overspill of threats and by surveillance over the dangerous, segregated and semiautonomous site. As the land does not legally belong to the Roma, and the space is not privatized, state intervention and control are legitimate.

Thus, the dominant hostile discourse toward the Kirtimai Roma community can be explained in the following way. The active stance of the Roma—attempts of Roma representatives to defend their property, their rights; the rise of a public voice and advocacy by human rights institutions—represented a transgression from the popular imaginary of Kirtimai taboras space. Policing, surveillance, compliance, and silence traditionally describe this space. Therefore, strong discursive attempts were made to secure a long-standing symbolic order to bring Roma back to silence and passivity, to counter any effort to pull this minority group out of the margins of social space. "Cleansing" of the mainstream public sphere meant restoration of the ordinary settled relationship between dominant and subordinated ethnic communities.[57]

During the analyzed period, the online space was a monologue in terms of representation of Roma. Practices of policing and surveillance of the Roma were considered on the basis of the interests of "the rest of the city community," which were incompatible with Roma interests. State policies to draw the Roma back to their own segregated life, to tame a source of disorder and threat to the localized and defined place, were supported by delfi.lt readers. The symbolic order of the Kirtimai site was seen as repugnant to the norms ruling the rest of the population.[58]

THE STATE IN (IN)ACTION

The popular imagery, and state policies toward the Roma minority, generated a closed circuit of permanent reproduction of social marginalization. In 2006 international human rights bodies presented a critical evaluation of Lithuanian governmental strategies to promote social integration of the Roma. The recent report of the European Commission Against Racism and Intolerance (ECRI) noted that the members of the Roma communities in Lithuania faced prejudice, disadvantage, and discrimination across many areas of life, spanning from education to employment, housing, health, access to personal documents, and relations with the police, although ECRI welcomed the adoption of the Programme for the Integration of Roma into Lithuanian Society 2000–2004.[59] However, it was noted that the involvement of Roma representatives in the elaboration of the program had been very limited.

Similar observations have been made by national human rights bodies, who argue that state attempts to elaborate a long-term comprehensive strategy to promote equal opportunities for the Roma communities of Lithuania have been relatively unsuccessful. The 2004–2006 national programs on social security and inclusion recognized refugees, immigrants, asylum seekers and Roma as socially vulnerable groups, but these groups are no longer included in policy documents for the period of 2006–2008.[60] The instruments to improve the situation of the Roma and other vulnerable social groups, presented in the National Anti-Discrimination Program, 2006–2008, are not active, direct, and sufficient.[61] ECRI recommends that any new program aimed at the integration of the Roma population be based on a concept of integration as a two-way process, where both majority and minority groups are seen as responsible for building a cohesive society. To this end, ECRI strongly recommends that the new program include measures targeted at the non-Roma population and aimed at countering societal prejudice and discrimination toward this part of the Lithuanian population.[62]

* * *

The above case study shows that the grotesque intermingling of the Roma identity and threat discourses was empowered by a complex of structural circumstances. An incongruency between the harm inflicted by the arson of the police station and the weight of official charges was not highlighted in the public sphere.

The lack of domestication of terror discourse on the national level, the availability of its discursive resources, chronic social marginalization, and permanently reproduced negative visibility of the Kirtimai Roma made them vulnerable to the implementation of drastic disciplining strategies. The popular indifference regarding the inefficiency of any social policies and positive state action toward the Roma community extends the field of legitimate maneuver of city authorities and police. Lithuanian experts on human rights note that "it seems unawareness of what to do about some social groups leads to their exclusion or disregard."[63] The important problems remain unsolved because of lack of the political will and self-determination to act.

The primary appeal to the security of "the rest" of the town community, and stress on one malady—drug trafficking—neglected the full scope of the problems that Roma face. The active and effective measures of positive social integration are replaced by negative practices of surveillance, taming, and ghettoizing. An enforced principle of self-control—the essence of Foucauldian panopticon—means transfer of the burden of urgent social issues onto the shoulders of the minority community itself.

Will the hope of "improved behavior" solve all hardship of structural violence? In autumn 2004, state authorities arbitrarily extended the discourse on terror to legitimate a dubious campaign of policing and to threaten that the resistance of the Roma would meet the strictest counteraction. It was a strategic speech act, committed to reduce the complexity of social space, a technique to deal with structural problems related to ethnic minority issues.

It is important to note that reference to "an act of terror" existentially diverges from any constructive policy because it allows and promotes destructive tactics and unilateral violent policies. It does not anticipate any communality or sensibility toward and responsibility for the "inside outsiders." This case study shows how present imperatives of globally saturating (anti)terror discourse disseminate and penetrate most distant social spaces and highlights how discursive resources can serve governmental practices of social disciplining.

APPENDIX: LIST OF ARTICLES ANALYZED

"Sostines cigonai su nerimu//laukia iskeldinimo" (20 September 2004)//www.delfi.lt (51 comments).

BNS, "Tabore irengta policijos posta cigonai skus Strasburui" (4 October 2004)//www.delfi.lt (433 comments).

BNS, "Vilniaus romams siulo dirbti viesuosius darbus" (5 October 2004)//www.delfi.lt (96 comments).

BNS, "Sulaikyti padegimu cigonu tabore itariami narkomanai" (6 October, 2004)//www.delfi.lt (440 comments).

BNS, "Sulaikyti nauji itariamieji padegimu cigonu tabore" (7 October 2004)//www.delfi.lt (61 comments).

BNS, "Vilniaus policija nepalieka ramybeje cigonu taboro" (8 October 2004)//www.delfi.lt (97 comments).

R. Cekutis, "A.Zuoko rinkimine akcija-atrakcija tabore" (12 October 2004)//www.delfi.lt (278 comments).

BNS, "Policijos postas tabore—brangus rinkimu triukas?" (13 October 2004)//www.delfi.lt (141 comments).

"*Prascau zodzio*: Kuo baigsis cigonu ir policijos karas?" (14 October 2004)//www.delfi.lt (74 comments).

"Policija neigia, kad veiksmai cigonu tabore—rinkimines kampanijos dalis" (15 October 2004)// www.delfi.lt (31 comments).

BNS, "Seimo kontroliere sustabde pastatu griovima tabore" (6 December 2004)//www.delfi.lt (146 comments).

TV3, "Romai is Vilniaus miesto savivaldybes reikalauja 200 tukst. Litu" (5 January 2005)//www. delfi.lt (180 comments).

LNK, "Cigonai uz nugriautus namus reikalauja 2 mln. Lt" (27 January 2005)//www.delfi.lt (216 comments).

K. Aleknaite, "Romu padetis Lietuvoje prasteja, ju pusen stoja teisininkai" (31 March 2005)// www.delfi.lt (143 comments).

ELTA, "Griaudama romu taboro bustus savivaldybe diskriminavo gyventojus, teigia Seimo kontrole" (1 September 2005)//www.delfi.lt (220 comments).

J. Vanagas, "Nuteistas Vilniaus tabore policijos posta padeges vyras" (5 June 2006)//www.delfi.lt (9 comments).

NOTES

1. BBC, *Germany Warns of Terrorist Threat* (August 20, 2006): http://news.bbc.co.uk/2/hi/europe/5267920.stm.

2. J. Galtung, "Violence, Peace, and Peace Research," *Journal of Peace Research* 6, no. 3 (1969): 167–191.

3. Y. Plasseraud, *Mazumos: tautiniu ir etniniu mazumu istudij vadas* (Vilnius: Apostrofa, 2006).

4. The data of the population 2001 census is presented by the Department of National Minorities and Lithuanians Living Abroad under the Government of the Republic of Lithuania: http://www.tmid.lt.

5. Historians agree the Roma arrived in Lithuania from Poland around the fourteenth century. In 1860s Lithuania there was a new migration wave of Roma from Romania and Hungary. The Roma of Lithuania heavily suffered Nazi holocaust and later underwent Soviet assimilation policies. Today the Roma community comprises three groups. Litovska Roma is the biggest group, encompassing the Roma of the Vilnius region that has named itself Polska Roma since the 1930s. Lotfitka Roma live in Northern Lithuania, in the towns of Zagaer, Mazeikiai, and Siauliai, and have affiliations in neighboring Latvia. The third group arrived in Lithuania from Moldova in the 1940s after World War II and settled in a Vilnius suburb. Later, the Roma of the Vilnius region and others of more distant regions started to establish themselves in the neighborhood. Therefore the present Kirtimai site encompasses two settlements of first and later newcomers. For more information see V. Toleikis, *Lietvos cigonai: tarp praeities ir dabarties* (Vilnius: Garnelis, 2001), and S. Vaitiekus, ed., *Cigonai Europoje ir Lietuvoje* (Vilnius: Tyto alba, 1998).

6. ELTA, *Tabore irengto posto padegima policija laiko teroro aktu* (October 6, 2007): http://www.omni.lt.

7. It is important to note a peculiar wording. In official and public discourses the word *taboras*, referring to mobile encampment (not a permanent settlement), has been used to describe the site of Kirtimai inhabited by the Roma community in Vilnius.

8. D. Saluga, *Vilniaus savivaldybe nepasiduos kovoje su narkotiku platintojais* (October 6, 2007): http://www.vilnius.lt.

9. Ibid.

10. S. Malinauskas and D. Nagele, "*Cigonau* kerstas policijai," *Vakaro zinios* (October 7, 2007): 4.

11. ELTA, "Policijos posta cigonai pakente tik para," *Lietuvos zinios* (October 7, 2007): p. 4.

12. A. Gurevicius, "Cigonu teroristai atakavo sostines policija," *Respublika* (October 7, 2007): p. 7.

13. M. Kuizinaite, "Cigonu atkirtis buvo zaibiskas," *Lietuvos rytas* (October 7, 2007): pp. 1, 6.

14. M. Kuizinaite, "Lusnyno gyventojai dega pykciu tvarkdariams," *Sostine* (October 9, 2007): pp. 1, 3.

15. "Cigonu ugnies kerstas nestabdo policijos uzmoju," *Lietuvos rytas* (October 9, 2007): p. 4.

16. J. Vanagas, "Nuteistas Vilniaus tabore policijos posta padeges vyras" (June 5, 2006): http://www.delfi.lt.

17. G. Borradori, *Philosophy in a Time of Terror: Dialogues with Jürgen Habermas and Jacques Derrida* (Chicago: University of Chicago Press, 2003).

18. J. Baudrillard, *In the Shadow of the Silent Majority* (New York: Semiotext, 1983): p. 51.

19. Just under one-half of the population (49%) responded that alleged terrorists should be rendered the same rights as indictable offenders. The numbers in Latvia and Estonia were, respectively, 60 and 70 percent. The global average is 62 percent. In Lithuania 51 percent of the population of do not agree or relatively disagree that military action is the most effective means to fight terrorism (Latvia, 56%; Estonia, 62%). The TNS-Gallup survey "Voice of the People 2004" was made in sixty states around the world in July–August 2004: http://www.tns-gallup.lt.

20. J. Damulyte, G. Sarafinas, "Lietuvoje nenubaustas n vienas teroristas," *Veidas* 43 (October 31, 1997).

21. A. Kuzmickas, "Valstybes diena—diversant ispuolis," *Lietuvos zinios* (July 7, 2001).

22. *The National Security Strategy*, adopted May 28, 2002.

23. A. Gutauskas, "Terorizmo baudziamasis teisinis ivertinimas pagal naujaji Lietuvos Respublikos baudziamj kodeksa," *Teise* 54 (2005): 1–13.

24. J. Habermas, *The Structural Transformation of the Public Sphere: An Inquiry into a Category of Bourgeois Society* (Cambridge: Polity, 1994).

25. J. Carey, *Communication as Culture: Essays on Media and Society* (Winchester: Unwin Hyman, 1989).

26. N. Couldry, *Media Rituals: A Critical Approach* (London: Routledge, 2003).

27. H. Molotch and M. Lester, "News as Purposive Behavior: On the Strategic Use of Routine Events, Accidents, and Scandals," *American Sociological Review* 39, no. 1 (1974): 101–112.

28. INNA/Trinity Mirror, "Negaliu gyventi be Beno," *Ekstra zinios* (February 13, 2006).

29. ELTA, *Cigonu taboro pasoneje irengto posto padegima pareigunai laiko teroro aktu* (October 6, 2004): http://www.elta.lt.

30. L. Carroll, *Alisa Stebuklu salyje ir Veidrodziu karalysteje* (Vilnius: Vyturys, 1991), p. 170.

31. Reports on Human Rights Condition in Lithuania, Human Rights Monitoring Institute, 2003, 2004, 2006: http://www.hrmi.lt.

32. Report, Discrimination of the Roma in the Employment Sector, Human Rights Monitoring Institute: http://www.hrmi.lt.

33. N. Kasatkina, ed., *Etninis nepakantumas: Etniskumo studijos*, 1 (Vilnius: Eugrimas, 2006), pp. 175–177.

34. The period of survey was June 13 to July 4, 2006. The results of the survey are presented by the Office of Equal Opportunities Ombudsperson: http://www.lygybe.lt.

35. N. Kasatkina, "Visuomeniniu normu dichotomija: tolerancija versus nepakantumas," in N. Kasatkina, ed., *Etninis nepakantumas. Etniskumo studijos*, 1 (Vilnius: Eugrimas, 2006), pp. 7–18.

36. Ibid.

37. V. Beresneviciute and M. Frejute-Rakauskiene, "Etnine tematika ir nepakantumas Lietuvos ziniasklaidoje: dienrasciu analize," in N. Kasatkina, ed., *Etninis nepakantumas: Etniskumo studijos*, 1 (Vilnius: Eugrimas, 2006), pp. 19–44.

38. A. Tereskinas, *Lietuvos ziniasklaida ir romai: tarp skandalo, policijos pranesimu ir besikartojanciu stereotipu* (2002): http://www.kulturosvartai.lt.

39. A. Tereskinas, *Minority Politics: Mass Media and Civil Society in Lithuania, Latvia, and Poland* (2002): http://www.policy.hu/tereskinas/Research 2002.html.

40. Beresneviciute and Frejute-Rakauskiene, note 38.

41. L. Donskis, *Be pykcio* (April 25, 2005), LTV (a program of the national television broadcaster); an online conference with Tadas Leoncikas, a head of the Human Rights Monitoring Institute (April 18, 2005).

42. L. Auskalniene, "Etninis nepakantumas Lietuvos internetineje ziniasklaidoje: komentarai internete," in *Etninis nepakantumas. Etniskumo studijos*, 1 (Vilnius: Eugrimas, 2006), pp. 45–58.

43. The data on the reach of delfi.lt is presented by an international communications company, "MediaHouse" (Spring 2007).

44. *Kompanija "Ekspress Group" isigijo naujienu portala "Delfi"* (August 2, 2007): http://verslas.banga.lt/lt/spaudai.full/46b1ec40f2a38.

45. Information provided by delfi.lt on http://www.delfi.lt/help/about .php?l=f. For the comprehensive data on demographic characteristics of internet users in Lithuania, see survey at http://www.tns-gallup.lt/lt/disp .php/lt_surveys/lt_surveys_116?ref=/lt/disp.php/lt_surveys?findsubm 1&srch=internet&okay=OK .

46. See the list of the articles in the appendix.

47. BNS, *Tabore irengta policijos posta cigonai skus Strasburui* (September 4, 2004): http://www.delfi.lt.

48. BNS, *Sulaikyti padegimu cigonu tabore itariami narkomanai* (October 6, 2004): http://www.delfi.lt.

49. BNS, *Vilniaus romams siulo dirbti viesuosius darbus* (October 5, 2004): http://www.delfi.lt.

50. The dailies and internet news sources promoted the idea. See R. Cekutis, A. *Zuoko rinkimine akcija-atrakcija tabore* (October 12, 2007): http://www.delfi.lt.

51. *Seimo kontroliere sustabde pastatu griovima tabore*, BNS (December 6, 2004).

52. However, the respective EU directives define positive discrimination and do not forbid member states to apply special measures to help vulnerable social groups.

53. BNS, note 51.

54. A. Fraser, *Cigonai* (Vilnius: Tyto alba, 2001).

55. M. Douglas, *Purity and Danger: An Analysis of the Concepts of Pollution and Taboo* (New York: Routledge, 1994).

56. T. Cresswell, "Weeds, Plagues, and Bodily Secretions: A Geographical Interpretation of Metaphors of Displacement," *Annals of the Association of American Geographers* 87 (1997): 330–345.

57. D. L. Horowitz, *Ethnic Groups in Conflict* (Berkeley: University of California Press, 1985).

58. A. Gurevicius, "Taboras—neiveikiamas mirties fabrikas," *Respublika* (October 7, 2004): 1, 4.

59. The report is available on the official ECRI website: http://www.coe.int/t/e/human_rights/ecri/1-ECRI/2-Country-by-country_approach/Lithuania/.

60. V. Beresneviciute, *Poziuris ietmines mazumas turetu buti lankstesnis ir kompetentingesnis* (May 5, 2007): http://www.bernardinai.lt.

61. The National Report, "Implementation of Human Right in Lithuania, 2006": http://www.balsas.lt.

62. ECRI, note 60.

63. Beresneviciute, note 61.

*Jurate Kavaliauskaite is a lecturer at the Institute of International Relations and Political Science, Vilnius University.